CATULLUS TO OVID:
READING LATIN LOVE ELEGY

GW00600847

Current titles in this series:

CATULLUS TO OVID: READING LATIN LOVE ELEGY

A Literary Commentary
with Latin Text

Joan Booth

Translations by Guy Lee and Joan Booth

Published by Bristol Classical Press
General Editor: John H. Betts

This impression 2003
This edition published in 1999 by
Bristol Classical Press
an imprint of
Gerald Duckworth & Co. Ltd.
90-93 Cowcross Street, London EC1M 6BF
Tel: 020 7490 7300
Fax: 020 7490 0080
inquiries@duckworth-publishers.co.uk
www.ducknet.co.uk

A catalogue record for this book is available
from the British Library

ISBN 1 85399 606 8

Acknowledgements

The translations of Catullus and Propertius are reprinted by kind permission
of Oxford University Press; they first appeared in *The Poems of Catullus*
and *Propertius: The Poems*, both edited and translated by Guy Lee
(1990 & 1994 respectively). Those of Ovid are reprinted by arrangement
with John Murray (Publishers) Ltd. from *Ovid's Amores* translated by
Guy Lee (1968). The translations of Tibullus are by Joan Booth
(in consultation with Guy Lee).

Cover illustration: Couple embracing on a couch. Campanian
terracotta group from Tarquinia; 2nd-1st century BC.
[© The British Museum]

Printed and bound in Great Britain by
Antony Rowe Ltd, Eastbourne

Contents

Abbreviations

AP = *Anthologia Palatina (The Greek Anthology)*
Catul. = Catullus
LIMC = *Lexicon iconographicum mythologiae classicae,*
     Zurich-Munich, 1981-
Ov. = Ovid
Am. = *Amores*
P. Oxy. = *Oxyrhynchus Papyri* 1898-
Prop. = Propertius
Tib. = Tibullus

The names of all other ancient authors and works are cited in full. References to editions and translations of fragmentary texts may be elucidated from the bibliography, as may all references by author-date to secondary literature in books and periodicals.

Preface

A version of this book first appeared in the BCP *Companions* series as *Latin Love Elegy* (1995). The present new edition is a response to the gratifying suggestion of reviewers and users of the earlier volume that its targeted readership should also include traditional students of Latin, to whom it could usefully offer a perspective beyond that of basic linguistic understanding. A Latin text of the poems translated and discussed now precedes the commentary, and all relevant Latin is quoted in the interpretative essays, which I hope will serve equally well those working with the original language and those reading exclusively in English translation. I must modify a loosely-worded claim in my Preface to the First Edition: the poems selected can more accurately be said to represent the considerable range of so-called *personal* Latin love elegy rather than Latin love elegy 'as a whole'. For practical reasons, I have excluded, for example, didactic and epistolary forms, but I hope that readers may in any case be encouraged by what is here to venture subsequently outside the current selection. There is substantial bibliographical updating throughout (in accordance with the principles of the original series, only items in English have been routinely cited, though important work in German has occasionally been mentioned). The general introduction in particular has been fully revised to take account of recent papyrological publications and renewed scholarly debate on the development of Latin love elegy. A new section ('The challenge') has been inserted to alert readers to the increased range of critical approaches currently applied to classical literature by modern scholars. I have corrected a number of errors and hope not to have introduced too many new ones, but wherever I have blundered the responsibility is my own.

My gratitude to the colleagues, friends and technical experts who helped in various ways with the original book remains, of course, undiminished. It is my pleasure, however, to record additional thanks here to those who have facilitated the new edition: to John Betts of BCP for initiating it and to Graham Douglas, Production Manager, for his technical ingenuity in solving typesetting problems; to the British Museum for permission to use the cover photograph; to Niklas Holzberg for swift access to certain secondary items; to Dr John Hilliard for his assistance with the preliminary computerising of the Latin text; and, as ever, to Guy Lee for his unfailingly generous academic and personal support.

J.B., Swansea 1999

Preface to the First Edition

The love poetry of Catullus has always been enthusiastically read in the modern world, both in Latin and in translation. And deservedly so. But the work of the Augustan elegists has never enjoyed such popularity – especially among non-Latinists, to many of whom Propertius and Tibullus have remained totally unknown (Ovid has fared slightly better). This has come about at least in part because of the lack of editions of translated texts to provide the student of Classical Studies with basic help and guidance, while preserving as much as possible of the academic rigour of traditional Classics. The present *Companion* is offered as a start towards remedying that deficiency. The poems included have been chosen to give some indication of the development and variety of Latin love elegy as a whole and the characteristics and range of its individual exponents. Each of Guy Lee's verse translations (different in style for each author; see 'Translator's Note') is followed by my commentary, which normally presents first a synopsis or brief paraphrase, with explanations of essential references and other factual matters, then a more detailed critical analysis (unashamedly subjective), and finally a series of deliberately provocative questions (in the case of Propertius 4. 7 and Ovid, *Amores* 3. 2 I have deviated slightly from this pattern). The selection from each poet is followed by a short retrospective survey. My main aim has been to give non-linguistic sixth-form and university students the means and encouragement to make informed critical judgements of their own. Generous cross-references to basic explanatory material (mostly in the Introduction) have been supplied to serve the needs of those readers who may not be tackling the whole book or even all the poems of an individual author.

I should like to record my gratitude to all of those who have helped with this undertaking. As always, I am much indebted to my father and to my friends, academic and non-academic, for their sustaining interest and practical support. On this occasion, however, I should particularly like to thank John Betts for inviting me to embark on the project; Jean Scott and the rest of the staff of Bristol Classical Press for overseeing its production; Roger Davies and Charles Fisher for assistance with the cover; Gloria Gunson for help with the proofs; successive classes of students for allowing themselves to be experimented on; and most of all, for his wisdom, patience and kindness, Guy Lee, *sine quo non*. Needless to say, the responsibility for any blunders or wrong-headedness still apparent is entirely mine.

J.B., *Swansea 1994*

Note on the translations

Of the versions by Guy Lee here offered those of the *Amores* are by far the freest. They are based on the following principles:

Exact translation of poetry is impossible.

One is not translating words but re-presenting meaning.

Aim at a version that can't be altered without loss.

Reach it by repeated revision.

Get the rhythm right and the length preferably less.

Imply what you can't state.

The translator of poetry is writing a poem of his own under the inspiration of his original.

The versions of Catullus are at the opposite extreme and based on the following principles:

The translator of poetry should be, like Aeneas, PIVS.

His problem is one of PIETAS.

Let him regard his original as a sacred text from which it is anathema to deviate.

Every live metaphor must be kept, no new metaphor foisted in.

Weigh each word of the original: is this an ordinary word? a rare word? a poetical word?

The translator must represent the primary meaning faithfully and resist the temptation to intrude himself.

Translation is an exercise in self-discipline.

Between these two extremes the versions of Tibullus by Joan Booth stand roughly midway; Guy Lee's versions of Propertius are closer to those of Catullus. The layout of the versions has been standardised. Except where indicated, all translations of Latin and Greek texts within the Introduction and Commentaries are by Joan Booth; those of elegiac lines, even though non-metrical, keep wherever possible to the layout of the original couplets.

A.G.L., *Cambridge 1999*
J.B., *Swansea 1999*

Introduction

1. The genre

(a) Content and characteristics

'Love elegy' is the name usually given to the poetry in elegiac metre[1] and on amatory themes composed during the last 30 years or so of the first century BC, in the principate of Augustus, by Propertius, Tibullus and Ovid. The Romans themselves also counted Cornelius Gallus[2] (69-26 BC) as a love elegist, and Catullus, in the first half of the century, was an important pioneer for them all. Six love elegies (of universally acknowledged dullness) by a poet who calls himself 'Lygdamus', but seems keen to pose as Ovid, and may in fact belong to the first century AD,[3] have survived as part of the *Corpus Tibullianum*.[4] So have six of probably Augustan date under the name of a woman, Sulpicia (these have attracted much interest from feminist critics in recent years[5] – though one scholar now argues that Sulpicia was a man![6]). The dominant personal form of the genre, however (i.e. the one in which the male poet himself plays the lover – the type of elegy exemplified in the present selection of poems) appears to have reached the end of its life with Ovid's *Amores*.

Post-Catullan personal love elegies vary from about 20 to just over 100 lines in length (though most are in between) and tend to revolve around a few stock characters and situations. The chief characters are the lover and his beloved; the beloved is normally a named woman, though Tibullus writes about a boy-friend in addition to his two mistresses. The lover is relatively poor and non-aristocratic, but sensitive and talented, relying on his poetry to win him the beloved's esteem and reciprocation. He is prepared to tolerate the odd lapse on her part but is grieved by chronic infidelity and is deeply jealous of any rival. He generally takes a romantic

---

[1] See pp. xv-xvii.

[2] See pp. xxvii-xxviii.

[3] For the vexed questions of his identity and dating and further discussion of his poems see Lee (1958-9), Parca (1986).

[4] See p. xxxix.

[5] See Wyke (1994) 114-15, with bibliography at 126, n. 1, and 127, n. 19.

[6] Holzberg (1999).

view of love, looking for spiritual and moral qualities in his beloved as well as sexual attractiveness, and he normally professes, for his own part, absolute fidelity and unfailing, subservient devotion (the Ovidian lover is an exception). The women themselves are invariably beautiful, intelligent, sophisticated, artistically accomplished and expensively dressed. To their lovers they are usually unfaithful and disobliging, grasping and imperious. They are also unavailable to those lovers on a permanent basis, either because they are married, or because they are cohabiting with some other man, or because they are controlled by a brothel-mistress; marriage with their lovers is out of the question. Time spent puzzling over whether a particular woman in Augustan love elegy is supposed to be an adulterous wife, a freedwoman-courtesan or a common prostitute is largely wasted. The distinctions were doubtless sometimes blurred even in real life,[7] and Propertius, Tibullus and Ovid simply do not bother about consistency in presentation of status, but just make the beloved unobtainable for whatever reason suits the situation they have chosen to explore in any given poem. It is equally pointless to try to construct a chronology for any real love-affairs in which the poets participated, or to make definitive judgements on their character, purely on the basis of the love-situations they portray in their poetry and the reactions to them they profess. For there is no reason whatever why everything they recount should have happened to them personally or happened exactly as told.[8] Nor, at the other extreme, is it necessarily right to follow the modern theoretical critics and deny any connection at all between the poet himself and the character he assumes in his elegies.[9] Common sense (which the theorists would argue cannot, by definition, exist) suggests that what we are offered by the writers of personal love elegy is most likely to be 'an amalgam of fact and fiction, convention and invention' (Lee [1962] 153).

The bedrock of post-Catullan personal Latin love elegy is a single stock situation: an 'eternal triangle' involving the lover, his beloved and a rival of some kind. The rival has various incarnations. The most common is that of a male admirer of the beloved who usurps her affections. His status may be completely unspecified, but we are sometimes told that he is rich – or, even worse, *nouveau* rich – that he travels abroad (on commercial or military business) and that he is emphatically not a poet. The reader

---

[7] See Griffin (1985) 28, and cf. p. xxix below.

[8] See Allen (1958).

[9] Those who adopt this position, following Veyne (1988), insist on speaking of 'The I person' or 'Ego' rather than, say, 'Tibullus' or 'Propertius'. Some take an even more radical 'anti-realist' line; see pp. xliv-xlv.

is to assume, though, that the beloved is herself attracted by him. This is not the case with another rival figure: the husband or recognised partner[10] who is the head of the beloved's household. He may be old or ugly (or both), and he is usually alleged to be stupid, but he frequently has to be deceived or outwitted before the lover and the beloved can get together. Yet another different type of rival is female – a girl other than the beloved, with whom the lover amuses himself. This girl is not at all the sort of self-assured, independent-minded creature who can command the lover's long-term commitment. Rather she is a common prostitute or a lady's maid, exploited on a casual basis when the lover wants consolation during rifts with his beloved, or to arouse her jealousy, or simply to enjoy 'a bit on the side'. Slaves of sundry kinds are well represented among the subsidiary stock characters of elegy; they include the doorkeeper, the chaperon, and the personal servant who acts as the go-between of the lover or beloved. Standard figures too are the crone who knows all about love-magic and the unscrupulous brothel-mistress. On an entirely different level there is also the lover's (male) friend, to whom poems are sometimes formally addressed. With the central threesome of lover, beloved and rival these other characters at various times interact (occasionally the supposed friend emerges as a rival himself).[11]

Many of the more notable stock situations of Augustan personal Latin love elegy are versions of the basic triangular set-up. For example, the beloved's husband or partner tends to make a nuisance of himself by locking the house-door and putting it and the beloved under guard to deter nocturnal visits from the lover. But the lover presents himself at the door by night all the same, usually the worse for drink, and hoping, in vain, to gain admittance through subterfuge, cajolery, bribery or intimidation. Sometimes it is not the measures taken by the husband which prevent his admittance, but the disinclination or greed of the beloved herself, who may demand a high price in money or presents, or favour a richer petitioner. At all events, the predicament of the 'locked-out lover' (*exclusus amator*) is one of the most pervasive of all stock elegiac situations. Others relevant to the present selection of poems are: (i) the lover's actual or threatened separation from his beloved (when she has gone away with the rival or the lover himself has to travel from home); (ii) his accusing her of infidelity, or being accused of it on his own part, in a face-to-face show-down; and (iii) his venturing to offer expert advice on amatory problems, as a veteran of them himself. Reflective and moralising themes not in themselves

---

[10] The Latin *uir* can indicate either of these; a freedwoman's *uir* could be her former master.

[11] Most, but not all, of these stock characters appear in the present selection of poems.

specifically amatory are also recurrent. Of special relevance to the poems here are the lover's complaint of the corrupting influence of wealth and his concern with the consequences of death – not just for love, but also for love *poets*. The standing and worth of love poetry is a general preoccupation of the Augustan elegists. 'Programmatic' poems, in which they air their views on the value of their chosen genre and their chosen way of life often stand in prominent places like the beginning or end of a book (and occasionally elsewhere).[12]

Augustan personal love elegy displays numerous features generally characteristic of ancient Greek and Roman literature, including what has become known as 'intertextuality'. Broadly defined, this is the use of direct or indirect allusion in one text to words or content in another text, or simple reliance on the reader's acquaintance with that other text, to convey a new message or create a new effect.[13] Even within the small selection of poems in this book many examples of it will be encountered.[14] Personal love elegy also shares a number of its standard techniques and elements of its subject-matter with other poetic genres, especially personal lyric (such as Horace's *Odes*), pastoral (such as Virgil's *Eclogues*) and epigram. Virtually all the notable surviving examples of love epigram before Catullus are Greek and are collected in Books 5 and 12 of the *Greek Anthology* (*Anthologia Palatina*).[15] Personal love elegy's favourite forms are narrative, soliloquy and direct address, but increasingly an interest is shown in dramatic monologue, in which a single speaker addresses one or more other parties, whose presence and (sometimes) responses are signalled by carefully contrived passing remarks. In common with all other stylistically elevated poetic genres of the time, love elegy draws frequently on Greek, and occasionally on Roman, mythology for decorative allusion or for illustration of a human phenomenon or experience. Some recurrent elegiac imagery, too, is universally common (e.g. the notions of love as fire, disease or madness). But some of the elegists' favorite metaphors, even if adumbrated earlier, are developed for maximum impact in the general Roman, or specifically Augustan, context. The portrayal of love as slavery will have been particularly striking in a society where slavery was a real, dreaded

---

[12] Cf. pp. 60, 69-70.

[13] The recognition of intertextual messages, as opposed to mere echoes or instances of imitation, in ancient literature, and especially in Latin poetry, is an important critical development of the last decade; see Hinds (1998).

[14] Some, but not all, will be signalled by mention of the word 'intertextual' or 'intertextuality' in the commentary or notes.

[15] See pp. xviii-xix.

and despised condition – self-abasement was not considered in any way ennobling in the pre-Christian era. The idea of love as a form of military service will have had special piquancy in the Augustan age, when soldiering proper was one of the careers which responsible citizens were encouraged to follow.[16]

A quintessential feature of all love elegy is of course its metre, the elegiac couplet (after which the genre is named). Any attempt at brief description of this runs the risk of over-simplification, but perhaps the following rather crude attempt may still convey something of the elegiac couplet's characteristic rhythm and melody.[17] The metres of classical Latin poetry are primarily based not on word-stress,[18] as in English verse, but on weight of syllables ('quantity'). 'Heavy' syllables are those with either a vowel naturally pronounced long or one which can count as long if it is immediately followed by two or more successive consonants (but *l* and *r* as the second of the two do not *always* artificially lengthen the preceding vowel). Heavy syllables (let us say *tum* to represent them) are conventionally indicated by the sign –. 'Light' syllables are those with a vowel naturally pronounced short; these are conventionally indicated by the sign ⌣ (let us say *ti* to represent these). Another basic feature is 'elision'. When a Latin word ending with a vowel (or a vowel plus *m*) is immediately followed by a word beginning with a vowel (or *h* plus a vowel), the syllable ending the first of these two words is 'elided', i.e. it is pronounced so lightly as to be discounted altogether for the purposes of the metre. Thus, for example, in the famous first line of Catullus 85 which begins *odi et amo*, *i* at the end of *odi* is elided before the following initial *e* of *et*: *od(i) et amo*.

Fairly fixed arrangements of long (heavy) and short (light) syllables make up specific types of poetic lines. The hexameter consists of six metrical units, conventionally called 'feet' (rather like musical bars), in which long and short syllables are distributed thus:

$$- \underset{\smile}{\smile} \mid - \underset{\smile}{\smile} \mid - \underset{\smile}{\smile} \mid - \underset{\smile}{\smile} \mid - \smile \smile \mid - \underset{\smile}{-}$$

---

[16] Cf. p. xxxi.

[17] The English versions of the poems selected for this volume all make some attempt to preserve the couplet's metrical character; see also p. ix.

[18] This is not to say that word-stress plays no part at all in Latin metre, but its exact role is too complex to be included in the present, very basic, synopsis, which is primarily intended to inform the non-linguistic reader.

The first four feet are variable, in each either two longs – – (a 'spondee')
or a long and two shorts – ⌣⌣ (a 'dactyl'), two shorts being the equivalent
of one long. The fifth foot, however, is regularly a dactyl and this results in
a distinctive rhythm at the end of the hexameter:

tum ti ti | tum tum

(or | *tum ti*; the very last syllable of the line is variable).[19] In addition there
is normally a break ('caesura'), indicated by the sign ||, roughly mid-line
where the end of a word comes after the first long syllable of the third, or
sometimes the fourth, foot.

The pentameter consists of five feet, falling into two units of two and a
half feet, sharply divided by a caesura, and heavy and light syllables are
distributed thus:

$$ - \overset{\smile}{\smile} \mid - \overset{\smile}{\smile} \mid - \mid\mid - \smile\smile \mid - \smile\smile \mid - $$

Again some variation is possible in the first half of the line, but the whole
of the second half is fixed: a peculiarly satisfying

tum ti ti | tum ti ti | tum.

These two lines together, hexameter and pentameter, form the elegiac cou-
plet. The couplet is normally the sense unit, with the pentameter in some
way resolving what the hexameter presents; it may complete, complement,
repeat or contrast with the hexameter's meaning.[20] The constant alterna-
tion of these two lines in a Latin elegy thus makes for an agreeable blend
of regularity and variation. Like all other classical Latin metres, the elegiac
couplet does not rhyme in the modern way; nor is it arranged, like some
Latin lyric metres, in a stanzaic pattern. The couple of samples below, with
the metre marked out,[21] may help to illustrate it.

Catullus 76. 19-20

$$ - \ \smile\smile \ \mid \ - \ \smile \ \smile\mid-\mid\mid-\mid - \ \mid \ - \smile \ \smile\mid - - $$

me miser(um) aspicit(e) et si uitam puriter egi

$$ - \smile\smile \ \mid \ - \ \ - \mid-\mid\mid- \ \smile \ \smile\mid \ - \ \ \smile \ \ \smile\mid- $$

eripit(e) hanc pestem perniciemque mihi

---

[19] Exceptions to this produce a strikingly unusual rhythm; see e.g. Catul. 76. 15, where the
fifth foot of the hexameter is a spondee.

[20] See further pp. 134-5.

[21] This marking out of the metre is technically known as 'scansion'; lines so marked are
said to be 'scanned'.

Ovid, *Amores* 2. 8. 27-8

$- \; \smile \smile \, | - \; - \, | - \; \smile \smile \, | - \| \smile \smile \, | - \; \smile \; \smile \, | - \; -$

quoque loco tecum fuerim quotiensque Cypassi

$- \; - \, | \; - \; \smile \; \smile \, | - \| \; - \; \smile \; \smile \, | -- \; \smile \; \smile \, | -$

narrabo dominae quotque quibusque modis.[22]

The elegiac couplet (which love elegy shares with the epigram, both ama-
tory and non-amatory) was in origin Greek. Indeed, most Roman poetic
genres were in entirety further developments of Greek ones; and when the
first-century AD critic Quintilian says 'In elegy too we challenge the
Greeks' (*elegia quoque nos Graecos prouocamus* [*Institutio Oratoria* 10.
1. 93]), it sounds as if the elegiac genre is no exception, for he seems to be
claiming for the Roman love elegists not so much originality as high qual-
ity. The issue, however, is a complex one, as we shall see, and it may be
that what we have from Quintilian is in fact an elegant understatement
which does his countrymen down.

(b) Development

Greek verse had been written in elegiacs for a very long time before the
couplet became one of the main vehicles for Roman personal love po-
etry.[23] As early as the seventh century BC Mimnermus had composed ele-
gies which covered a wide range of subjects, including love.[24] Is im-
possible to know, however, because of the fragmentary state of the extant
texts, whether the love there was supposed to be the poet's own, (as was
the case in Greek lyric of the seventh/sixth century BC written by, for ex-
ample, Sappho[25]) or that of some other character, real or mythological.
External sources tell us that Mimnermus was himself in love with a flute-
girl called Nanno and that he gave her name to one of his poems or
collections, but again it is uncertain whether the work in question was
about his love for her, or whether the use of her name as a title was merely
a gracious compliment. From at least as early as the fifth century BC sur-
vives a collection of certainly personal love poems in elegiacs attributed to
Theognis (though not in fact by him). They are short pieces (most no more

---

[22] For more detail on the metre see Kenney (1990) xxvii-xxix.

[23] The other form in which it was written was lyric, such as Catullus' polymetrics and
Horace's *Odes*. Cf. n. 60 below.

[24] For the most famous surviving fragment see p. 27. n. 24.

[25] See pp. xxxv, 29.

than half a dozen lines[26]) dealing exclusively with male homosexual love. The fifth century also saw the production of the *Lyde*, an elegiac poem at least two books long by Antimachus of Colophon. It was named, like Mimnermus' *Nanno*, after a woman he reputedly loved. The content was clearly predominantly, and perhaps exclusively, mythological, though the possibility that the mythological element was somehow framed by reference to Antimachus' own love cannot be ruled out.[27]

Evidence for Greek poetry in elegiacs on amatory subjects in the Hellenistic period (third to first century BC) is much more plentiful, but still incomplete. Most of what survives is in the form of epigrams, very short in length (rarely more than ten lines and usually between two and six), humorously ironic in tone and ostentatiously witty in style. They regularly depict what is ostensibly the writer's own love, and the male homosexual relationship features quite as often as the heterosexual one. Here are a few examples from the extensive collection in the *Greek Anthology* (the translations, though non-metrical, keep to the layout of the original elegiac lines).[28]

> If you burn my scorched soul often,
>> Love, it will flee. It too, villain, has wings.
>>
>> Meleager, *AP* 5. 57

> Child Love, you are really killing me. Empty on me
>> all your quiver-stock, leaving not an arrow more.
> That way you would kill me alone with your shafts, and wanting
>> to shoot at another, you would no longer have a barb.
>>
>> Archias, *AP* 5. 58

> Snow, hail, be dark, lighten, thunder,
>> shake out all your purple clouds over the earth!
> If you kill me, then I will stop; but if you let me live,
>> though I go through worse than this, I will come serenading.
> For the god who drives me is your master too, Zeus; at his bidding
>> you turned into gold and breached the tower of bronze.
>>
>> Asclepiades, *AP* 5. 64

---

[26] Some scholars, however, think that some of the surviving blocks of text are extracts from longer poems.

[27] So argues Cairns (1979) 219-20.

[28] More examples on pp. 23, 37, 51-2, 139.

The night is long and wintry and sets in with the Pleiad in mid-course;
   and I, drenched, go back and forth by her threshold,
wounded by desire for that treacherous one. For not with love
   did Cypris strike me, but with a tormenting dart from the fire.

Asclepiades, AP 5. 189

Didyme has carried me off with her twig [of inducement]. Alas! I
   melt like wax before the fire, when I look upon her beauty.
And if she is black, what of it? So are the coals, but when we
   light them, they glow like rosebuds.

Asclepiades, AP 5. 210

Sweet is the boy and sweet to me also the name Myiscus
   and full of charm. What excuse do I have for not loving?
For, by Cypris, he's beautiful, utterly beautiful. And if he gives pain –
   Love knows how to mix bitterness with honey.

Meleager, AP 12. 154

Enough to demonstrate that the unobliging beloved, the locked-out lover, the imagery of fire and sickness and the mythological example were all the stock-in-trade of these neat but – in emotional depth as well as compass – insubstantial elegiac poems.

Longer Greek poems in elegiacs, however, were also widely written, on various subjects, in the Hellenistic period. None was more influential than the *Aetia* ('Causes') of Callimachus of Cyrene (c. 305–c. 240 BC), poet and scholar at Alexandria, and also the writer of *Hymns*, *Iambi*,[29] love epigrams and a mythological narrative, the *Hecale*. The four books of the *Aetia* covered a wide range of personal and non-personal topics, but, as their name suggests, their unifying feature was their attempt to account for the existence of various names, cults, practices, artefacts or phenomena by reference to mythological stories. 'Aetiological' poetry was a general fashion of Callimachus' time; but it was poetic manner as much as matter which interested him. He made a hero of the eighth-century BC Greek poet Hesiod,[30] who wrote didactic works in hexameters on farming (*Works and Days*) and on the genealogy of the gods (*Theogony*). The *Theogony* provided Callimachus with a precedent for divinely sanctioned didactic poetry

---

[29] See p. xxiv.

[30] See Callimachus, *AP* 9. 507. Cameron (1995) 362-86, however, contests the claim of Callimachus' general reverence for Hesiod.

(Hesiod had claimed to have been directly inspired by the Muses[31]), but Callimachus sought to outshine Hesiod in every aspect of style. He cultivated polish, erudition, and fine attention to detail, and displayed all these features in relatively small-scale works rather than aiming at the monumental compass and bombastic manner of traditional heroic epic. He was memorably belligerent about these aesthetic principles of his, and nowhere more so than in the preface to his *Aetia*. Here are some of the most telling lines (frag. 1. 13-38 Trypanis;[32] for the sake of maximum clarity in English no attempt has been made in the case of this fragmentary text to keep to the layout of the original elegiacs):

> (And this I [say] to the Telchines) 'Let the crane, which takes pleasure in the blood of the pygmies, [fly] from Egypt to the land of the Thracians, and let the Massagetae shoot from afar (15) at the [Medes]; but [nightingales] are so much the sweeter. Be off with you, destructive tribe of Jealousy! From now on [judge] skill by art, and not by the Persian measure. And do not look to me to produce a song loudly roaring; thundering is not for me, but for Zeus.' (20)
>
> For, when I first placed a writing-tablet upon my knees, Lycian Apollo said to me:
>
> '[...] poet, [feed your] sacrificial victim to be as fat as possible, but your Muse, my good friend, keep slender. This too I bid [you]: tread the ground which wagons are not forever traversing (25) and do not [drive your chariot] in the same ruts as others, nor along the broad road, but on [unworn] paths, though your course be narrower. For we sing among those who like the sweet sound of [the cicada], and not the din of the [...] asses.' (30)
>
> Let [others] bray like the long-eared beast, but let me be the small, the winged one – yes, yes indeed! – so that I may sing, living on dew-drops, [free] food from the divine air, and at once shed old age, which weighs upon me (35) like the triangular island upon deadly Enceladus. [But no matter], for those whom the Muses have not looked askance at as children they do not cast off as friends when they are grey.

---

[31] See p. 57, n. 102.

[32] Even the lines which survive are incomplete; the square brackets mark editorial supplements or remaining lacunae.

The cryptic expression and ostentatious learning of this poetic manifesto is itself a good example of the 'Alexandrian' style which Callimachus commended. It also sets forth the key Alexandrian stylistic principles – the criteria by which Callimachus wished poetic 'skill' (line 18) to be judged. These can be summarised as follows. (i) Smallness of scale: the far-flying cranes, the far-shooting Massagetae and the Persian measure (this was supposed to be about 60 stades) all symbolise rejected protraction of length. (ii) Restraint and delicacy: nightingales (if that supplement is correct), slenderness, the sweet song and airy wings of the tiny cicada, with its ability to live on dew-drops, stand for the exquisite refinement to be desired, while thunder, fatness and braying asses stand for the repudiated grandiloquence and bombast. (iii) Avoidance of the commonplace: the broad road and the common tracks symbolise the ruck which is to be shunned, and the narrow, wagon-free path the difficult and *recherché* which are to be pursued.

The preoccupation with Jealousy (the name of the Telchines, a mythical island people, seems intended to stand for 'spiteful critics') reveals an almost paranoid streak. Similar pronouncements are made by Callimachus elsewhere.[33] These words give the impression that their author believes himself to be one hundred per cent right and, what is more, in a minority of one. In all probability, though, he was not unique. The name of Philitas[34] of Cos (born c. 320 BC) is on several occasions coupled with Callimachus' in programmatic and inspirational contexts as model *par excellence* for non-epic, and especially amatory, poetry in the Alexandrian style,[35] and he may well have shared many of Callimachus' stylistic views without making such a fuss about them.[36] But Callimachus' fuss was to prove very appealing to the New Poets of Republican Rome[37] and, for different reasons, also to the Augustans after them, who made a *leitmotiv* in particular of Apollo's warning to the poet.[38]

The commended Alexandrian style of the *Aetia* to all intents *is* the style of the Augustan elegiac poets, and, along with other Roman poets of

---

[33] See p. 70, n. 172.

[34] Probably a more correct form of the poet's name than 'Philetas', which is also found from Augustan times onwards and used to be preferred by modern scholars; see Bowie (1985) 72, n. 27.

[35] See e.g. Prop. 3. 1. 3-6, 3. 3. 52.

[36] See Knox (1985), Cameron (1991).

[37] See pp. xxv-xxvi.

[38] See pp. xxxii-xxxiii.

their time, they showed considerable interest in one of this poem's episodes, the mythological love of Acontius and Cydippe in Book 3 (67-75 Trypanis).[39] It is clear enough in fact that mythological love of all kinds featured frequently in longer Hellenistic poems in elegiacs (longer, that is, than epigrams). But did these Greek poets write about personal love in separate longer elegies? Or did their longer elegiac poems involving mythological love also contain an element of personal love? And was either type of composition the chief model for the content and form of Latin personal love elegy? These are all points of very long-running debate, still unresolved because of the desperately fragmentary state of surviving Hellenistic elegy. Except for the personal element, almost all the basic features of Latin love elegy – its stock situations, characters, forms and imagery – are quite easily paralleled in Greek or heavily Greek-influenced genres which survive much more intact than Hellenistic elegy. Variations of the basic triangular situation, the confrontation scene, erotic teaching, the slave accomplice, the brothel-mistress, and the favourite metaphors of love (some, admittedly, in only rudimentary form) are all to be found in New Comedy, exemplified in Greek by Menander (fourth/third century BC) and in Latin by Plautus and Terence (third/second century BC), who followed Greek originals closely. This form of drama was generally characterised by its everyday atmosphere and its concentration on the experiences and problems of the individual rather than on political, philosophical or religious issues, as had been the case in Old Comedy. Stock elegiac situations, such as the separation of lover and beloved, also appear in later Greek prose writing – non-personal erotic letters[40] and erotic fiction.[41] Early twentieth-century German scholars, doubting, as many still do, the Roman creation of anything truly original in literature, attempted to explain the similarities between Latin love elegy, New Comedy and late Greek epistolography and fiction by positing a common source for them all in a competely lost corpus of Hellenistic personal love elegy, separate from that concerned with mythological love. The more open-minded, however, realised that there is no reason why the Latin elegists should not have drawn directly on New Comedy – Roman as well as Greek – or why the comic dramatists and the later Greek epistolographers and novelists should themselves be denied all originality. The 'common source' theory

---

[39] See Kenney (1983).

[40] E.g. those of Alciphron (second/third century AD), Philostratus (third century AD) and Aristaenetus (fourth/fifth century AD).

[41] E.g. the novels of Chariton (first century AD), Longus (second/third century AD) and Heliodorus (third/fourth century AD). See further Holzberg (1995).

subsequently came to be regarded with justifiable scepticism in the absence of firm evidence for the existence of a corpus of Hellenistic elegy of the type posited.[42] The case of Philitas well illustrates the instability of the ground. He certainly wrote elegiac poems containing episodes of mythological love, and he was reputedly in love himself with a woman named Bittis.[43] It has often been suggested, on the basis of external factors, that he also wrote about his own love in elegiacs, possibly within a pastoral context,[44] but no more than about 40 lines of his poetry are extant, many of them disembodied or incomplete, and none contain anything to substantiate the elaborate speculation.[45]

Recently published papyri, however, justify yet another rethink on the whole vexed issue of what kind(s) of Hellenistic love elegy existed and how much, if at all, the Latin form of the genre was directly influenced by it. Four papyrus fragments from Oxyrhynchus (discussed and conveniently translated by Butrica [1996]) are of some relevance. All of them are obviously, even in their severely mutilated state, from elegiac poems longer than the average epigram, and their date of composition is almost certainly Hellenistic.[46] The content of two of them of special interest. (i) *P. Oxy.* 3723 offers 23 incomplete lines containing a reference to the story of Hercules and Hylas and perhaps one to a similar erotic liaison involving Dionysus and a boy; the last line apparently contains some sort of despairing self-address by the speaker. (ii) *P. Oxy.* 2885 offers 21 incomplete lines which contain a series of references to mythological women, includeing Medea and Scylla, daughter of Nisus, who all murdered for love, followed by four lines in which a woman appears to be accused by the speaker of being too consumed by love herself to listen. It thus seems quite possible – but is by no means inevitable – that the speaker in each case is supposed to be the poet himself who is in love – in love with the addressee

---

[42] See e.g. Day (1938), Griffin (1985) 198-210.

[43] Knox (1993) assumes that she was his wife.

[44] See e.g. Luck (1969) 38-9, and for the pastoral theory Cairns (1979) 25-7, Hunter (1983) 76-83, Bowie (1985), Thomas (1992); Knox (1993) 68 and Cameron (1995) 418-20 are among those who contest it. Cf. also p. 133, n. 17. All the extant Hellenistic poetry which does treat love in a pastoral context – by Theocritus (third century BC) and his imitator Bion (perhaps writing c. 100 BC) – is written in hexameters and from a non-personal point of view.

[45] How much of Philitas' work was actually known first hand to later generations of either Greek or Roman writers is another matter of debate; contrast e.g. Bulloch (1973) 84 with Knox (1993).

[46] See the detailed arguments in Butrica (1996) 298-312. I am grateful to Professor Wolfgang Luppe for correspondence on this point.

in (ii) and with some boy, or even some girl, in (i).[47] If all this surmise is correct, the belief that the Hellenistic Greeks wrote about personal love in elegiac poetry must be reinstated. The chances, however, that the personal element dominated to anything like the extent that it did in the Latin form of the genre still seem slim. It is more likely that the Greek poets used the personal element, if they used it at all, as a frame for relatively extended treatment of mythological love.[48] In short, the combination of subject-matter, slant, technique, length and metre found in Augustan Latin love elegy still appears to have been something new.

This is not of course to deny all direct Greek or even other Roman influence on Augustan love elegy. Dramatic monologue, ironic tone, and complaints of lovers being corrupted by wealth are all to be found in the *Iambi* of Callimachus, a collection of thirteen poems (not all extant, and most very incomplete) on miscellaneous themes and unified only by their iambic or choliambic metre and sharp, lively manner. *Iambus* 3, which obviously dealt in part with wealth's corrupting influence on a boy-beloved, seems likely to have directly inspired Tibullus 1. 8 and 1. 9.[49] Elegy's dramatic monologues and confrontation scenes also have clear affinities with a heterogeneous corpus of material rather imprecisely called 'mime'. This included both literary compositions (poems and scripted sketches) and improvised knockabout performances. The literary form at its most polished is exemplified by the Greek *Mimiambi* of Hero(n)das (third century BC), poems which present scenes supposedly from real life and often with an amatory slant; for example, one concerns a woman chastising a slave ex-lover for sleeping with somebody else, and another an old procuress trying to interest a young woman in a new lover. There is usually one main speaker, but other speaking or silent characters may also participate. Some of the *Idylls* of Theocritus (or those attributed to him) are cast in much the same mould. Whether these poems were intended purely for reading or were performed, in public or in private, is much debated.[50] The prose or prose-and-verse scripted sketch seems to have been a low-level

---

[47] J.M. Bremer and P.J. Parsons, the original editors of *P. Oxy.* 3723, felt that the possible use of allusions to the loves of mythological characters to point the writer's own amatory experience in a manner not unlike Propertius' suggested a post-Augustan rather than Hellenistic date of composition (so also Parsons separately in an article written in German [1988]).

[48] Such, in essence, is Butrica's judicious conclusion ([1996] 312-16), though much of his preceding discussion is tendentious.

[49] See pp. 116 and 119, and further Dawson (1946).

[50] See Hutchinson (1988) 241-2, Cameron (1995) 89-90.

literary counterpart to the improvised type of sketch, doubtless presenting many of the same themes and characters.[51] It became a popular form of entertainment in the Hellenistic and later especially the Augustan theatre. Most frequently a single speaker presented a series of dramatically related episodes in quick succession and without explicit connection;[52] the catching of a wife red-handed with an adulterer was one regular ingredient.[53] Enough to suggest, at all events, that the influence of mime of every kind on the themes and structure of Augustan love elegy should not be underestimated.

The Hellenistic love epigram itself had Latin imitators around 100 BC. Here are a couple of surviving examples (the translation, though again non-metrical, keeps to the layout of the original elegiac lines):

> When I try to tell you, Pamphila, of the troubled love in my heart,
>> the words to say what I seek from you desert my lips.
> A sudden sweat courses over my breast, aroused as I am;
>> so, struck silent and aroused, I am ashamed and I am lost.
>>>> Valerius Aedituus, frag. 2 Büchner

> You who are the guardians of lambs, the tender progeny of sheep,
>> do you seek fire? Come here. You [still] seek it? The fire is a man.
> I shall set the whole wood on fire at once, if I lay a finger on it.
>> The whole flock is ablaze – everything I set eyes on.
>>>> Porcius Licinus, frag. 6 Büchner

As in the Hellenistic Greek examples, the emphasis here is on irony and wit. Both the substance and the imagery are essentially conventional. Neither lover nor beloved has any individuality, and there is no attempt to give the impression of real emotional involvement.[54]

In the wake of these early epigrammatists, however, came the 'New' (or 'neoteric') 'Poets', operating between about 70 and 45 BC. This is the label usually given to the group of which Catullus is really the only survivor

---

[51] Laberius (c.106–43 BC) is the best-known Roman exponent, but the surviving fragments of his work are not informative.

[52] See Hubbard (1974) 52-3.

[53] See McKeown (1979), Fantham (1988-9).

[54] The six books of 'Playful Erotics' (*Erotopaegnia*) by Laevius (writing early in the first century BC) are the only other pre-Catullan Latin poetry on love known to us. Mythological, not personal, love was again the subject, and not elegiacs but various lyric metres (see n. 60 below) were used. See further Ross (1969) 155.

(though the work of other members of it, such as C. Helvius Cinna and Catullus' close friend Licinius Calvus, was clearly held in high regard). Theirs was the generation of Romans which really 'discovered' Alexandrianism in the sense that they deliberately chose to make that style their own and, moreover, to make an issue of it. The existence of Alexandrian Greek poetry must have been well known for some considerable time, and its manner certainly influenced others earlier,[55] if in a less wholesale and less dramatic way. Why did the New Poets, then, latch on to it as they did? Doubtless because its real newness in its own time and the revolutionary spirit associated with it through the truculent pronouncements of Callimachus in particular were exactly the sort of features which would appeal to a group of like-minded Young Turks with literary inclinations. Swimming against the tide and being ahead of popular taste were an essential part of the fun, and if their work, as is alleged, drew the scorn of Cicero,[56] as a dyed-in-the-wool adherent of the 'old' poets,[57] the New Poets would no doubt have been delighted. They did not seek mass adulation, but were an élite coterie, a 'set' rather than a formal school, who were out to please each other and enjoyed each other's support. Catullus never gives the Callimachean impression of embattled isolation.[58]

The inclinations of the New Poets led to a vogue for relatively short narrative hexameter poems in the Alexandrian style on mythological and non-heroic themes. The only surviving example is Catullus 64 (*The Marriage of Peleus and Thetis*), which is 408 lines long and suggests that nonheroic themes in effect meant love themes.[59] Along with this new interest in narrative poems on mythological love – if again Catullus is anything to go by – developed an interest in poetry on love from a personal point of view. To explore an affair with the woman he calls Lesbia Catullus turned to the two genres in which personal love was traditionally treated: lyric,[60] and elegiac epigram (72 and 85 are examples of the latter). One poem (76), however, seems by virtue of its combination of emotional depth with greater-than-epigrammatic length to be on the borderline between epigram

---

[55] See Cameron (1995) 28-9.

[56] See Cicero, *Tusculan Disputations* 3. 45.

[57] E.g. Q. Ennius; see p. 65.

[58] See further Quinn (1969) 44-69.

[59] Cinna's *Smyrna* and Calvus' *Io* were probably similar in type of content and tone, though their length is uncertain.

[60] For an example see pp. 31-2. The term 'lyric' is here used to cover short poems in Greek metres, including Sapphic stanzas, Phalaecian hendecasyllables and 'limping iambics' (properly called choliambics or scazons).

and elegy. Poem 68 is another Catullan composition of immense pioneering importance. Within this longer elegiac poem[61] personal love, which had been primarily associated (at least in elegiac metre) with the epigram, is treated more seriously, *and* it is illustrated by mythological love, which had been primarily associated with Hellenistic narrative elegy, such as the Acontius and Cydippe episode of the *Aetia*. Though the recently published papyri now suggest that the Hellenistic poets may not have kept the two types of love as separate as had previously been imagined, there is still no reason to suppose that Catullus 68 is anything but the first poem to connect them in such an intricate and yet oblique way. Nothing as complex as Catullus 68 seems to have been ever attempted again, but similar things in a simpler, scaled-down form do appear in, for example, Propertius.

Between Catullus and Propertius, however, intervened the shadowy figure the Romans themselves seem to have counted as the first elegist:[62] Cornelius Gallus, soldier-poet and friend of Virgil, who committed suicide in 26 BC when he fell from grace with Augustus as a result of his self-aggrandizement as Prefect of Egypt. He is not *quite* so shadowy now as he once was. Until 1978 only one uninteresting pentameter of his poetry was known, but in that year nine lines of elegiacs confidently identified as his came to light in a papyrus from the Nubian desert (the Qaṣr Ibrîm fragment).[63] These lines suggest that he was, if anything, even 'rougher' than Quintilian implies,[64] and that compliments to 'Caesar' (possibly Augustus[65] but probably Julius Caesar[66]), whether sincere or not, occasionally issued from his pen. Unfortunately, however, the recently published lines tell us nothing at all about the role that he played in the development of love elegy during the period after Catullus and before the emergence of Propertius and Tibullus. For this we still have to rely mostly on surmise from what Virgil says about him in *Eclogues* 6 and 10 and what Virgil's fourth-century AD commentator Servius says about Virgil (how closely the real Gallus resembled the Virgilian Gallus we just cannot tell). From Servius (on *Eclogue* 10. 1) we gather that Gallus composed four books of poems, probably entitled *Amores* ('Loves'), about a woman he calls Lycoris.

---

[61] 120 or 160 lines; 1-40 may belong to a separate poem.

[62] See Ov. *Tristia* 4. 10. 51-4.

[63] Text and translation in Anderson, Parsons and Nisbet (1979) (= Nisbet [1995] 101-31, with updated bibliography at 432).

[64] See p. xliv.

[65] So e.g. Crowther (1983) 1646-7.

[66] So e.g. Nisbet (1979) 151-2 (= *id.* [1995] 124-5).

This was a pseudonym for the actress Cytheris, who was reputedly also the mistress of Mark Antony. Virgil implies too at *Eclogue* 6. 64-73 that Gallus wrote some sort of aetiological poetry in the Callimachean-Hesiodic style, and Servius tells us that Parthenius of Nicaea provided him with a prose handbook of sad mythological love-stories[67] to use as the basis of his poetry. So it looks as if Gallus wrote personal love poems in elegiacs and some sort of mythological love poetry. It has generally been assumed that these were separate compositions, though to insist on this now seems unwise in the light of what the recent papyri have suggested about Hellenistic elegy.[68] The temptation is to speculate further on whether anything Gallus wrote could have somehow bridged the gap between the personal and the mythological rather less precariously than does Catullus 68, and so prepared the way for the likes of Propertius 1. 1 and 2. 13.[69] But the evidence at present allows only inconclusive conjecture.

(c) Context

Gallus is a particularly interesting figure in that he managed to be simultaneously (at least in the earlier part of his career) a love poet, a soldier and a respected member of the governing establishment. Such a combination of roles became increasingly difficult under Augustus. The late Republic, on the other hand, was in some ways a most tolerant society. Admittedly, firmly entrenched in traditional social and moral thinking was the idea that a middle- or upper-class young man's duty was to serve his country in politics or the army, marry a woman of similar social standing and duly produce heirs. Similarly entrenched was the idea that excessive indulgence in leisure and pleasure, particularly of a Greek kind, was decadent and dangerous, be it material (liking for luxury in food, clothes and artefacts) or emotional (sybaritic satisfaction of the sexual appetite).[70] But men had no need, if they so chose, to let these views interfere much with their private lives. Marriage was in theory by consent and therefore potentially able to accommodate both romantic and sexual love, but in practice it was more often than not dynastically motivated and not based on what the modern world would call love at all (if this developed later, it was generally just extremely good luck!). Pre-marital and extra-marital liaisons for

---

[67] *Erotica Pathemata*; these had in turn been collected from Euphorion, a writer of Alexandrian mythological narratives in the third century BC.

[68] Ross (1975) already disputes this assumed dichotomy, but cf. the review by Zetzel (1977).

[69] See pp. 35-44 and 55-64.

[70] See e.g. Livy 34. 4. 1 ff., 39. 6, Polybius 31. 25, and cf. Griffin (1985) 4-15.

upper-class men were thus not condemned, provided that they were not indulged in with unmarried girls, other men's wives or supposedly respectable widows. Sexual pleasure with either common prostitutes or more classy Greek courtesans, often freedwomen (either freelance or run from an up-market brothel), was considered perfectly acceptable, provided it was kept within bounds. Many well-known statesmen availed themselves of this permissive attitude (e.g. Scipio Aemilianus). Society was not, however, nearly so tolerant where women were concerned. The lives of upper-class women were in practice exceedingly circumscribed. Child-bearing was primarily what a Roman wife was for, and beyond that housekeeping and spinning wool were all that was expected of her. A famous epitaph[71] commemorates a woman for exactly these occupations; another exemplary wife in this tradition was Cornelia, the mother of the Gracchi.[72] If a married woman strayed from this boring round, her reputation was at risk, but no wonder that some well-born women of intelligence did – especially when they were able to see the much more attractive lifestyle enjoyed by the courtesan-class. Some aristocratic women simply indulged in the courtesans' leisure activities (e.g. Sempronia, an associate of the conspirator Catiline and probably the mother of Brutus, Caesar's assassin, who was said to sing and dance better than she should have been able to[73]), while others took up their lifestyle more radically (e.g. Clodia the wife of Q. Metellus Celer, alleged to have poisoned her husband and dispensed her sexual favours to half of Rome[74]). The very sophistication of such women and also the exciting whiff of scandal and nonconformity about them would have made them very attractive to the likes of the New Poets. The existence of this type of woman allowed the development of the concept of romantic love, where the beloved inspired devotion through qualities other than purely sexual attractiveness, but remained unobtainable on a permanent basis.[75] She represented in fact the ideal marriage-partner in emotional, not practical, terms. The involvement of a man like Catullus with such a woman may have provoked gossip and muttering,[76] but this – the

---

[71] *Laudatio Turiae*; see Horsfall (1983).

[72] She justifies her own life from beyond the grave in Prop. 4. 11.

[73] Sallust, *Catiline* 25.

[74] See Cicero, *Pro Caelio* 32, and cf. p. xxxiv.

[75] This is well defined and discussed by Rudd (1981).

[76] See e.g. Catul. 5 and 7.

pointing of the disapproving but fairly powerless finger of the moralists in his direction – was on the whole the worst that could happen.[77]

Upper-class adult males of the time could also indulge without censure in certain sorts of homosexual liaisons before or outside marriage. Being the lover of an adolescent boy as well as a girl, or depicting oneself as such in poetry, would have raised few eyebrows on moral grounds, provided that the boy was of inferior social status. A sexual relationship with a male was not thought to be qualitatively different from one with a female in terms of the emotions it could excite and the satisfaction it could offer. The Romans differed from the Greeks, however, in their attitude to the passive partner in a homosexual relationship – the one who was penetrated. Greek convention dictated that the active partner was to reward the boy for the sexual pleasure that he gave him (like a woman, the passive was assumed not to derive much himself) by becoming his sponsor, mentor and friend as he outgrew the relationship on reaching full manhood.[78] But among the Romans the passive was regarded with scorn and derision, and was cast off without a qualm when his adolescent appeal expired. A slave or a freedman might be expected to submit, willingly or under duress, but no freeborn Roman citizen should take on what amounted to 'the woman's role' in sexual intercourse.[79]

Politics intruded little on the life which a man like Catullus could enjoy in this relatively free and easy milieu. It is particularly interesting that he could openly mock, insult or dismiss with indifference important public figures of the time – Cicero (Poem 49), Mamurra, Julius Caesar's notorious engineer (Poems 29 and 57) and even Caesar himself (Poem 93).[80] Why could the Augustans apparently not do the same? The chief reason was Augustus. A series of civil wars in the 40s and 30s BC had left him, the great nephew and adopted son of Julius Caesar,[81] almost by default, the sole ruler of the Roman world following his defeat of Mark Antony at the battle of Actium in 31 BC. He subsequently embarked on consolidating his position and encouraging in various ways the creation of a new personal image. His general policy was to pose as the restorer of the old rather than the bringer-in of the new, and accordingly he gave his

---

[77] The foregoing discussion is indebted to Lyne (1980) 1-18; see also Pomeroy (1975) 150-204, Treggiari (1991), 5-13, 83-124, 229-61.

[78] See Dover (1978), especially 49-51, 81-91.

[79] See further Wiseman (1985) 10-13, Williams (1995), Booth (1996) 245-6.

[80] An anecdote offered by Suetonius has it that Caesar was in fact upset, but, after Catullus had made some sort of token gesture, Caesar invited him to dinner.

[81] 'Augustus' was the honorific title taken by C. Julius Caesar Octavianus (Octavian) in 27 BC.

enthusiastic support to traditional moral values and institutions. Under him private luxury was officially frowned upon and private austerity approved. Soldiering, public service and religious observance were all officially encouraged. The romantic, free-wheeling life was officially discouraged in a drive for sexual probity which was presented as a moral crusade but was in fact politically and economically motivated (the 'Julia-laws' of 18 BC were designed to strengthen marriage and boost the birthrate of legitimate Roman citizens). Sophisticated intellectual and artistic activity was expected to have an edifying function and some practical usefulness. Whether these developments represent a concerted 'agenda' devised and ruthlessly implemented by Augustus himself or, rather, reflect the mostly spontaneous response of his citizens to his standing and influence (*auctoritas*) is yet another matter of huge debate;[82] but whatever the truth, a remarkably coherent official ethos there certainly was. What Augustus really thought of the intrinsic worth of sophisticated literary activity is impossible to discern, but he avoided any inflammatory moves to suppress it. Doubtless he saw that it *could* flourish to his own advantage, since writers of the time as a matter of course gave public exposure to the persons, views and interests of their friends and associates. Doubtless, too, for this reason he was glad to have as his own close friend and political adviser (though he never held political office) Gaius Maecenas, a man who was much involved in the literary scene. This wealthy and cultured aristocrat had already drawn to him during the 30s BC a group of outstanding Roman poets, including Virgil and Horace, and Propertius was to join them in the 20s. The terms 'patronage' and 'circle' conventionally used with reference to Maecenas' relations with the Augustan poets are probably misleading. The poets were neither as beholden to him as were clients to a patron nor on such an equal footing with him – or even necessarily with each other – as membership of a 'circle' suggests. Rather, the relationship was the warm and reciprocal one of 'friendship' (*amicitia*[83]), but a friendship of unequals and of individuals who had some, but not all, interests and views in common. Never could the poets match what Maecenas could give by dint of his wealth and influence, but what they could offer him was a continued place in the public eye through the medium of their poetry.[84] In

---

[82] The two positions outlined are extremes, the former adopted by Syme (1939) 440-75 and the latter by Galinsky (1996). The majority view is somewhere between the two; see e.g. Zanker (1988), who examines the ethos of the period as seen through its iconography and plastic arts.

[83] See also p. 25.

[84] So, persuasively, White (1993) 3-34.

this milieu it is easy to envisage Maecenas functioning as a useful kind of 'interface' between Augustus and the poets. From seeing how the poets portrayed Maecenas, Augustus would know what poets as 'friends' could do, and through Maecenas the poets would know what *his* friend would like, and hence what their own friend would like from them to please him, namely, for them to keep Augustus also in the public eye as a matter of course and to portray him in the same edifying and sympathetic light. For Maecenas or even Augustus in person, when he later counted Virgil and Horace among his own 'friends', to have conveyed such desires to the poets falls far short of directing or commissioning them to write something. The pressure exerted by friendship was more subtle, but pressure of a kind it undoubtedly was none the less.[85]

So, although all artists worthy of the name wish to be free to follow their own inclinations, most of the poets who wrote under Augustus are likely, for the reasons outlined above, to have felt under an obligation of politeness to him at the very least. There is another factor to consider, too, if we are to be realistic about human nature. Augustus had come to power on a tide of blood and was to all intents and purposes in sole power. He must have seemed a distinctly frightening figure; the situation was unprecedented, and nobody knew what he might do. It would be understandable if the poets, who had attracted his attention and perhaps even given him ideas through their association with Maecenas, felt uneasy about offending or disappointing him. It was in this context that they seized upon the motif of Apollo's warning to the poet from Callimachus' *Aetia* and adapted it to make a humorous, elegant and gracious excuse for not providing what they were aware that Augustus would have *really* liked (whether or not he actually said so): a traditional epic about his own exploits. That adaptation has become known as the 'refusal' (*recusatio*) and is one of the favourite programmatic motifs of the Augustans.[86] The Callimachean stance appealed to them just as much as to the New Poets, but not because they were themselves stylistic revolutionaries. The 'refusal' is their means of begging themselves off the *subject-matter* they find distasteful. Style by this time was probably no longer a burning issue, for the learned, obliquely allusive and exquisitely refined Callimachean style was by now the only style that any self-respecting poet would adopt, even if he did write epic, as Virgil in the *Aeneid* showed. Arguably also the Callimachean

---

[85] Cf. Griffin (1984) for a somewhat different approach but essentially the same conclusion. Along with others, I have sometimes in the past described Maecenas as a kind of 'unofficial Minister for the Arts'; I now consider this misleading.

[86] See pp. 69-71, 132-4.

motif particularly appealed because its associations with belligerent independence could lend the illusion of spirit to the Augustans' own careful apologetics. One cannot help wondering, though, what Callimachus himself would have made of non-epic in the Alexandrian manner being presented not as the best in itself, but as the type of poetry fit for poets who could manage nothing more![87]

2. The poets

In the absence of the equivalent of a dust-jacket note on the author in the case of most ancient poets, we have to rely for information about their lives and circumstances on a mixed bag of sources: such supposedly autobiographical references as they do make from time to time, deductions from other details in their work, comments by contemporary authors, and ancient biographies sometimes written centuries later, when a 'mythology' had had time to grow up. This means that the picture may be generally sketchy or deficient in certain fundamentals. When judging from what a poet himself says, it always has to be taken into account that circumstances can be invented and points exaggerated or minimised to suit the artistic purpose of the moment. On the other hand it is perverse to take the view that all anecdotal evidence is by definition worthless, or that a detail is bound to be fictitious just *because* it appears in a work of art.[88] What is more, the commonplace can be invented and the unusual true – and vice versa. It is with those cautions, therefore, that the following summaries are offered of what is known or might be surmised about the lives of Catullus, Propertius, Tibullus and Ovid and about the dating of their work. For convenience we can refer to a book's 'publication', but it is as well to remember that there was no formal launching of a written version in the ancient world; rather the poet's work was first presented to his public when he himself read such parts of it as he chose to an invited audience.

---

[87] Cameron (1995) 454-7 is right to stress that the poet's belittling of his own talent is not a Callimachean motif. He may also be right to suggest (456) that the inspiration for this feature is more likely to be four lines of the Greek pastoral poet Bion (6. 8-11).

[88] The pages which immediately follow, and especially citation of Apuleius' (in)famous recording of the supposed real names of Lesbia, Delia and Cynthia, will be no doubt be anathema to theoretical critics of Latin personal love elegy (cf. pp. xii and xliv-xlv, with nn. 9 and 144). Yet they can no more prove the information wrong than anyone else can prove it right.

(a) Catullus

Gaius Valerius Catullus is the only one of the four love poets here represented who belongs to the pre-Augustan age. We can deduce from comments by the fourth-century AD Christian writer Jerome and a reference to Julius Caesar's expedition to Britain in 55 BC in what was probably one of Catullus' last poems (11) that he was born in 84 BC and died in 54 BC. His family home, before he moved to Rome and became one of the smart set,[89] was Verona in Cisalpine Gaul, and his father was a wealthy local landowner,[90] said to be in the habit of entertaining Julius Caesar. Catullus himself was doubtless also comfortably off (the pennilessness he complains of in Poem 13 sounds more like a temporary cash-flow problem than real hardship). He mentions several times a brother, buried in the Troad (Poem 101), whose premature death devastated him (Poems 65, 68). In his late teens Catullus apparently did the sort of thing well-brought-up young men were supposed to do in preparation for a conventionally respectable and prosperous career, for he alludes to serving on the staff of Memmius, governor of the province of Bithynia in 57-56 BC (Poems 10, 31, 46). After that, if the picture of his life presented in his work is remotely authentic, he appears to have done practically nothing that would have 'counted' in conservative eyes, but rather to have given himself up completely to the 'New Poetry' and to love of an exceptionally intense and romantic kind for an utterly riveting but (in his eyes) unworthy woman.

Who was Lesbia? According to Apuleius, writing in the second century AD and using at least third-hand information, the name was a pseudonym for one Clodia.[91] There was indeed a notorious woman of this name in the Rome of Catullus' time, who lived her life very much in the manner of the Lesbia of the poems. This was the wife, and subsequently widow, of Q. Metellus Celer;[92] she was also the sister of the notorious tribune P. Clodius Pulcher.[93] This Clodia had an affair with the young protégé of Cicero, M. Caelius Rufus, and in Poem 58 Catullus talks bitterly to a Caelius about 'our' Lesbia, as if both of them had a stake in her. Yet there are problems in identifying Lesbia with this Clodia. The most serious of them is that Catullus confesses to being an adulterer in his relationship

---

[89] See pp. xxv-xxvi.

[90] Perhaps a businessman; see Wiseman (1985) 100.

[91] Apuleius, *Apology* 10.

[92] See p. xxix.

[93] Both Clodius and Clodia (together with Clodia's two sisters) had adopted plebeian versions of their respective original patrician family names Claudius and Claudia.

with Lesbia, but none of his poems about her can securely be dated before 56 BC, by which time Metellus' Clodia was no longer his wife, because he was dead. Either Clodia had remarried before her affair with Catullus; or his Lesbia was not Metellus' Clodia, but one of her two sisters, who *were* married at the time in question; or Lesbia was not any of them at all, the identification being mere gossip or guess.[94] But whoever Lesbia was or was not, why that particular pseudonym? It literally means 'woman of Lesbos', and might be thought to be an appropriate sobriquet for any Greek or Greek-style courtesan, but there is more to it than that. The most famous of all 'women of Lesbos' was the female poet Sappho,[95] whose home the island was, and Catullus makes it doubly clear that thoughts of her lie behind his choice of pseudonym for his own mistress by writing what are probably chronologically his first and last poems about her (51 and 11 respectively) in the Sapphic metre.[96] His choice sets an enduring fashion for giving a poetic beloved a name which itself in some way connotes poetry.

The extant single collection of 116 poems, ranging from epigrams of only two lines to a narrative poem of over 400 (Poem 64), is ordered not by subject-matter (of which there is a considerable variety) or by chronology, but by metre. Whether the order is Catullus' own, however, is an unresolved question.

(b) Propertius

Sextus Propertius[97] obviously had enough self-confidence to think that an autobiographical note of some sort would be required to satisfy the curiosity of his readers when his Book 1 of his elegies began to circulate.[98] For he closes it with a ten-line epigram announcing his birthplace as Umbria and mentions that he had a kinsman killed in the siege of Perusia (in

---

[94] See further Lee (1991) xx-xxii, Wiseman (1969) 50-60.

[95] Cf. p. xvii.

[96] In Poem 51 he follows closely a poem of Sappho's own; cf. p. 29.

[97] There is no record of a third name, a *cognomen*, for Propertius; not all Romans had one of these extra personal names.

[98] Book 1 has also come to be known as the *Monobiblos* ('Single Book'), a title which appears in some but not all of the MSS, and it is generally thought to have circulated under this name before the later books were 'published', probably all together. Heyworth (1995) 175-8 challenges this assumption, arguing that *Monobiblos* is the title of a bookseller's anthology of the whole of Propertius. Certainly there seems to be reason to doubt that the title is Propertius' own, but it is still possible for it to refer to the first book only and for that book to have originally circulated separately. Was the *Monobiblos* perhaps a special, bookseller's reissue of Book 1 in response to popular demand?

neighbouring Etruria), which took place in 41 BC.[99] In the first poem of Book 4 (lines 119-34) he fills out the picture a little more. His reputation, he says, has brought fame to Assisi, which suggests that he was born in this particular Umbrian town. He implies that his family had 'old money', but he does not specifically claim equestrian or aristocratic status. His father had died when he was a boy, and his family's property had been diminished by land confiscations. Presumably he means those of 41-40 BC following the defeat of the murderers of Julius Caesar by Octavian and Mark Antony at the battle of Philippi in 42 BC. All this happened before he really grew up or, as he says, 'assumed the toga of manhood' (*toga uirilis*), a ritual which normally took place between the ages of fourteen and seventeen. From this it may be deduced that he cannot have been born before 57 BC; and it was probably no later than 50 BC, given that first publication could be expected when he was in his twenties, and his earliest datable poems belong to about 30 BC. He says himself that he opted for full-time poetry in preference to oratory (which would naturally have led to a career in law or politics) when he was quite young. He seems therefore to have done even less 'proper' work than Catullus. He may have been married, for the younger Pliny mentions one Passennus Paullus as a descendant of his; but he could have just adopted an heir.

Various roughly datable references in his poems point to Book 1 (22 or 23 poems) being published around 30 BC,[100] Book 2 (the MSS present 34 poems[101]) around 26 BC, Book 3 (25 poems) around 23 BC and Book 4 (11 or 12 poems) around 16 BC.[102] He may have died soon after this, but was certainly dead by AD 2, when Ovid, referring to that year at *Remedia Amoris* 763, speaks of him in the past tense.[103] Already in Book 1 Propertius is prepared to defend his preference for the life of love rather than the life of action (1. 6) and for love poetry rather than war poetry (1. 7 and 1. 9), but he does not at this stage address his remarks directly to Maecenas,[104] as he does in Books 2 (Poem 1) and 3 (Poem 9). This suggests that it was after, and perhaps on the strength of, the appearance of Book 1 that

---

[99] The poem (1. 22) can be read as an indication of anti-Caesarian feeling.

[100] By this time, if his remark at 1. 11. 21-4 reflects his own real circumstances, his mother was also dead.

[101] Their poem-division, however, is unreliable, and Book 2 is in any case almost certainly an amalgamation of two original books; see Heyworth (1995), Lyne (1998a) 21-2, and cf. pp. 60-61.

[102] For the character of each of these books see p. 94.

[103] For the dating of his poems in relation to Tibullus' see pp. xxxviii-xxxix below.

[104] See pp. xxxi-xxxii.

he was accepted into Maecenas' group.[105] It is generally assumed from Horace's sneering remarks about the sort of poet who calls another 'a Callimachus'[106] as an extravagant but meaningless form of compliment that he did not like Propertius, for the 'Roman Callimachus' was exactly what Propertius himself claimed to be at 4. 1. 64. This, however, probably singles out Propertius unfairly, for Horace also sneers at the idea of contemporary Roman poets calling each other 'an Alcaeus' and 'a Mimnermus', but no specific targets have been identified behind these.

A woman he calls Cynthia was Propertius' poetic equivalent of Catullus' Lesbia. Before her, he claims (1.1.1-2), he did not know what love was; an old flame of sorts called Lycinna, whose existence he admits to in 3.15, simply did not count.[107] But Cynthia is even harder to identify than Lesbia, though Apuleius again[108] comes up with a name: Hostia. There may be something in it (Cynthia in the poems has a more or less consistent character), but if Hostia *was* the name of a real woman in Propertius' life, this woman is totally unknown.[109] At all events, the name Cynthia, like the Catullan Lesbia, is symbolic: it was emphatically a woman with *poetic* possibilities who 'first captivated' Propertius (1. 1. 1), for 'Cynthian', after Mt Cynthus on the island of Delos, was a cult-title of Apollo, god of poetry, who was born there.[110]

(c) Tibullus

Albius Tibullus was as reticent about himself as Propertius was forthcoming. We do not even know his first name (*praenomen*), Albius being his family name (*nomen*) and Tibullus his extra personal name (*cognomen*). He mentions a mother and sister in 1. 3, but whether these represent his real family again we do not know. There exists a very brief anonymous ancient *Life* of Tibullus, probably derived from the first/second-century AD biographer Suetonius, but everything in it could well be inferred from

---

[105] Another point against the idea that Book 1 never did circulate separately in advance of the other books; cf. n. 98 above.

[106] Horace, *Epistles* 2. 2. 100.

[107] Lycinna, he implies, obligingly introduced him to sex, but Cynthia to unrequited passion. Possibly he invented the pre-Cynthia affair at the later stage in order to be able to explore the idea of the beloved's jealousy of a predecessor.

[108] See nn. 88 and 91 above.

[109] The extreme view is that Cynthia is entirely fictitious; so Wyke (1987), though even she is prepared to concede a possible whiff of reality about the woman behind the name in Book 1.

[110] See also p. 41, n. 29.

Tibullus' own poetry[111] or from other sources. The most important of these is Horace, *Epistles* 1. 4, addressed to one 'Albius', who has a country estate in Latium at Pedum between Tibur and Praeneste. This fits with the beloved country property which features in Tibullus' own poetry,[112] but there is no mention of a 'Tibullus' in Horace's poem. The identification is made on the strength of another Horatian poem, *Odes* 1. 33, in combination with the *Epistle*. The *Ode* is addressed to an 'Albius' who writes love elegies lamenting his own amatory suffering. Horace counsels him to stop and to understand that the eternal triangle is a fact of life.[113] The chances of the Albius of the *Ode* not being Albius Tibullus the elegist, and the Albius of the *Epistle* not being the same as the Albius of the *Ode* seem remote. Tibullus the elegiac lover claims that his family property has fallen on hard times and is considerably smaller than it used to be.[114] This could indicate that the real Tibullus' property suffered, as Propertius claims that his did, from the land confiscations of 41-40 BC.[115] Horace teases the Albius of the *Epistle* about his comfortable circumstances, and he could have been prompted to this by Tibullus' affectation of poverty in many of his elegies. At all events, if Horace's Albius is our Tibullus, it is clear that Horace liked him ('fair judge [*candide iudex*] of my *Sermones*', he calls the epistolary addressee) and was on terms of fairly close friendship with him. His poetry does at times seem to allude to Horace's,[116] and his generally modest manner would have been likely to commend him to a senior.

Tibullus' life cannot be dated with any more certainty than Propertius'. An Augustan epigram by Domitius Marsus commemorating his death implies that it took place around the same time as Virgil's, i.e. in 19 BC. If Tibullus was indeed, as it says, 'a young man' when he died (*iuuenis* is a fairly elastic term in Latin covering anything from sixteen to forty-five), he could have been born as early as 64 BC. Probably, though, it was

---

[111] E.g. from Tib. 2. 3. 81-4 the fact that he was a bit of a dandy; see p. 121.

[112] Especially Tib. 1. 1 and 1. 5; see pp. 100-101 and p. 125.

[113] Interestingly Horace gives as an example a set-up in some respects reminiscent of that in Tibullus 1. 8 and uses one of the same names, Pholoe.

[114] Tib. 1. 1. 19-24, 33-42.

[115] When, however, Horace hints at something similar at *Epistles* 2. 2. 49-51 and Virgil could at least be thought to be doing so in *Eclogues* 1 and 9, there must be a slight suspicion that fashion rather than fact was behind all this 'personal suffering' at the hands of the powerful. Did it somehow enhance a poet's credibility – rather in the way that some sort of childhood trauma has become an almost essential ingredient in autobiography of modern times?

[116] See p. 107.

later, perhaps about 57 BC, for Ovid intimates at *Tristia* 4. 10. 31-4 that Tibullus was older than Propertius. We can surmise that Book 1 (10 poems) was published soon after the Triumph awarded to Messalla Corvinus (see below) in 27 BC for his victory in Aquitaine, since 1. 7, which celebrates his birthday, marks that event. This means it would have appeared slightly later than Propertius' Book 1.[117] But it is fairly clear that Tibullus' Book 1 was complete and circulating before Propertius' Book 2, since Propertius at 2. 5. 21-6 seems to allude to Tibullus 1. 10. 59-62. An official list from 18 BC suggests that the appointment of the *quindecimuir* which Tibullus celebrates in his second book (see below) was in 18 BC a recent event, and it therefore looks as if Book 2 might be dated to the year of Tibullus' death, 19 BC. The short length of Book 2 (6 poems) is certainly in keeping with a sudden, unplanned curtailment of poetic activity.[118] A third book (divided into two by Renaissance scholars) has been transmitted under Tibullus' name but is not by him. The three books together (or sometimes just the spurious Book 3) are now known as the *Corpus Tibullianum* ('Tibullan Collection'). Propertius and Tibullus never mention each other directly, but Propertius implies criticism of Tibullus at 2. 5. 21-6, and Tibullus arguably ventures one or two slyly ironic correctives of Propertius' overblown attitudes in his first book.

Unlike Catullus and Propertius, Tibullus, if he is representing himself at all authentically in his poetry, does seem to have had something in the way of a conventional career, and even continued to pursue it, if without enthusiasm, while writing poetry. Surprisingly he was (like Cornelius Gallus[119]) apparently a professional soldier, accompanying his supporter and benefactor M. Valerius Messalla Corvinus, a distinguished aristocratic statesman, orator and man of letters, as well as a successful military commander, on an overseas campaign in Gaul[120] and on an expedition to the Levant.[121] The ancient *Life* even claims that he won military distinctions.[122] Messalla is conventionally described as Tibullus' patron, and yet the relationship between them was clearly every bit as much a 'friendship'

---

[117] See further Murgatroyd (1980) 13-15.

[118] But cf. p. 109, with n. 49.

[119] See pp. xxvii-xxviii.

[120] See Tib. 1. 7.

[121] See Tib. 1. 3, where he says he fell ill on the outward journey and had to be left behind in Corcyra.

[122] This, however, may be just an inference from Tib. 1. 7. 9 (addressed to Messalla): 'not without me was your glory gained' (*non sine me est tibi partus honos*).

as that between Maecenas and any of his literary group.[123] Tibullus expresses both affection and respect for him, and he builds a whole poem (2. 5) around the installation of his son, Messallinus, as one of the fifteen priestly officials (*quindecimuiri*) who looked after the sacred Sibylline books. Messalla had the distinction of having retained his standing under Augustus, even though he had fought on the Republican side at Philippi (42 BC). Indeed, he was enough of a turncoat to be found fighting on Octavian's side at Actium as consul for 31 BC. Still, he gathered a flourishing literary group around him in the 20s BC which rivalled that of Maecenas, with *his* very different history. Messalla's deeply Republican past[124] would appear to have attracted especially those poets not prepared to pay lip-service to the Augustan ethos. Not only did it include Tibullus, who never even mentions Augustus once, but also the irreverent Ovid, who mentioned him often enough, but from his own point of view would have done better to keep quiet.[125]

Tibullus is unusual among the four love poets here represented not only in being apparently a man with a job and a relatively local Latin rather than a provincial, but also in that he writes about not one but three named beloveds – two women, Delia in Book 1 and Nemesis in Book 2, and in Book 1 also a boy, Marathus. The name Marathus is attested as that of one of Augustus' freedmen and is probably used by Tibullus for his boy-friend as an indication of the lowly origins and status of persons of his type.[126] Both Delia and Nemesis are invented, and certainly symbolic, names. Delia most immediately suggests 'Delian' Apollo, god of poetry, so-called after his birthplace.[127] It seems likely enough that Tibullus deliberately chose a name with the same sort of poetic associations as Lesbia and Cynthia, but without something more it does not offer a satisfying contrast with Nemesis, which in Greek means 'retribution'. Possibly Delia is supposed to suggest light and joy through the associations of Apollo and his Delos-born sister Artemis (Diana) with sun and moon respectively, while Nemesis, as the name of the daughter of Night in Hesiod's

---

[123] See pp. xxxi-xxxii.

[124] This is possibly reflected in Tibullus' association of him in 1. 7 with the continuation of ancient Roman tradition.

[125] On Messalla and his group see further Williams (1978) 65-9.

[126] See p. xxx. The name may also have some symbolic significance; see Murgatroyd (1980) 9.

[127] See p. xxxvii.

Theogony, is supposed to evoke darkness and sorrow.[128] For, whether Tibullus conceives of two different women in Books 1 and 2, or is merely showing us two sides of the same woman, in his Delia-book he clings to the possibility, however remote, of his love being reciprocated, but in his Nemesis-book concentrates on the grim prospect of endless suffering and rejection. Apuleius[129] claims that behind the name Delia was a real Roman woman called Plania. The Latin *planus* in fact means much the same as the Greek *delos*, i.e. 'clear', and for Tibullus to have been able to choose a name which plays on this, as well as having the poetic and emotional associations discussed above, really seems just too good to be true. But then, truth sometimes *is* stranger than fiction.

(d) Ovid

Publius Ovidius Naso has left us something more than the equivalent of a dust-jacket note: he has left us a complete CV – in the form of a poem (*Tristia* 4. 10). It was written from Tomis, a remote outpost of the Roman Empire on the Black Sea, to which Ovid was banished from the capital in disgrace in AD 8, and its ostensible purpose was to guard against the possibility of his officially becoming, in Orwell-speak, an 'un-person'. He obviously believes that his *poetry* at least will not be destroyed,[130] but will continue to be popular enough for his readers to care who he was. Anti-biographical critics are sceptical of almost every word in *Tristia* 4. 10[131] (even, in the most radical case, of Ovid's very claim to have been sent into exile), but although the poem is stylised in some respects[132] and as carefully honed as 'an entry in *Who's Who*' (Booth [1991] 1), it is difficult to see what Ovid could have had to gain from falsifying the most basic of its information, such as his date and place of birth (20 March, 43 BC, at Sulmo – modern Sulmona – in the Abruzzi). He belonged, he says, to a family of old equestrian rank, and he had a brother a year older to the day (a coincidence so curious that it sounds absolutely authentic), Before he died at the age of twenty, Ovid's brother set him an example in every way, doing well at school in Rome, where the two of them were sent, in the usual manner of the sons of the propertied classes, to be trained in rhetoric, i.e. the art of

---

[128] Bright (1978) 118-19.

[129] See nn. 88 and 91 above.

[130] This is somewhat illogical, for if any systematic attempt to obliterate his memory were going to be made, this would surely be the first step to be taken.

[131] See e.g. Holzberg (1997).

[132] See Fairweather (1987).

public speaking. This education was supposed to prepare them for a career in law or politics, towards which Ovid's brother duly progressed, but Ovid himself was even at this stage, he says, diverted by poetry.[133] His father was put out about this because he thought no poet ever made any money. So Ovid took himself in hand and assumed the 'toga of manhood' (*toga uirilis*) with his brother at the usual age of about sixteen.[134] They were both given the privilege of wearing the broad purple stripe (*latus clauus*), which theoretically proclaimed their candidature for the series of magistracies which would eventually lead to their elevation from equestrian to senatorial rank. In other poems[135] we are told that Ovid had a spell in Athens and travelled abroad with a friend after finishing his education in Rome; this was the 'done thing' for young men of his social rank. After his brother's premature death Ovid did hold some minor public offices (to compensate his parents for the loss of their more promising son?). But this 'reform' did not last long: he soon gave up the idea of upward-mobility for good and devoted the rest of his life to poetry.[136] First he made a point of hanging around all the prominent poets of the time in Rome. He specifically mentions Horace and Propertius as well as less famous figures and says death prematurely deprived him of Tibullus. We gather from elsewhere[137] that he was eventually accepted into the literary group of Messalla Corvinus, to which Tibullus also belonged. He saw himself as the natural successor of Propertius and first made his name with the *Amores* ('Loves'), the three books of love elegies mainly about a woman he calls Corinna. He had three successive wives, he reports, of whom the first was neither use nor ornament (*nec digna nec utilis* [*Tr.* 4. 10. 69]), the second was 'all right' (*sine crimine* [*Tr.* 4. 10. 71]) and the third was a paragon, who stood by him in his exile; he also claims one daughter and two grandchildren. Both his parents luckily died, he says, before he was banished to the place where he is now resigned to ending his days. Even he, for all his method, cannot supply the date of his death, but fortunately Jerome records it as AD 17.

---

[133] We learn from the elder Seneca and Quintilian that in his poetry he indulged the ingenuity which his teachers of rhetoric thought excessive for their discipline, good performer in the schools though he was judged to be; cf. p. 157.

[134] Cf. p. xxxvi on Propertius.

[135] *Tristia* 1. 2. 77, *Ex Ponto* 2. 10. 21-6, *Fasti* 6. 421-4.

[136] A familiar pattern by now, (cf. pp. xxxiv, xxxvi) but not for that reason necessarily untrue.

[137] *Ex Ponto* 2. 3. 75-8.

Three issues relating to Ovid are the subject of endless scholarly debate. The first is the cause of his exile. He himself says it was brought about by 'a poem and a mistake' (*carmen et error*[138]). The poem was the *Ars Amatoria* ('Art of Love'), a guide to how to pick up and prevail upon a woman.[139] This was alleged to incite women to adultery, and Ovid's own opening insistence that it was not meant for the eyes or ears of *married* women, predictably, cut no ice with Augustus. He is never explicit about the mistake. It seems to have been some unwitting involvement in the scandal surrounding the adultery of Augustus' granddaughter Julia in AD 8. This was perhaps the excuse Augustus needed to punish Ovid for the irritating *Ars*, against which he had been harbouring resentment ever since its appearance (to have exiled Ovid for a book alone would have been unprecedented and would have looked like extreme over-reaction).

The second area of persisting uncertainty about Ovid concerns the dating of his works. Besides the *Amores* he also wrote in the elegiac metre the *Heroides*, a collection of imaginary letters from mythological heroines to the lovers or husbands who had deserted them, the pseudo-didactic *Ars Amatoria* and its companion piece the *Remedia Amoris* ('Remedies for Love'), the *Fasti*, a kind of religious calendar, two collections of poems from exile, the *Tristia* ('Sorrows') and *Epistulae ex Ponto* ('Letters from the Black Sea'), and the *Ibis*, a curious piece of personal invective. In hexameters he composed the celebrated mythological epic the *Metamorphoses*; and he had a tragedy, *Medea*, to his name too, but it is now lost. To complicate matters, the *Amores* circulated in two different forms (according to Ovid himself in his prefatory epigram to the collection): five successive books first appeared (not exactly a first 'edition' in our sense of the term, but for convenience that is what it is usually called) and then later a kind of abridged omnibus edition of three books. Only the second edition survives, and how like or unlike the first edition it was is unknown but much discussed. Neither edition can be dated with any certainty; suffice it to say here that there is reason to suppose that the five books of the first appeared some time between 19 and 11 (or possibly 8 BC) and the three of the second by 2 BC at the latest.[140]

The third hotly debated issue is the identity of Corinna. Her obviously fictitious name is of the same symbolic nature as those of the other elegiac mistresses in that it is that of a third-century BC female Greek writer of

---

[138] *Tristia* 2. 207.

[139] Book 3 instructs a girl on how to go about getting a man.

[140] See further Booth (1991) 2-4. Holzberg (1997) 10-19 argues that the second 'edition' of the *Amores* and the *Medea* are both fictitious.

lyric poetry.[141] But, unlike the other poets, Ovid actively encourages his readers on occasions to believe that his mistress was a fictitious figure altogether, though at others he teasingly implies that maybe she was not. At all events, it clearly gave him satisfaction to think that nobody at the time could settle the matter;[142] and it might have given him even more, had he known that some people were still just as fruitlessly trying two thousand years on.

3. The challenge

'Tibullus is in my opinion the most polished and elegant writer [of elegy]. There are some who prefer Propertius. Ovid is more playful than both, just as Gallus is rougher' (*mihi tersus atque elegans maxime uidetur auctor Tibullus. sunt qui Propertium malint. Ouidius utroque lasciuior, sicut durior Gallus*). Such was the famous judgement of Quintilian (*Institutio Oratoria* 10. 1. 93) on the foursome of elegists in the recognised canon. In this volume you do not have Gallus, but you do have Catullus (and you may ask why Quintilian does not include him in the canon too). It is up to you now, reader, to sample these poets for yourself and make judgements of your own.

But before you do, and from wherever you start – with or without Latin – a word of encouragement: 'reading', in the fashionable sense of 'interpreting what has been written', is not only a more exciting but also a more individual business than reading in the literal sense of 'processing the written words by using the eye or the fingers'. All 'readers' will to some extent find what they look for in a classical text. Classical philologists and classical humanists will look for what they think the author wanted to communicate, believing it possible to discover this on the basis of their own linguistic and literary knowledge and their experience of human behaviour and emotion; they will often seek assistance from what social and political historians in turn believe to be objective truth about circumstances and events.[143] Theoretical critics will deny that objective truth of any kind is possible and will tend to discountenance every empathetic and historicist (or so-called 'realist') response to literature (termed

---

[141] Corinna the lyricist was once thought to belong to the fifth century BC; the name is also that of a prostitute in a late Greek dialogue (Lucian, *Dialogi Meretricii* 6).

[142] Even Apuleius (see nn. 88 and 91 above) has nothing to offer.

[143] See Rudd (1996).

'discourse' by theorists themselves). In their concern with the politics (in the broadest sense of that word) and the psychology of reader-response, they will look primarily for the social, political and intellectual structures and conditioning which alone, they believe, make a piece of writing 'mean' anything to anybody, anywhere, at any time. Some (the 'deconstructionists') will overturn even this position by maintaining that any identification of structures and conditioning is itself rendered unobjective by the structures and conditioning which have affected the identifier, and so *ad infinitum*.[144] Feminist criticism is a special branch of the theoretical approach, and in recent times it has naturally been much applied to Latin love elegy – writing almost exclusively by men about emotional and sexual relationships with women. When feminist critics 'read', they look for textual signals, sometimes explicit, sometimes oblique, of male attitudes towards females of every class and disposition; and any of these 'readings', like those of theoretical critics in general, can be turned inside out and upside down so that what was 'read' positively by one feminist critic as male 'empowerment' of the female can be 'read' negatively by another as mere depiction of unorthodox male subservience.[145]

The 'readings' of personal Latin love elegy which are offered in the present volume are essentially philological and humanist in their approach, but, even so, you are occasionally encouraged to consider another perspective, in particular the feminist one; and there is nothing to prevent you from doing it more often, if you wish. In any case, reader, now 'read', with confidence and with pleasure.

---

[144] See e.g. Kennedy (1993) and cf. n. 9 above. In theoretical criticism nothing ever *is*; everything is merely an indication of, or stands for, something else. A balanced and lucid survey of the theoretical approach to classical literature is offered by D.P. and P.G. Fowler (1996), and a lively counterblast to radical literary theory in general by Washington (1989).

[145] Contrast e.g. Hallett (1973) with Wyke (1989) 42-3, (1994) 118.

Latin Texts

CATVLLI CARMINA

LXXII

Dicebas quondam solum te nosse Catullum,
  Lesbia, nec prae me uelle tenere Iouem.
dilexi tum te non tantum ut uulgus amicam
  sed pater ut gnatos diligit et generos.
nunc te cognoui. quare etsi impensius uror,   5
  multo mi tamen es uilior et leuior.
'qui potis est?' inquis? quod amantem iniuria talis
  cogit amare magis sed bene uelle minus.

LXXVI

Siqua recordanti benefacta priora uoluptas
  est homini cum se cogitat esse pium
nec sanctam uiolasse fidem nec foedere in ullo
  Diuum ad fallendos numine abusum homines,
multa parata manent in longa aetate, Catulle,   5
  ex hoc ingrato gaudia amore tibi.
nam quaecumque homines bene cuiquam aut dicere possunt
  aut facere, haec a te dictaque factaque sunt.
omnia quae ingratae perierunt credita menti.
  quare iam te cur amplius excrucies?   10
quin tu animum offirmas atque istinc teque reducis
  et Dis inuitis desinis esse miser?
difficile est longum subito deponere amorem.
  difficile est, uerum hoc qualubet efficias.
una salus haec est. hoc est tibi peruincendum.   15
  hoc facias, siue id non pote siue pote.
o Di, si uestrum est misereri aut si quibus umquam
  extremam iam ipsa in morte tulistis opem,
me miserum aspicite et, si uitam puriter egi,
  eripite hanc pestem perniciemque mihi,   20

1

quae mihi subrepens imos ut torpor in artus
  expulit ex omni pectore laetitias.
non iam illud quaero, contra me ut diligat illa,
  aut, quod non potis est, esse pudica uelit.
ipse ualere opto et taetrum hunc deponere morbum.   25
  o Di, reddite mi hoc pro pietate mea.

LXXXV

Odi et amo. quare id faciam fortasse requiris?
  nescio sed fieri sentio et excrucior.

S. PROPERTI ELEGIARVM

LIBER PRIMVS

I

Cynthia prima suis miserum me cepit ocellis
  contactum nullis ante cupidinibus.
tum mihi constantis deiecit lumina fastus
  et caput impositis pressit Amor pedibus,
donec me docuit castas odisse puellas   5
  improbus, et nullo uiuere consilio.
et mihi iam toto furor hic non deficit anno,
  cum tamen aduersos cogor habere deos.
Milanion nullos fugiendo, Tulle, labores
  saeuitiam durae contudit Iasidos.   10
nam modo Partheniis amens errabat in antris
  ibat et hirsutas ille uidere feras;
ille etiam Hylaei percussus uulnere rami
  saucius Arcadiis rupibus ingemuit.
ergo uelocem potuit domuisse puellam: 15
  tantum in amore preces et bene facta ualent.
in me tardus Amor non ullas cogitat artis
  nec meminit notas, ut prius, ire uias.
at uos, deductae quibus est fallacia lunae
  et labor in magicis sacra piare focis,   20

en agedum dominae mentem conuertite nostrae
    et facite illa meo palleat ore magis!
tunc ego crediderim uobis et sidera et amnis
    posse Cytaeines ducere carminibus.
aut uos, qui sero lapsum reuocatis, amici,   25
    quaerite non sani pectoris auxilia.
fortiter et ferrum saeuos patiemur et ignis,
    sit modo libertas quae uelit ira loqui.
ferte per extremas gentis et ferte per undas
    qua non ulla meum femina norit iter.   30
uos remanete, quibus facili deus annuit aure,
    sitis et in tuto semper amore pares.
in me nostra Venus noctes exercet amaras,
    et nullo uacuus tempore defit Amor.
hoc, moneo, uitate malum: sua quemque moretur   35
    cura, neque assueto mutet amore locum.
quod si quis monitis tardas aduerterit auris,
    heu referet quanto uerba dolore mea!

III

Qualis Thesea iacuit cedente carina
    languida desertis Cnosia litoribus,
qualis et accubuit primo Cepheia somno
    libera iam duris cotibus Andromede,
nec minus assiduis Edonis fessa choreis   5
    qualis in herboso concidit Apidano,
talis uisa mihi mollem spirare quietem
    Cynthia non certis nixa caput manibus,
ebria cum multo traherem uestigia Baccho
    et quaterent sera nocte facem pueri.   10
hanc ego nondum etiam sensus deperditus omnis
    molliter impresso conor adire toro.
et quamuis duplici correptum ardore iuberent
    hac Amor hac Liber, durus uterque deus,
subiecto leuiter positam temptare lacerto   15
    osculaque admota sumere et arma manu,
non tamen ausus eram dominae turbare quietem,
    expertae metuens iurgia saeuitiae;
sed sic intentis haerebam fixus ocellis
    Argus ut ignotis cornibus Inachidos.   20

et modo soluebam nostra de fronte corollas
  ponebamque tuis, Cynthia, temporibus,
et modo gaudebam lapsos formare capillos,
  nunc furtiua cauis poma dabam manibus;
omniaque ingrato largibar munera somno,   25
  munera de prono saepe uoluta sinu.
et quotiens raro duxti suspiria motu,
  obstupui uano credulus auspicio
ne qua tibi insolitos portarent uisa timores
  neue quis inuitam cogeret esse suam –   30
donec diuersas praecurrens luna fenestras,
  luna moraturis sedula luminibus,
compositos leuibus radiis patefecit ocellos.
  sic ait in molli fixa toro cubitum:
'tandem te nostro referens iniuria lecto   35
  alterius clausis expulit e foribus?
namque ubi longa meae consumpsti tempora noctis,
  languidus exactis, ei mihi, sideribus?
o utinam talis perducas, improbe, noctes
  me miseram qualis semper habere iubes!   40
nam modo purpureo fallebam stamine somnum
  rursus et Orpheae carmine, fessa, lyrae;
interdum leuiter mecum deserta querebar
  externo longas saepe in amore moras –
dum me iucundis lapsam sopor impulit alis,   45
  illa fuit lacrimis ultima cura meis.'

LIBER SECVNDVS

XIII

Non tot Achaemeniis armantur Susa sagittis
  spicula quot nostro pectore fixit Amor.
hic me tam gracilis uetuit contemnere Musas
  iussit et Ascraeum sic habitare nemus,
non ut Pieriae quercus mea uerba sequantur   5
  aut possim Ismaria ducere ualle feras,
sed magis ut nostro stupefiat Cynthia uersu:
  tunc ego sim Inachio notior arte Lino.
non ego sum formae tantum mirator honestae
  nec si qua illustris femina iactat auos;   10

me iuuet in gremio doctae legisse puellae
  auribus et puris scripta probasse mea.
haec ubi contigerint, populi confusa ualeto
  fabula: nam domina iudice tutus ero.
quae si forte bonas ad pacem uerterit auris,   15
  possum inimicitias tunc ego ferre Iouis.
quandocumque igitur nostros mors claudet ocellos
  accipe quae serues funeris acta mei.
nec mea tunc longa spatietur imagine pompa,
  nec tuba sit fati uana querela mei,   20
nec mihi tunc fulcro sternatur lectus eburno,
  nec sit in Attalico mors mea nixa toro.
desit odoriferis ordo mihi lancibus, adsint
  plebei paruae funeris exsequiae.
sat sit magna mihi, si tres sint pompa libelli   25
  quos ego Persephonae maxima dona feram.
tu uero nudum pectus lacerata sequeris
  nec fueris nomen lassa uocare meum,
osculaque in gelidis pones suprema labellis
  cum dabitur Syrio munere plenus onyx.   30
deinde ubi suppositus cinerem me fecerit ardor
  accipiat Manis paruula testa meos,
et sit in exiguo laurus super addita busto
  quae tegat exstincti funeris umbra locum,
et duo sint uersus: QVI NVNC IACET HORRIDA PVLVIS   35
  VNIVS HIC QVONDAM SERVVS AMORIS ERAT.
nec minus haec nostri notescet fama sepulcri
  quam fuerant Pthii busta cruenta uiri.
tu quoque si quando uenies ad fata, memento,
  hoc iter ad lapides cana ueni memores.   40
interea caue sis nos aspernata sepultos;
  non nihil ad uerum conscia terra sapit.
atque utinam primis animam me ponere cunis
  iussisset quaeuis de Tribus una Soror!
nam quo tam dubiae seruetur spiritus horae?   45
  Nestoris est uisus post tria saecla cinis;
cui si longaeuae minuisset fata senectae
  barbarus Iliacis miles in aggeribus,
non ille Antilochi uidisset corpus humari
  diceret aut 'O mors, cur mihi sera uenis?'   50
tu tamen amisso non numquam flebis amico;
  fas est praeteritos semper amare uiros.
testis cui niueum quondam percussit Adonem

uenantem Idalio uertice durus aper;
illis formosum lauisse paludibus, illic   55
  diceris effusa tu, Venus, isse coma.
sed frustra mutos reuocabis, Cynthia, Manis,
  nam mea qui poterunt ossa minuta loqui?

LIBER TERTIVS

III

Visus eram molli recubans Heliconis in umbra
  Bellerophontei qua fluit umor equi,
reges, Alba, tuos et regum facta tuorum,
  tantum operis, neruis hiscere posse meis
paruaque iam magnis admoram fontibus ora   5
  unde pater sitiens Ennius ante bibit
et cecinit Curios fratres et Horatia pila,
  regiaque Aemilia uecta tropaea rate,
uictricesque moras Fabii pugnamque sinistram
  Cannensem et uersos ad pia uota deos,   10
Hannibalemque Lares Romana sede fugantis
  anseris et tutum uoce fuisse Iouem,
cum me Castalia speculans ex arbore Phoebus
  sic ait aurata nixus ad antra lyra:
'Quid tibi cum tali, demens, est flumine? quis te   15
  carminis heroi tangere iussit opus?
non hinc ulla tibi speranda est fama, Properti;
  mollia sunt paruis prata terenda rotis,
ut tuus in scamno iactetur saepe libellus
  quem legat exspectans sola puella uirum.   20
cur tua praescriptos euecta est pagina gyros?
  non est ingenii cumba grauanda tui.
alter remus aquas alter tibi radat harenas,
  tutus eris: medio maxima turba mari est.'
dixerat, et plectro sedem mihi monstrat eburno   25
  quo noua muscoso semita facta solo est.
hic erat affixis uiridis spelunca lapillis
  pendebantque cauis tympana pumicibus,
orgia Musarum et Sileni patris imago
  fictilis et calami, Pan Tegeaee, tui;   30
et Veneris dominae uolucres, mea turba, columbae

tingunt Gorgoneo punica rostra lacu
　diuersaeque nouem sortitae iura Puellae
　exercent teneras in sua dona manus.
haec hederas legit in thyrsos, haec carmina neruis　　　　35
　aptat, at illa manu texit utraque rosam.
e quarum numero me contigit una dearum
　(ut reor a facie, Calliopea fuit):
'Contentus niueis semper uectabere cycnis
　nec te fortis equi ducet ad arma sonus.　　　　40
nil tibi sit rauco praeconia classica cornu
　flare, nec Aonium tingere Marte nemus;
aut quibus in campis Mariano proelia signo
　stent et Teutonicas Roma refringat opes,
barbarus aut Sueuo perfusus sanguine Rhenus　　　　45
　saucia maerenti corpora uectet aqua.
quippe coronatos alienum ad limen amantis
　nocturnaeque canes ebria signa fugae,
ut per te clausas sciat excantare puellas
　qui uolet austeros arte ferire uiros.'　　　　50
talia Calliope, lymphisque a fonte petitis
　ora Philitea nostra rigauit aqua.

XXIV

Falsa est ista tuae, mulier, fiducia formae;
　olim oculis nimium facta superba meis.
noster amor talis tribuit tibi, Cynthia, laudes:
　uersibus insignem te pudet esse meis.
mixtam te uaria laudaui saepe figura　　　　5
　ut, quod non esses, esse putaret amor;
et color est totiens roseo collatus Eoo
　cum tibi quaesitus candor in ore foret –
quod mihi non patrii poterant auertere amici
　eluere aut uasto Thessala saga mari.　　　　10
haec ego non ferro, non igne coactus, et ipsa
　naufragus Aegaea uera fatebor aqua:
correptus saeuo Veneris torrebar aeno;
　uinctus eram uersas in mea terga manus.
ecce coronatae portum tetigere carinae;　　　　15
　traiectae Syrtes, ancora iacta mihi est.
nunc demum uasto fessi resipiscimus aestu
　uulneraque ad sanum nunc coiere mea.

7

Mens Bona, si qua dea es, tua me in sacraria dono.
   exciderant surdo tot mea uota Ioui.   20

LIBER QVARTVS

VII

Sunt aliquid Manes: letum non omnia finit
   luridaque euictos effugit umbra rogos.
Cynthia namque meo uisa est incumbere fulcro,
   murmur ad extremae nuper humata uiae,
cum mihi somnus ab exsequiis penderet amoris   5
   et quererer lecti frigida regna mei.
eosdem habuit secum quibus est elata capillos,
   eosdem oculos; lateri uestis adusta fuit
et solitum digito beryllon adederat ignis
   summaque Lethaeus triuerat ora liquor.   10
spirantisque animos et uocem misit; at illi
   pollicibus fragiles increpuere manus.
'Perfide, nec cuiquam melior sperande puellae,
   in te iam uires somnus habere potest?
iamne tibi exciderant uigilacis furta Suburae   15
   et mea nocturnis trita fenestra dolis
per quam demisso quotiens tibi fune pependi,
   alterna ueniens in tua colla manu?
saepe Venus triuio commissa est, pectore mixto
   fecerunt tepidas pallia nostra uias.   20
foederis heu taciti, cuius fallacia uerba
   non audituri diripuere Noti!
at mihi non oculos quisquam inclamauit euntis:
   unum impetrassem te reuocante diem.
nec crepuit fissa me propter harundine custos   25
   laesit et obiectum tegula curta caput.
denique quis nostro curuum te funere uidit,
   atram quis lacrimis incaluisse togam?
si piguit portas ultra procedere, at illuc
   iussisses lectum lentius ire meum.   30
cur uentos non ipse rogis, ingrate, petisti?
   cur nardo flammae non oluere meae?
hoc etiam graue erat, nulla mercede hyacinthos
   inicere et fracto busta piare cado?

Lygdamus uratur – candescat lamina uernae –   35
  sensi ego, cum insidiis pallida uina bibi.
ut Nomas arcanas tollat uersuta saliuas,
  dicet damnatas ignea testa manus.
quae modo per uilis inspecta est publica noctes
  haec nunc aurata cyclade signat humum,   40
at grauiora rependit iniquis pensa quasillis
  garrula de facie si qua locuta mea est;
nostraque quod Petale tulit ad monumenta coronas,
  codicis immundi uincula sentit anus,
caeditur et Lalage tortis suspensa capillis,   45
  per nomen quoniam est ausa rogare meum.
te patiente meae conflauit imaginis aurum
  ardente e nostro dotem habitura rogo.
non tamen insector, quamuis mereare, Properti;
  longa mea in libris regna fuere tuis.   50
iuro ego Fatorum nulli reuolubile carmen –
  tergeminusque canis sic mihi molle sonet –
me seruasse fidem. si fallo, uipera nostris
  sibilet in tumulis et super ossa cubet.
nam gemina est sedes turpem sortita per amnem   55
  turbaque diuersa remigat omnis aqua.
unda Clytaemnestrae stuprum et stuprum altera Cressae
  portat mentitae lignea monstra bouis.
ecce coronato pars altera rapta phaselo
  mulcet ubi Elysias aura beata rosas,   60
qua numerosa fides, quaque aera rotunda Cybebes
  mitratisque sonant Lydia plectra choris.
Andromedeque et Hypermnestre sine fraude maritae
  narrant historiae tempora nota suae.
haec sua maternis queritur liuere catenis   65
  bracchia nec meritas frigida saxa manus.
narrat Hypermnestre magnum ausas esse sorores,
  in scelus hoc animum non ualuisse suum.
sic mortis lacrimis uitae sanamus amores;
  celo ego perfidiae crimina multa tuae.   70
sed tibi nunc mandata damus, si forte moueris,
  si te non totum Chloridos herba tenet.
nutrix in tremulis ne quid desideret annis
  Parthenie; potuit, nec tibi auara fuit.
deliciaeque meae Latris, cui nomen ab usu est,   75
  ne speculum dominae porrigat illa nouae.
et quoscumque meo fecisti nomine uersus,

ure mihi. laudes desine habere meas.
pone hederam tumulo mihi quae praegnante corymbo
  mollis contortis alliget ossa comis 80
ramosis Anio qua pomifer incubat aruis
  et numquam Herculeo numine pallet ebur.
hic carmen media dignum me scribe columna,
  sed breue, quod currens uector ab urbe legat:
HIC TIBVRTINA IACET AVREA CYNTHIA TERRA; 85
ACCESSIT RIPAE LAVS, ANIENE, TVAE.
nec tu sperne piis uenientia somnia portis;
  cum pia uenerunt somnia, pondus habent.
nocte uagae ferimur, nox clausas liberat umbras
  errat et abiecta Cerberus ipse sera. 90
luce iubent leges Lethaea ad stagna reuerti;
  nos uehimur, uectum nauta recenset onus.
nunc te possideant aliae. mox sola tenebo.
  mecum eris et mixtis ossibus ossa teram.'
haec postquam querula mecum sub lite peregit 95
  inter complexus excidit umbra meos.

TIBVLLI CARMINVM

LIBER PRIMVS

I

Diuitias alius fuluo sibi congerat auro
  et teneat culti iugera magna soli
quem labor assiduus uicino terreat hoste,
  Martia cui somnos classica pulsa fugent:
me mea paupertas uitae traducat inerti 5
  dum meus assiduo luceat igne focus.
ipse seram teneras maturo tempore uites
  rusticus et facili grandia poma manu;
nec Spes destituat, sed frugum semper aceruos
  praebeat et pleno pinguia musta lacu. 10
nam ueneror seu stipes habet desertus in agris
  seu uetus in triuio florida serta lapis,
et quodcumque mihi pomum nouus educat annus
  libatum agricolam ponitur ante deum.
flaua Ceres, tibi sit nostro de rure corona 15

spicea quae templi pendeat ante fores,
pomosisque ruber custos ponatur in hortis
  terreat ut saeua falce Priapus aues.
uos quoque, felicis quondam, nunc pauperis agri
  custodes, fertis munera uestra, Lares.   20
tunc uitula innumeros lustrabat caesa iuuencos:
  nunc agna exigui est hostia parua soli.
agna cadet uobis, quam circum rustica pubes
  clamet 'io, messes et bona uina date'.
iam modo, iam possim contentus uiuere paruo   25
  nec semper longae deditus esse uiae,
sed Canis aestiuos ortus uitare sub umbra
  arboris ad riuos praetereuntis aquae.
nec tamen interdum pudeat tenuisse bidentem
  aut stimulo tardos increpuisse boues;   30
non agnamue sinu pigeat fetumue capellae
  desertum oblita matre referre domum.
at uos exiguo pecori, furesque lupique,
  parcite; de magno est praeda petenda grege.
hic ego pastoremque meum lustrare quotannis   35
  et placidam soleo spargere lacte Palem.
adsitis, diui, neu uos e paupere mensa
  dona nec e puris spernite fictilibus.
fictilia antiquus primum sibi fecit agrestis,
  pocula de facili composuitque luto.   40
non ego diuitias patrum fructusque requiro
  quos tulit antiquo condita messis auo;
parua seges satis est, satis est requiescere lecto
  si licet et solito membra leuare toro.
quam iuuat immites uentos audire cubantem   45
  et dominam tenero continuisse sinu!
aut gelidas hibernus aquas cum fuderit Auster
  securum somnos igne iuuante sequi!
hoc mihi contingat: sit diues iure furorem
  qui maris et tristes ferre potest pluuias.   50
o quantum est auri pereat potiusque smaragdi
  quam fleat ob nostras ulla puella uias!
te bellare decet terra, Messalla, marique
  ut domus hostiles praeferat exuuias:
me retinent uinctum formosae uincla puellae   55
  et sedeo duras ianitor ante fores.
non ego laudari curo, mea Delia; tecum
  dum modo sim, quaeso segnis inersque uocer.

11

te spectem suprema mihi cum uenerit hora;
  te teneam moriens deficiente manu.   60
flebis et arsuro positum me, Delia, lecto
  tristibus et lacrimis oscula mixta dabis.
flebis; non tua sunt duro praecordia ferro
  uincta, nec in tenero stat tibi corde silex.
illo non iuuenis poterit de funere quisquam   65
  lumina non uirgo sicca referre domum.
tu manes ne laede meos, sed parce solutis
  crinibus et teneris, Delia, parce genis.
interea, dum Fata sinunt, iungamus amores:
  iam ueniet tenebris Mors adoperta caput;   70
iam subrepet iners aetas, neque amare decebit
  dicere nec cano blanditias capite.
nunc leuis est tractanda Venus, dum frangere postes
  non pudet et rixas inseruisse iuuat.
hic ego dux milesque bonus. uos, signa tubaeque,   75
  ite procul; cupidis uulnera ferte uiris.
ferte et opes: ego composito securus aceruo
  dites despiciam despiciamque famem.

VIII

Non ego celari possum quid nutus amantis
  quidue ferant miti lenia uerba sono,
nec mihi sunt sortes nec conscia fibra deorum
  praecinit euentus nec mihi cantus auis.
ipsa Venus magico religatum bracchia nodo   5
  perdocuit, multis non sine uerberibus.
desine dissimulare: deus crudelius urit
  quos uidet inuitos succubuisse sibi.
quid tibi nunc molles prodest coluisse capillos
  saepeque mutatas disposuisse comas?   10
quid fuco splendente genas ornare? quid ungues
  artificis docta subsecuisse manu?
frustra iam uestes, frustra mutantur amictus
  ansaque compressos colligat arta pedes.
illa placet, quamuis inculto uenerit ore   15
  nec nitidum tarda compserit arte caput.
num te carminibus, num te pallentibus herbis
  deuouit tacito tempore noctis anus?
cantus uicinis fruges traducit ab agris,
  cantus et iratae detinet anguis iter,   20

cantus et e curru Lunam deducere temptat,
  et faceret si non aera repulsa sonent.
quid queror, heu, misero carmen nocuisse? quid herbas?
  forma nihil magicis utitur auxiliis;
sed corpus tetigisse nocet, sed longa dedisse   25
  oscula, sed femori conseruisse femur.
nec tu difficilis puero tamen esse memento;
  persequitur poenis tristia facta Venus.
munera nec poscas; det munera canus amator
  ut foueat molli frigida membra sinu.   30
carior est auro iuuenis cui leuia fulgent
  ora nec amplexus aspera barba terit.
huic tu candentes umero suppone lacertos
  et regum magnae despiciantur opes.
at Venus inuenit puero concumbere furtim,   35
  dum timet et teneros conserit usque sinus,
et dare anhelanti pugnantibus umida linguis
  oscula et in collo figere dente notas.
non lapis hanc gemmaeque iuuant quae frigore sola
  dormiat et nulli sit cupienda uiro.   40
heu sero reuocatur amor seroque iuuentas
  cum uetus infecit cana senecta caput.
tum studium formae est; coma tum mutatur ut annos
  dissimulet uiridi cortice tincta nucis;
tollere tum cura est albos a stirpe capillos   45
  et faciem dempta pelle referre nouam.
at tu, dum primi floret tibi temporis aetas,
  utere: non tardo labitur illa pede.
neu Marathum torque. puero quae gloria uicto est?
  in ueteres esto dura, puella, senes.   50
parce, precor, tenero. non illi sontica causa est
  sed nimius luto corpora tingit amor.
uel miser absenti maestas quam saepe querelas
  conicit, et lacrimis omnia plena madent.
'quid me spernis?' ait. 'poterat custodia uinci;   55
  ipse dedit cupidis fallere posse deus.
nota Venus furtiua mihi est – ut lenis agatur
  spiritus, ut nec dent oscula rapta sonum.
et possum media quauis obrepere nocte
  et strepitu nullo clam reserare fores.   60
quid prosunt artes, miserum si spernit amantem
  et fugit ex ipso saeua puella toro?
uel cum promittit subito sed perfida fallit

et mihi nox multis est uigilanda malis?
dum mihi uenturam fingo, quodcumque mouetur   65
  illius credo tunc sonuisse pedes?'
desistas lacrimare, puer. non frangitur illa,
  et tua iam fletu lumina fessa tument.
oderunt, Pholoe, moneo, fastidia diui
  nec prodest sanctis tura dedisse focis.   70
hic Marathus quondam miseros ludebat amantes,
  nescius ultorem post caput esse deum.
saepe etiam lacrimas fertur risisse dolentis
  et cupidum ficta detinuisse mora.
nunc omnes odit fastus, nunc displicet illi   75
  quaecumque opposita est ianua dura sera.
et te poena manet, ni desinis esse superba.
  quam cupies uotis hunc reuocare diem!

LIBER SECVNDVS

IV

Sic mihi seruitium uideo dominamque paratam;
  iam mihi, libertas illa paterna, uale.
seruitium sed triste datur, teneorque catenis
  et numquam misero uincla remittit Amor,
et seu quid merui seu nil peccauimus, urit.   5
  uror; io, remoue, saeua puella, faces.
o ego, ne possim tales sentire dolores,
  quam mallem in gelidis montibus esse lapis
stare uel insanis cautes obnoxia uentis
  naufraga quam uasti tunderet unda maris!   10
nunc et amara dies et noctis amarior umbra est;
  omnia nunc tristi tempora felle madent.
nec prosunt elegi nec carminis auctor Apollo:
  illa caua pretium flagitat usque manu.
ite procul, Musae, si non prodestis amanti: 15
  non ego uos ut sint bella canenda colo
nec refero Solisque uias et qualis, ubi orbem
  compleuit, uersis Luna recurrit equis.
ad dominam faciles aditus per carmina quaero:
  ite procul, Musae, si nihil ista ualent.   20
at mihi per caedem et facinus sunt dona paranda

ne iaceam clausam flebilis ante domum;
aut rapiam suspensa sacris insignia fanis,
   sed Venus ante alios est uiolanda mihi.
illa malum facinus suadet dominamque rapacem   25
   dat mihi: sacrilegas sentiat illa manus.
o pereat quicumque legit uiridesque smaragdos
   et niueam Tyrio murice tingit ouem!
hic dat auaritiae causas et Coa puellis
   uestis et e Rubro lucida concha Mari.   30
haec fecere malas, hinc clauim ianua sensit
   et coepit custos liminis esse canis.
sed pretium si grande feras, custodia uicta est
   nec prohibent claues et canis ipse tacet.
heu quicumque dedit formam caelestis auarae,   35
   quale bonum multis attulit ille malis!
hinc fletus rixaeque sonant, haec denique causa
   fecit ut infamis nunc deus esset Amor.
at tibi quae pretio uictos excludis amantes
   eripiant partas uentus et ignis opes.   40
quin, tua tunc iuuenes spectent incendia laeti
   nec quisquam flammae sedulus addat aquam.
heu, ueniet tibi mors, nec erit qui lugeat ullus
   nec qui det maestas munus in exsequias.
at bona quae nec auara fuit, centum licet annos   45
   uixerit, ardentem flebitur ante rogum;
atque aliquis senior, ueteres ueneratus amores,
   annua constructo serta dabit tumulo
et 'bene' discedens dicet 'placideque quiescas
   terraque securae sit super ossa leuis.'   50
uera quidem moneo, sed prosunt quid mihi uera?
   illius est nobis lege colendus Amor.
quin etiam sedes iubeat si uendere auitas,
   ite sub imperium sub titulumque, Lares.
quicquid habet Circe, quicquid Medea ueneni,   55
   quicquid et herbarum Thessala terra gerit,
et quod, ubi indomitis gregibus Venus afflat amores,
   hippomanes cupidae stillat ab inguine equae,
si modo me placido uideat Nemesis mea uultu,
   mille alias herbas misceat illa, bibam.   60

P. OVIDI NASONIS AMORVM

LIBER PRIMVS

I

Arma graui numero uiolentaque bella parabam
  edere, materia conueniente modis.
par erat inferior uersus; risisse Cupido
  dicitur atque unum surripuisse pedem.
'quis tibi, saeue puer, dedit hoc in carmina iuris?   5
  Pieridum uates, non tua, turba sumus.
quid si praeripiat flauae Venus arma Mineruae,
  uentilet accensas flaua Minerua faces?
quis probet in siluis Cererem regnare iugosis,
  lege pharetratae uirginis arua coli?   10
crinibus insignem quis acuta cuspide Phoebum
  instruat, Aoniam Marte mouente lyram?
sunt tibi magna, puer, nimiumque potentia regna:
  cur opus affectas ambitiose nouum?
an, quod ubique, tuum est? tua sunt Heliconia tempe?   15
  uix etiam Phoebo iam lyra tuta sua est?
cum bene surrexit uersu noua pagina primo,
  attenuat neruos proximus ille meos.
nec mihi materia est numeris leuioribus apta,
  aut puer aut longas compta puella comas.'   20
questus eram, pharetra cum protinus ille soluta
  legit in exitium spicula facta meum
lunauitque genu sinuosum fortiter arcum
  'quod'que 'canas, uates, accipe' dixit 'opus.'
me miserum! certas habuit puer ille sagittas.   25
  uror, et in uacuo pectore regnat Amor.
sex mihi surgat opus numeris, in quinque residat;
  ferrea cum uestris bella ualete modis.
cingere litorea flauentia tempora myrto,
  Musa per undenos emodulanda pedes.   30

II

Esse quid hoc dicam, quod tam mihi dura uidentur
  strata, neque in lecto pallia nostra sedent,

et uacuus somno noctem, quam longa, peregi
   lassaque uersati corporis ossa dolent?
nam, puto, sentirem, si quo temptarer amore –   5
   an subit et tecta callidus arte nocet?
sic erit: haeserunt tenues in corde sagittae
   et possessa ferus pectora uersat Amor.
cedimus, an subitum luctando accendimus ignem?
   cedamus: leue fit, quod bene fertur onus.   10
uidi ego iactatas mota face crescere flammas
   et uidi nullo concutiente mori.
uerbera plura ferunt quam quos iuuat usus aratri,
   detrectent prensi dum iuga prima boues.
asper equus duris contunditur ora lupatis: 15
   frena minus sentit quisquis ad arma facit.
acrius inuitos multoque ferocius urget
   quam qui seruitium ferre fatentur, Amor.
en ego, confiteor, tua sum noua praeda, Cupido;
   porrigimus uictas ad tua iura manus.   20
nil opus est bello: pacem ueniamque rogamus;
   nec tibi laus armis uictus inermis ero.
necte comam myrto, maternas iunge columbas;
   qui deceat currum uitricus ipse dabit;
inque dato curru, populo clamante triumphum   25
   stabis et adiunctas arte mouebis aues.
ducentur capti iuuenes captaeque puellae:
   haec tibi magnificus pompa triumphus erit.
ipse ego, praeda recens, factum modo uulnus habebo
   et noua captiua uincula mente feram.   30
Mens Bona ducetur manibus post terga retortis
   et Pudor et castris quicquid Amoris obest.
omnia te metuent, ad te sua bracchia tendens
   uulgus 'io' magna uoce 'triumphe' canet.
Blanditiae comites tibi erunt Errorque Furorque,   35
   assidue partes turba secuta tuas.
his tu militibus superas hominesque deosque;
   haec tibi si demas commoda, nudus eris.
laeta triumphanti de summo mater Olympo
   plaudet et appositas sparget in ora rosas.   40
tu pinnas gemma, gemma uariante capillos
   ibis in auratis aureus ipse rotis.
tum quoque non paucos, si te bene nouimus, ures;
   tum quoque praeteriens uulnera multa dabis.
non possunt, licet ipse uelis, cessare sagittae;   45

feruida uicino flamma uapore nocet.
talis erat domita Bacchus Gangetide terra:
tu grauis alitibus, tigribus ille fuit.
ergo cum possim sacri pars esse triumphi,
parce tuas in me perdere uictor opes. 50
aspice cognati felicia Caesaris arma:
qua uicit, uictos protegit ille manu.

LIBER SECVNDVS

VII

Ergo sufficiam reus in noua crimina semper?
ut uincam, totiens dimicuisse piget.
siue ego marmorei respexi summa theatri,
eligis e multis unde dolere uelis;
candida seu tacito uidit me femina uultu, 5
in uultu tacitas arguis esse notas.
si quam laudaui, miseros petis ungue capillos;
si culpo, crimen dissimulare putas.
siue bonus color est, in te quoque frigidus esse;
seu malus, alterius dicor amore mori. 10
atque ego peccati uellem mihi conscius essem:
aequo animo poenam qui meruere ferunt.
nunc temere insimulas credendoque omnia frustra
ipsa uetas iram pondus habere tuam.
aspice ut auritus miserandae sortis asellus 15
assiduo domitus uerbere lentus eat.
ecce, nouum crimen: sollers ornare Cypassis
obicitur dominae contemerasse torum.
di melius, quam me, si sit peccasse libido,
sordida contemptae sortis amica iuuet! 20
quis Veneris famulae conubia liber inire
tergaque complecti uerbere secta uelit?
adde quod ornandis illa est operosa capillis
et tibi per doctas grata ministra manus.
scilicet ancillam, quae tam tibi fida, rogarem? 25
quid, nisi ut indicio iuncta repulsa foret?
per Venerem iuro puerique uolatilis arcus
me non admissi criminis esse reum.

VIII

Ponendis in mille modos perfecta capillis,
  comere sed solas digna, Cypassi, deas,
et mihi iucundo non rustica cognita furto,
  apta quidem dominae sed magis apta mihi,
quis fuit inter nos sociati corporis index?   5
  sensit concubitus unde Corinna tuos?
num tamen erubui? num uerbo lapsus in ullo
  furtiuae Veneris conscia signa dedi?
quid quod, in ancilla si quis delinquere possit,
  illum ego contendi mente carere bona?   10
Thessalus ancillae facie Briseidos arsit,
  serua Mycenaeo Phoebas amata duci.
nec sum ego Tantalide maior, nec maior Achille.
  quod decuit reges, cur mihi turpe putem?
ut tamen iratos in te defixit ocellos,   15
  uidi te totis erubuisse genis.
at quanto, si forte refers, praesentior ipse
  per Veneris feci numina magna fidem.
(tu, dea, tu iubeas animi periuria puri
  Carpathium tepidos per mare ferre Notos!)   20
pro quibus officiis pretium mihi dulce repende
  concubitus hodie, fusca Cypassi, tuos.
quid renuis fingisque nouos, ingrata, timores?
  unum est e dominis emeruisse satis.
quod si stulta negas, index ante acta fatebor   25
  et ueniam culpae proditor ipse meae,
quoque loco tecum fuerim quotiensque, Cypassi,
  narrabo dominae quotque quibusque modis.

LIBER TERTIVS

II

'Non ego nobilium sedeo studiosus equorum –
  cui tamen ipsa faues, uincat ut ille, precor.
ut loquerer tecum, ueni, tecumque sederem
  ne tibi non notus quem facis esset amor.

tu cursus spectas, ego te: spectemus uterque   5
  quod iuuat atque oculos pascat uterque suos.
o, cuicumque faues, felix agitator equorum!
  ergo illi curae contigit esse tuae?
hoc mihi contingat, sacro de carcere missis
  insistam forti mente uehendus equis,   10
et modo lora dabo, modo uerbere terga notabo,
  nunc stringam metas interiore rota.
si mihi currenti fueris conspecta, morabor
  deque meis manibus lora remissa fluent.
a, quam paene Pelops Pisaea concidit hasta   15
  dum spectat uultus, Hippodamia, tuos!
nempe fauore suae uicit tamen ille puellae –
  uincamus dominae quisque fauore suae.
quid frustra refugis? cogit nos linea iungi;
  haec in lege loci commoda Circus habet.   20
tu tamen a dextra, quicumque es, parce puellae:
  contactu lateris laeditur ista tui.
tu quoque, qui spectas post nos, tua contrahe crura,
  si pudor est, rigido nec preme terga genu.
sed nimium demissa iacent tibi pallia terra;   25
  collige – uel digitis en ego tollo meis.
inuida uestis eras, quae tam bona crura tegebas!
  quoque magis spectes – inuida uestis eras!
talia Milanion Atalantes crura fugacis
  optauit manibus sustinuisse suis;   30
talia pinguntur succinctae crura Dianae
  cum sequitur fortes fortior ipsa feras.
his ego non uisis arsi; quid fiet ab ipsis?
  in flammam flammas, in mare fundis aquas.
suspicor ex istis et cetera posse placere   35
  quae bene sub tenui condita ueste latent.
uis tamen interea faciles arcessere uentos
  quos faciet nostra mota tabella manu?
an magis hic meus est animi, non aeris, aestus
  captaque femineus pectora torret amor?   40
dum loquor, alba leui sparsa est tibi puluere uestis –
  sordide de niueo corpore puluis abi!
sed iam pompa uenit: linguis animisque fauete.
  tempus adest plausus: aurea pompa uenit.
prima loco fertur passis Victoria pinnis –   45
  huc ades et meus hic fac, dea, uincat amor.
plaudite Neptuno, nimium qui creditis undis –

nil mihi cum pelago; me mea terra capit.
plaude tuo Marti, miles – nos odimus arma;
   pax iuuat et media pace repertus amor.   50
auguribus Phoebus, Phoebe uenantibus adsit;
   artifices in te uerte, Minerua, manus.
ruricolae, Cereri teneroque assurgite Baccho;
   Pollucem pugiles, Castora placet eques.
nos tibi, blanda Venus, puerisque potentibus arcu   55
   plaudimus: inceptis annue, diua, meis
daque nouae mentem dominae, patiatur amari –
   annuit et motu signa secunda dedit.
quod dea promisit, promittas ipsa, rogamus –
   pace loquar Veneris, tu dea maior eris.   60
per tibi tot iuro testes pompamque deorum
   te dominam nobis tempus in omne peti.
sed pendent tibi crura: potes, si forte iuuabit,
   cancellis primos inseruisse pedes.
maxima iam uacuo praetor spectacula Circo   65
   quadriiugos aequo carcere misit equos.
cui studeas uideo; uincet cuicumque fauebis.
   quid cupias ipsi scire uidentur equi.
me miserum! metam spatioso circumit orbe.
   quid facis? admoto proximus axe subit.   70
quid facis, infelix? perdis bona uota puellae.
   tende, precor, ualida lora sinistra manu.
fauimus ignauo. sed enim reuocate, Quirites,
   et date iactatis undique signa togis.
en reuocant; ac ne turbet toga mota capillos,   75
   in nostros abdas te licet usque sinus.
iamque patent iterum reserato carcere postes;
   euolat admissis discolor agmen equis.
nunc saltem supera spatioque insurge patenti;
   sint mea, sint dominae fac rata uota meae.   80
sunt dominae rata uota meae – mea uota supersunt;
   ille tenet palmam – palma petenda mea est.'
risit et argutis quiddam promisit ocellis.
   'hoc satis hic, alio cetera redde loco.'

Translations and Commentaries

CATULLUS
(translations by Guy Lee)

Catullus 72

You said one day you'd only know Catullus, Lesbia,
  And you'd refuse to embrace even Jove instead of me.
I loved you then, not just as common men a girl-friend
  But as a father loves his sons and sons-in-law.
I know you now. So though my passion's more intense   5
  Yet for me you're much cheaper and lighter-weight.
'How can that be?' you ask. It's because such hurt compels
  A lover to love more but to like less.

In all three poems selected for this edition (72, 76 and 85) Catullus the
tormented lover attempts to express his pain. Here in Poem 72 he explores
the contrast between what Lesbia[1] claimed ('you said' [*dicebas*, 1]) and
what he himself has realised to be the truth ('I know', [*cognoui*, 5]). The
English translation preserves the emotive juxtaposition of the two lovers'
names in the first line. Catullus' Poem 70 is similar:

> Nulli se dicit mulier mea nubere malle
>   quam mihi, non si se Iuppiter ipse petat.
> dicit – sed mulier cupido quod dicit amanti
>   in uento et rapida scribere oportet aqua.

> My woman says there's no one she would rather wed
>   Than me, not even if asked by Jove himself.
> Says – but what a woman says to an eager lover
>   One should write on the wind and the running water.[2]

(trans. Lee)

---

[1] See pp. xxxiv-xxxv.

[2] Catullus' writing it on papyrus perhaps underlines the irony.

That poem is similar again to a Hellenistic Greek epigram by Calli-machus:[3]

> Swore Callignotus to Ionis he would never
>   Hold boy or girl dearer than her.
> He swore, but the saying's true that the ears of the immortals
>   Are deaf to lovers' promises.
> So now his flame is male, but of the wretched girl,
>   Like Megara, 'no word or reckoning'.[4]
>
> AP 5. 6 (trans. Lee)

Layers of 'intertextuality'[5] help to make Catullus' point here. What Callimachus observes as an outsider Catullus in Poem 70 experiences himself, but what Callimachus states as a fact Catullus there merely hints at. The further new feature here in Catullus 72 is the combination of the poet's personal involvement with the *certainty* of his beloved's untruthfulness.

Antithesis gives the poem a satisfyingly balanced structure, the first half pointedly contrasting with the second – past with present ('one day', *quondam* [1]; 'now', *nunc* [5]) and illusion with reality. Underlying both these contrasts is yet another – between spiritual and sexual love.[6] To Lesbia is attributed a profession of exclusive and exceptional commitment to Catullus (1-2). This, like her professed desire to marry him in Poem 70, we eventually discover he took completely seriously, expecting of her, his mistress, no less than the absolute fidelity and selfless devotion of a conventional Roman wife. But there is enough to tell the reader straightaway that Lesbia was just exaggerating, for her favourable comparison of her lover with god almighty is a mere commonplace.[7] The *physical* emphasis in what she has allegedly said is also significant: *nosse* (1) is used in the biblical sense of 'know', (i.e. 'have sexual relations with'), and *tenere* (2), literally 'hold', can also euphemistically connote sexual activity (hence the translation 'embrace'). Catullus' description of his own feelings, on the other hand, hits quite a different note. He apparently expected wifely devotion from Lesbia, but he does not explicitly claim husbandly concern for her. Rather he says, even more strikingly, that he looked upon her not as a

---

[3] See pp. xix-xxi.

[4] The last line is cryptic but seems to mean that she has ceased to be of importance.

[5] See p. xiv.

[6] The Latin verb used for 'love' in lines 3-4 is *diligere* and in line 8 *amare*; Catullus clearly intended to distinguish the two here (see Wiseman (1985) 166), though the distinction is not maintained in subsequent Latin, nor, indeed, consistently in the rest of Catullus' own poetry.

[7] Cf. Catul. 70. 2 (quoted on p. 22), Plautus, *Casina* 323-4, Ov. *Metamorphoses* 7. 801. Perhaps the cliché sprang from Jupiter's reputation as the arch-philanderer.

mere 'girl-friend',[8] but with affection like a father's for his 'sons and sons-in-law' (*gnatos...et generos* [4]). Emphatically *non*-physical affection, then; but if that is all, why not 'sons and daughters', as the modern reader would expect? Some scholars have argued that this must be (more or less) what Catullus meant, since the Latin masculines would include the feminine equivalents. But though 'sons' could plausibly stand for 'sons and daughters', it is very doubtful whether 'sons-in-law' could include 'daughters-in-law'; and why mention any sort of 'in-laws' anyway? The answer probably lies in the conventional attitudes of upper-class Roman men of Catullus' time. Sons they saw as the essential means of preserving a family's name and status and safeguarding its property,[9] while a strategic choice of son-in-law could help to cement political and other alliances between individuals.[10] Catullus would thus appear to be using the language of family relationships boldly and uniquely to convey not just the spiritual as opposed to the physical element in his affection for Lesbia but also the *seriousness* with which he regarded their liaison.[11] His worst anguish stems from the realisation that *she* did not regard it in anything like the same way: Catullus now 'knows' her (5) in a poignantly different sense from that in which she professed to want to 'know' him (1).

Verbal echo and correspondence point the antithesis between spiritual and sexual love throughout the second half of the poem, where Catullus attempts to analyse his now ambivalent feelings toward Lesbia. His 'passion' has become more intense (literally he says 'although I *burn* [*uror*, 5] more intensely', using the well-worn fire metaphor[12] for what he regards as the commonplace kind of love), but she has become 'cheaper' and 'lighter-weight' (*uilior et leuior* [6]) in his eyes (the Latin *impensius* [5], 'more intensely', is etymologically connected with the verb *pendere*, which can mean both 'pay' and 'weigh', and so perhaps counterpoints 'cheaper' and 'lighter-weight' more than can be obvious in English translation). A question (7), somewhat artificially attributed to Lesbia herself and as starkly prosaic in Latin (*qui potis est?*) as it is in English, then paves the way for the final effort to explain (7-8): the 'hurt' (*iniuria*) she has inflicted on Catullus makes him 'love more' (*amare magis*), but 'like less' (*bene*

---

[8] The Latin *amica* here seems to signify a partner in a distinctly casual relationship, perhaps even a prostitute.

[9] See e.g. Cicero, *Pro Cluentio* 32.

[10] As it did, at least for a time, in the case of Julius Caesar and Pompey, after Pompey married Caesar's daughter Julia in 59 BC; cf. p. xxviii.

[11] At 68. 119-24 Catullus turns to the idea of family feeling to convey the intensity of a young bride's love for her husband; he compares it with that of an aged grandfather for a son and heir born 'in the nick of time' to his daughter.

[12] Cf. Callimachus *AP* 5. 6. 5 (quoted on p. 23), and see p. xiv.

uelle minus), i.e. it results in an increase of sexual but a decrease of spiritual love. The cause of the 'hurt' can be nothing but Lesbia's infidelity,[13] and the jealousy which this prompts will be what makes Catullus desire her more. The Latin *iniuria*, however, is also the term for any act dishonouring the obligations of friendship (*amicitia*),[14] and *bene uelle minus* suggests a diminishing of the benevolent regard (*beneuolentia*) of one man for another which was essential to the maintenance of that friendship. So for the second time in the poem Catullus carefully employs language evocative of conventional Roman upper-class attitudes towards social relations to articulate his own very *un*conventional attitude towards an erotic affair. This is something new in extant ancient love poetry,[15] though Catullus could conceivably have taken a cue from more casual uses of some of the same vocabulary. Terence, *Eunuchus* 58-61 provides an example of the kind of thing he could have heard or read: 'There are all these evils in love: wrongs (*iniuriae*), suspicions, enmities (*inimicitiae*), reconciliations, war, then peace again'.

Catullus 76

If in recalling former kindnesses there's pleasure
  When a man reflects that he has been true,
Not broken solemn promise nor in any pact abused
  The Gods' divinity to fool his fellow men,
Then many joys remain in store for you, Catullus,   5
  Throughout a long lifetime from this thankless love.
For whatever kind things men can say or do
  To anyone, these you have said and done,
But invested in a thankless mind they have all been wasted.
  So now why torture yourself any more?   10
Why not harden your heart and tear yourself away from her
  And stop being wretched against the Gods' will?
It's difficult to cast off long love suddenly.
  It's difficult, but this you must somehow do.
This is your only chance. To this you must win through   15
  Possible or not, this you must achieve.

---

[13] For *iniuria* in this sense cf. Prop. ii. 24. 39, iv. 8. 27.

[14] Well-born Romans saw *amicitia* as a fairly formal commitment to provide mutual support and assistance in both public and private matters – lawsuits, candidatures for political office, and all manner of personal calamities.

[15] The importance to Catullan love poetry of terminology associated with *amicitia* was first pointed out by R. Reitzenstein in 1912; see further Lyne (1980) 24-6, 39-40, 291-2, Ross (1969) 80-92, Fitzgerald (1995) 117-20, 128-34.

O Gods, if you can pity or have ever brought
  Help at last to any on the point of death,
Look on my wretchedness and if I have led a decent life
  Take away from me this deadly disease,   20
Which like a paralysis creeping into my inmost being
  Has driven from my heart every happiness.
I do not now ask this, that she love me in return,
  Or, what's impossible, that she be chaste.
I pray to be well myself and cast off this foul sickness.   25
  O Gods, grant me this for my true dealing.

The essence of Poem 76 is self-pity (a note sounded early on by the pa-
thetic self-address in line 5). Catullus begins with what at first looks like a
reflection on his own religious rectitude. The references to being 'true'
(*pium*[16] [2]), to the 'solemn promise' (*sanctam fidem*) and to the 'pact'
(*foedere*) made without 'the Gods' divinity' (*Diuum numine*) being
'abused', i.e. without swearing falsely, (3-4) all contribute to the impres-
sion that religious observance is the issue. But it is mistaken. The mention
of 'kindnesses' (*benefacta* [1]) points to the real underlying concept here,
for these are the services expected by one upper-class Roman friend of
another, and when Catullus talks of being 'true' in this context, the word
connotes fulfilment of friendship's obligations.[17] All the other terms, too,
which at first sight seem religious can be associated with the bond of
friendship or the bond of marriage.[18] These concepts of friendship and
marriage have already been used by Catullus in Poems 70[19] and 72 to con-
vey the seriousness and commitment with which he approached his rela-
tionship with Lesbia,[20] and the reader who is aware of both this and the fact
that 'abusing the Gods' divinity' is a common failing of lovers[21] may well
realise that love is what Catullus is actually talking about in lines 1-6.

---

[16] Cf. 'true dealing'·for *pietate* in line 26.

[17] See p. 25 with n. 14, and cf. Catul. 73, where the poet explicitly claims to have lost faith generally in people being 'true' because a man friend has proved false.

[18] Marriage in Catullus' time was not a sacrament or normally a love-match, but a pledge of mutual support based on consent and goodwill; see p. xxviii.

[19] Quoted on p. 22.

[20] Cf. also for the key terms *fides* ('faith'), *foedus* ('pact') and *amicitia* ('friendship') Catul. 87. 3-4 'No faith there ever was in any pact as great / as was found on my part in love of you' (*nulla fides ullo fuit umquam in foedere tanta / quanta in amore tuo ex parte reperta mea est*), 109. 5-6 '(Gods, grant) That we may be allowed to keep through the whole length of our life / this eternal pact of sacred friendship' (*ut liceat nobis tota perducere uita / aeternum hoc sanctae foedus amicitiae*).

[21] See e.g. Callimachus, *AP* 5. 6 (quoted on p. 23 above) Ov. *Am.* 2. 8. 17-20 with discussion on p. 146.

When he speaks of 'a man' (*homini*) and 'men' (*homines*) in lines 2 and 4, however, the sense is the general one of 'human being(s)', not 'member(s) of the male sex', and love is not explicitly mentioned until line 6. It becomes clear enough in that line that Catullus' feelings of hurt and betrayal are due to his unusually committed love having proved 'thankless' (*ingrato*), i.e 'unreciprocated', but the *tone* of his opening remains elusive. Some critics have accused him of repellent self-righteousness in his attempt to console himself with the thought of some pleasure he can look forward to from recalling his own proper conduct. But this is probably to misunderstand him. The idea of satisfaction to be had from recalling one's past with pride was a commonplace of moral philosophy,[22] and a *sceptical* allusion to that seems likely here, for it is obvious that the only thing Catullus *really* thinks can bring him 'pleasure' (1) and 'joys' (5) is requited love. What he is implying may well be: 'This is what the philosophers say, but personally I don't believe a word of it'.[23] If so, there is an oblique restatement here of the old adage that a life without love is a life not worth living.[24]

In lines 7-9 Catullus no longer concerns himself with the (un)likelihood of future compensation for his present situation, but simply confirms that the situation is as he has implied: 'For the fact is that I have done everything I could have and should have, and I have got nothing in return'. He is not the first ancient poet to complain of this; cf. the writer's feelings in one of the Greek elegiac pieces addressed to a boy-beloved and attributed to Theognis[25] (1263-6 West):

> Boy, you have given poor return to one who acted with goodwill
> toward you;
> there is no gratitude on your part for good deeds.
> You have never done me any service, and I, who have already often
> acted with goodwill toward you, have never won any respect.

The Greek poet, however, is complaining simply of the boy's refusal to 'play the game' of (Greek) homosexual love,[26] whereas Catullus' couching of the complaint in language which evokes the concept of Roman friendship

---

[22] See further Powell (1990) 199-200, who notes the phraseological similarity between Catullus' opening line and Cicero, *De Senectute* 9. Booth (1997) 165.

[23] There is perhaps irony in the very words Catullus uses in Latin for 'pleasure' and 'joys' (*uoluptas* and *gaudia*), since they often denote specifically amatory gratification.

[24] The sentiment is first attested in the early Greek elegiacs of Mimnermus (see p. xvii): 'What life would there be, what joy, without golden Aphrodite? / May I die when I no longer care for these things – / clandestine love, sweet gifts and a couch' (frag. 1. 1-3 West).

[25] See p. xvii. For the layout of this non-metrical translation see p. ix.

[26] See p. xxx.

gives it a much more serious tone. He has said and done, he claims, all the 'kind things' (7) men can say or do to anyone (the dogged simplicity of the verbal repetition is striking). Reciprocal goodwill (*gratia*) was precisely what the performance of 'kindnesses' (*benefacta*) was supposed to generate between friends,[27] but Catullus' kindnesses have been invested in the wrong place (the translation of *credita* [9] as 'credited' perserves the commercial metaphor) – in a 'mind' (*menti* [9]) which was 'thankless' (*ingratae* here means 'unreciprocating'; cf. the same word in line 6). 'So why prolong the agony?' ('torture yourself', *te...excrucies* [10]), Catullus asks, with a painful logicality accentuated by the prosaic plainness of the expression. The somewhat cryptic (and much debated) sequence of thought in lines 1-10 would thus seem to be: why does Catullus persist with his special kind of love for Lesbia,[28] when, whatever its dubious long-term moral rewards, it brings him in the present nothing but pain?

'Why don't you just pull yourself together? Put it all behind you? Snap out of it?', a suddenly objective Catullus asks himself in the next breath; 'Make a clean break? If only I could!', replies his tormented soul. 'You must – no "can't"'s – your very survival is at stake!', counters the other voice. So do Catullus' head and heart tussle with each other in lines 11-16. At first (11-12) he is pointedly indirect (a convincing indication of his anguish?), saying only 'tear yourself away *from there*' (*istinc*[29] [11]), when he means 'from your infatuation with Lesbia', and 'stop being wretched against the will of the gods' (12), when he means 'stop brooding over your unreciprocated affection and desire, for it is morally inappropriate'. In lines 14-16, however, Catullus brings himself to spell out his problem and its remedy. His initial statement is almost identical to one found in a fragment of the fourth-century BC Greek comic playwright Menander (544 Körte): 'It is hard to break up intimacy in a short time'. We know nothing of the context in Menander, but the same sentiment here in Catullus, as part of the attempt to reflect a mental struggle, has a unique emotional power. It derives from several sources: the grim repetition of 'it's difficult' (*difficile est* [13, 14]), the insistent four-fold 'this' (*hoc...haec...hoc...hoc* [14-16]) and an unusually weighty rhythm at the end of line 15[30] (the effect of the four long syllables of *peruincendum* is well conveyed in the translation by the string of monosyllables 'you must win through'). Again there is a harrowing, prosy ordinariness about the vocabulary, the Latin expressions for 'from (t)her(e)' (*istinc* [11]), 'somehow (or other)' (*qualubet* [14)]) and

---

[27] See Lyne (1980) 24-5.

[28] She is not named, but it would be perverse to think of the woman in question as anyone else.

[29] Even the English translation 'from her' is more direct than the Latin.

[30] A 'spondaic' hexameter; see p. xvi with n. 19.

'possible or not'[31] (*siue id non pote siue pote* [16]) all being more at home in the colloquial language than in elevated poetry. In the middle of Catullus' desperate attempt at self-counselling there emerges for the first time the notion of sickness and recovery which is to dominate the rest of the poem: 'chance' (15) translates Latin *salus*, which means both 'salvation' and 'health'.

'To be well' (*ualere*) is what Catullus prays for in line 25. He implies that he is 'on the point of death' (*ipsa in morte* [18]), and he refers to his love-anguish as a 'deadly disease' (*pestem perniciemque* [20]) and a 'foul sickness' (*taetrum...morbum*) which he wishes to 'cast off' (*deponere* [25]; the same Latin word in line 13). Unrequited love was already being depicted as a morbid condition in seventh-century BC Greek lyric, most notably (in the surviving texts) by Sappho,[32] who records the abnormal physical symptoms she experiences at the sight of her beloved.[33] Catullus himself (51. 9-12) follows her closely in recording his own reactions to the sight of Lesbia:

> lingua sed torpet, tenuis sub artus
> flamma demanat, sonitu suopte
> tintinant aures, gemina teguntur
> lumina nocte.

> But my tongue's paralysed, invisible flame
> Courses down through my limbs, with din of their own
> My ears are ringing and twin darkness covers
> The light of my eyes.[34]   (trans. Lee)

The Roman comic dramatists before Catullus, like the Augustan elegists after him, frequently use the idea of love as a sickness in the form of a simple metaphor without reference to any physical symptoms, but when they do so, the tone is always essentially light-hearted.[35] Catullus here in Poem 76, however, combines a non-physical conception of love-sickness

---

[31] Cf. English 'no such word as "can't"'.

[32] See pp. xvii, xxxv.

[33] Frag. 31. 9 ff. Campbell

[34] 'Every departure that Catullus has made from his model is a change for the worse' opines Jenkyns (1982) 21. For other variations on the same theme see Callimachus, *AP* 12. 71. 3, 150. 6, Theocritus, *Idyll* 2. 85-90, Valerius Aedituus, frag. 1 Büchner (quoted on p. xxv; this too seems directly indebted to Sappho).

[35] See e.g. Plautus, *Cistellaria* 74, Terence, *Eunuchus* 225-6, Tib. 2. 5. 109-10, Prop. 2. 1. 57-8, and the whole of Ovid's *Remedia Amoris* ('Remedies for Love'). Further discussion in Booth (1997) 157-8.

with intense gravity of tone. By *likening* his 'disease' to a general and progressive physical 'paralysis' (*torpor*), instead of claiming to *be* bodily crippled in some transient and localised way (as at 51. 9, quoted above[36]), he emphasises both the mental and the total nature of his incapacitation, pointing, perhaps, not just to the obsessiveness of his love but also to the function-numbing depression which results from its frustration.[37] Finally Catullus appeals to the gods to effect his cure (25-6).[38] In what spirit is this appeal made? Many see it as a genuinely hopeful recourse at the last to trust in divine justice and mercy on the conventional *quid pro quo* basis of Roman religion.[39] In other words, the gods, *since* they have it in their power to pity and aid (17-18), should release Catullus from his suffering, *seeing that* he has 'lived a decent life' (19) and been 'true' (26).[40] 'Since' and 'seeing that' are how the 'if's in lines 17-18 and 19 have to be taken for this interpretation to work, and conditional clauses do indeed often have such a force in formal Latin prayers. There is some difficulty, however, in understanding lines 17-26 in this light. As some scholars have perceived,[41] 'O Gods' in Latin does not have a reverential tone but an emotive colloquial one, less suited to a formal prayer than to a cry of despair (cf. English 'God help me!', intimating not that God will, or should, but rather that nobody else can). It thus seems possible that the 'if' clauses in lines 17-18 and 19 are not expressions of faith, but of doubt and desperation: 'If gods exist who respond to human suffering, I need a miracle from them now; if anyone has deserved one, surely it is I'. If *this* interpretation is valid, hardly a flicker of hope illuminates the blackness of Catullus' mental torment. Yet he has by the end of the poem progressed to accepting what initially seemed unacceptable: life and pleasure will be impossible for him unless love and its devastating consequences (he now treats cause and effect as one) *are taken away.*[42]

Not until the penultimate couplet does Catullus bring himself to speak of his beloved directly, and even then he does not mention her name. He

---

[36] Intertextual play (see p. xiv) with his own earlier poem as well as with Sappho's is a possibility here.

[37] See further Booth (1997) 157, 167-8.

[38] Calls simply for an end to love were already quite common; see e.g. 'Theognis' 1323-6 West, Meleager *AP* 5. 215, Philodemus, *AP* 11. 41. 7-8.

[39] E.g. Luck (1969) 67-8.

[40] Both of these claims may be interpreted as references to Catullus' irreproachable behaviour in love on the principles outlined in 1-4, though his claim to have lived 'decently' (*puriter* [19]) has also been thought to allude to his freedom from some of the more offensive sexual habits of Lesbia's current circle; see Wiseman (1985) 171-2.

[41] E.g. Williams (1968) 411.

[42] Cf. p. 27, with n. 24 above.

confesses, again with prosaic simplicity ('what's impossible', *quod non potis est* [24]), that he has given up all hope of his spiritual love ever being reciprocated[43] or of her being 'chaste' (*pudica* [24]; this in Latin often implies absolute fidelity to a single partner, not complete sexual abstinence). His only concern now is for his own mental survival. Contrast especially one of Catullus' non-elegiac poems on Lesbia:

Miser Catulle, desinas ineptire
et quod uides perisse perditum ducas.
fulsere quondam candidi tibi soles
cum uentitabas quod puella ducebat
amata nobis quantum amabitur nulla.
ibi illa multa cum iocosa fiebant
quae tu uolebas nec puella nolebat,
fulsere uere candidi tibi soles.
nunc iam illa non uult; tu quoque, impotens, noli
nec quae fugit sectare nec miser uiue,
sed obstinata mente perfer, obdura.
uale, puella. iam Catullus obdurat
nec te requiret nec rogabit inuitam.
at tu dolebis cum rogaberis nulla.
scelesta, uae te, quae tibi manet uita?
quid nunc te adibit? cui uideberis bella?
quem nunc amabis? cuius esse diceris?
quem basiabis? cui labella mordebis?
at tu, Catulle, destinatus obdura.   Catullus 8

Wretched Catullus, you should stop fooling
And what you know you've lost admit losing.
When you kept following where a girl led you,
The sun shone brilliantly for you, time was,
Loved by us as we shall love no one.
There when those many amusing things happened
Which you wanted nor did the girl not want
The sun shone brilliantly for you, truly.
Now she's stopped wanting, you must stop, weakling.
Don't chase what runs away nor live wretched
But with a mind made up be firm, stand fast.
Goodbye, girl. Catullus now stands fast,
Won't ask or look for you who're not willing.

---

[43] He uses the same Latin word (*diligere*) for 'love' here as he used of the non-physical affection he felt for Lesbia in 72; see p. 23 with n. 6.

But you'll be sorry when you're not asked for.
Alas, what life awaits you now, devil?
Who'll find you pretty now? What type touch you?
Whom will you love and whose be called henceforth?
Whom will you kiss? and you will bite whose lips?
But you, Catullus, mind made up, stand fast.   (trans. Lee)

Is Catullus' reason for wanting to break with Lesbia the same in this poem as in 76? And does he really envisage it being final in either case?

Catullus 85

I hate and love. Perhaps you're asking why I do that?
I don't know, but feel it happening, and am tortured.

In Poem 85 the neatness and brevity of Hellenistic Greek epigram[44] are combined with characteristically Catullan intensity of feeling. Here the emotional conflict of Poem 72, and to some extent also of Poem 76, is more starkly expressed. Instead of the careful distinction between spiritual love and sexual desire and the anxious groping for strikingly new methods of expression, the bald facts: 'I hate and love' (*odi et amo* [1]). The ultimate economy is omission of something to indicate who or what is the recipient of the hate and the love.[45] A doggedly prosaic question from an obtuse imaginary interrogator then allows Catullus to claim the situation to be inexplicable, but real, and utterly excruciating. 'You ask why I *do* it?' he says, using an active verb (*faciam* [1]), which implies that the whole thing is within his own control,[46] but his reply, by way of a passive verb (*fieri* [2]), that it is just 'happening' clearly proclaims his helplessness. The poem's emotional power is rooted in its very simplicity (six first person verbs and no nouns or adjectives) and in the final climactic 'I am tortured' (*excrucior* [2]). The root-meaning of *excrucior* is 'I suffer on the cross', and the agony of crucifixion sprang from the unrelenting pull of counteracting forces on the hands and the feet of the victim. Such is the pain Catullus feels that the opposing forces of 'hate' and 'love' inflict on him, since he cannot escape from either. Of course, the coexistence of these two conflicting emotions may seem unlikely, but it is in fact very familiar to us (the 'love-hate relationship') and was evidently familiar to the

---

[44] See pp. xviii-xix.

[45] See further Small (1983) 40.

[46] He almost convinced himself that it was within his control in Poem 76.

ancients too, judging from earlier poets' exploration of it. Note, for example, 'Theognis' 1090-94 West:

> My heart is troubled about your friendship.
> For I can neither hate nor love,
> recognising that when one is a man's friend it's difficult
> to hate, but difficult love him when he is averse.[47]

The singularity of Catullus is that he makes the familiar and understandable paradox appear strange and enigmatic.[48]

Catullus: Retrospect

Few short Latin poems generate, severally or collectively, as much debate and dissension as these three, Catullus 72, 76 and 85. Which, for example, is emotionally, and which artistically, the most successful? Catullus' plain *cri de cœur* in 85? His attempt to explain the inexplicable in 72? Or his effort to reason and will away his racking pain in 76? A German critic has declared Poem 85 to be more artful than it seems, and the touch of inexplicitness in it has been judged a fault.[49] Poem 72 has been called both 'fumbling' in its expression (Copley [1949] 29) and 'the precise formulation of a lost ideal' with a tone of 'icy detachment' (Quinn [1970] 400, 403).[50] But the alleged 'fumbling' has also been forgiven on the grounds that Catullus did at least 'succeed in presenting a clear picture of the psychological conflict which that love occasioned' (Copley [1949] 33), while the alleged precision and analytical detachment have been pronounced unwelcome because 'analysis and poetry are essentially conflicting occupations' (Lyne [1980] 41). For its author's degree of emotional involvement Poem 76 has won praise: 'We are *intended* to feel that Catullus has lost his sense of proportion' (Quinn [1970] 407); but also criticism: 'Catullus is not distanced from feeling in the way that an artist should be' (Lyne [1970] 32). It has been seen both as a spontaneous composition[51] and as one 'managed with perfect timing and sense of drama' (Williams [1968] 410). All three poems can be understood independently, and it is hard to deduce

---

[47] For the layout of this non-metrical translation see p. ix. Cf. Meleager. *AP* 5. 24. Evenus. *AP* 12. 172. Terence. *Eunuchus* 70-74.

[48] For an interesting collection and discussion of a wide variety of English versions of the poem see Rudd (1976) 183-9.

[49] See Lyne (1980) 41.

[50] Cf. Commager (1965) 95.

[51] So the German commentator W. Kroll.

anything definite about the sequence of their composition; but it is worth considering whether any one of them gains (or loses) anything from the reader's knowledge of the others. We can ask, too, whether they all explore the same mental conflict, and whether any of them is more of an elegy than an epigram.[52]

What, also, of Poems 72, 76 and 85 as a group? Does the marked prosiness of all three pieces make them inferior to, say, Poem 8? Is it inaccurate to call the unusual terminology which Catullus draws upon to articulate his emotions 'imagery'? Or, to put it another way, does he, instead of merely *likening* his involvement with Lesbia to a friendship, an ideal marriage or an illness, regard it as actually *being* one or more of these things?[53] Are these poems indeed 'brilliantly original' (Lyne [1980] 41), or are they substantially indebted to earlier poetry? How much in their turn do the Augustan love elegies in the present selection owe to these Catullan compositions? And do Catullus' subject-matter and vocabulary, his forms, style and tone, and above all his attitudes to love, ever appear again?

---

[52] For conflicting views on this point and its importance contrast Ross (1969) 110 with Wheeler (1934) 170-71.

[53] Lyne (1980) 25, speaking of the language of friendship, claims that 'there is not really any question of metaphor'. Cf. Kennedy (1993) 46-63.

PROPERTIUS
(translations by Guy Lee)

Propertius 1. 1

Cynthia first, with her eyes, caught wretched me
  Smitten before by no desires;
Then, lowering my stare of steady arrogance,
  With feet imposed Love pressed my head,
Until he taught me hatred of chaste girls –   5
  The villain – and living aimlessly.
And now, for a whole year, this mania has not left me,
  But still I am forced to suffer adverse Gods.
Milanion by facing every hardship, Tullus,
  Conquered the cruelty of Atalanta.   10
Sometimes, deranged, he roamed the glens of Parthenius
  And was gone to watch the long-haired beasts.
Stunned by that blow from Hylaeus' club he even
  Groaned in anguish to Arcadian crags.
So he was able to master his swift-footed girl;   15
  Such power in love have prayers and kindnesses.
For me, though, Love is slow, can think of no devices
  And forgets to go his legendary way.
But you who know the trick of drawing down the moon
  And the task of atonement on magic altars,   20
Here is your chance, come, change my mistress' thinking
  And make her face paler than mine.
Then I could believe you have the power to move
  Rivers and stars with Colchian sorcery.
Or you, friends, who (too late) call back the fallen,   25
  Seek remedies for a heart diseased.
Bravely will I suffer blade and cruel burning,
  Given liberty to speak as anger bids.
Bear me through farthest nations, bear me over the waves
  Where no woman will know my way.   30
Stay home, all you to whom God nods with easy ear,
  And be paired in love forever true.
On me our Venus levies nights of bitterness,

And empty love is ever present.
I warn you, shun this evil. Let each man's darling hold him   35
Nor quit when love has grown familiar.
But if to warnings anyone should turn slow ears,
Alas, how bitterly he'll rue my words!

Cynthia has Propertius for the first time in his life well and truly smitten. Love, through her, has taught him a lesson. Although he has been in this deranged state for a year now, he says, the gods are still hostile to him (1-8). Slipping in the name of his principal addressee, Tullus (almost certainly the nephew of L.Volcacius Tullus who was consul with Octavian in 33 BC[1]), he then abruptly recalls the mythological lover Milanion, who by 'prayers and kindnesses' (*preces et bene facta* [16]) overcame the unresponsiveness of Atalanta (9-16). She was an unbendingly chaste huntress (her name in Greek means 'unyielding'), exposed at birth on Mt Parthenius[2] in Arcadia and allegedly once lecherously set upon by two Centaurs (fabled half-man, half-horse creatures); Hylaeus[3] is the name of one of them. Propertius here intimates that Milanion's assistance against them won him Atalanta's gratitude and compliance,[4] but in his own case, he claims, Love does not come up with any schemes or follow the pattern of such old and familiar stories (17-18). Next, abruptly again, he challenges practitioners of magic (traditionally credited with aphrodisiac influence)[5] to prove to him the power of their 'Colchian sorcery'[6] (Colchis was the home of the witch Medea) by working a miracle: making Cynthia 'become paler' (*palleat... magis* [22]) with love than he is himself (19-22).[7] Then he appeals to unnamed 'friends' (*amici* [25]), who are 'too late' (*sero* [25]) to save him from love altogether, to find some means of releasing him from his current suffering, either by subjecting him to painful treatment or taking him physically well out of harm's way (25-30). Finally, he warns those blessed in their present love to stay where they are and not seek change for

---

[1] The identification is based on Prop. 1. 6. 19-20; see further Hubbard (1974) 24-5, Syme (1978) 98-9, 179-80.

[2] The name of the mountain itself means 'virginal'.

[3] *Hylaei* is the generally accepted conjectural correction of the nonsensical reading of the MSS at this point.

[4] Cf. Ov. *Ars Amatoria* 2. 191, a passage clearly influenced by Propertius'.

[5] Cf. Prop. 1. 12. 9-10, Tib. 1. 2. 43-64, 5. 41-2, 8. 17-18, 2. 4. 55-60 and, especially, Theocritus, *Idyll* 2.

[6] *Cytaeines carminibus* (24) literally means 'the spells of the Cytaean woman'; Cytaea (or Cyta) was a mythical city in Colchis.

[7] For pallor as a traditional symptom of amatory affliction cf. Tib. 1. 8. 51, Ov. *Am.* 2. 7. 10.

change's sake. Above all they should avoid the 'evil' (*malum* [35]) which Love inflicts on him. Anyone who does not listen will end up regretting his mistake (31-8).

A suffering lover and an unobliging, exotically named woman[8] who dominates his life: this basic situation is familiar enough from Catullus. But, whereas Catullus focusses obsessively on the emotions and behaviour of lover and beloved, Propertius adopts a wider perspective, bringing into his opening poem a string of other parties: the personified Love (and Venus), the gods *en masse*, Milanion and Atalanta, Tullus, witches, unnamed friends, and fellow-lovers. The animate and aggressive Love he imports from Hellenistic epigram.[9] Lines 1-4 recall in particular Meleager, *AP* 12. 101:

> When I was unwounded by Desires, Myiscus,
>   shooting me in the heart with his eyes, uttered this cry:
> 'I have caught the boaster; and look, that supercilious air
>   of sceptred wisdom I am trampling underfoot'.
> But, getting my breath back, I replied: 'Dear boy, why the surprise?
>   Love brought down Zeus himself from Olympus'.[10]

'Intertextuality'[11] is hard at work here, with superficial similarity serving to highlight significant difference. In Propertius it is not the lover but the beloved – female and not male – who gets first mention. The lover himself is 'wretched' (*miserum* [1]) instead of nonchalant and witty. The personified Love as well as the beloved plays a part in subjugating him. He is not tritely shot and wounded, nor is he even just 'caught' like a prisoner of war, but also 'smitten' (*contactum* [2]), as if with disease.[12] Nor in his case is it philosophic wisdom[13] which Love has mocked, but the cock-sureness of inexperience.[14]

---

[8] See p. xxxvii.

[9] See pp. xviii-xix.

[10] For the layout of this non-metrical translation see p. ix. Cf. also Meleager, *AP* 12. 48.

[11] See p. xiv.

[12] Not in itself a new idea; see pp. xiv, 29-30.

[13] The Hellenistic thinkers, both Stoic and Epicurean, regarded love as a sickness of the soul caused by a wrong attitude of mind and curable by the self-help which their philosophy offered.

[14] This idea is conveyed through imagery interestingly reminiscent of that used by the Epicurean poet-philosopher Lucretius to illustrate Epicurus' emancipation of human beings from fear of the gods by means of philosophy at *De Rerum Natura* 1. 62-6: 'When human life ...was lying on the ground, oppressed by the weight of religion, whose head loomed out of the sky, making mortals cower under its terrible stare, a Greek man for the first time dared to raise his mortal eyes in defiance' (*humana...cum uita iaceret / in terris oppressa graui sub religione*

Love's conquest of Propertius is thus depicted as something unique and terrifying rather than typical and insignificant, and as no momentary triumph, but one with lasting consequences for his whole existence.[15] It has taught him to 'hate chaste girls' (*castas odisse puellas* [5]) and 'to live aimlessly' (*nullo uiuere consilio* [6]).

What does this much-discussed remark mean? Probably that Propertius has come to have no interest in traditionally virtuous women, who would always say 'no' out of moral rectitude, and has no thoughts of arranging to marry one of them, as would be expected of a young Roman of his social status.[16] This does not inappropriately imply that Cynthia is hardly better than a whore, as many who have rejected such a line of interpretation have thought, but rather that she is excitingly unpredictable. She too may say 'no', if she feels like it (as she obviously does much of the time), but in her case there is always the enticing possibility that she will say 'yes' (and Propertius gives no reason to suppose that she has not at least occasionally already done so by this stage).[17] Love, then, has affected not so much Propertius' body as his mind – his capacity for rational judgement. The idea that it was a kind of madness had long been popular with both poets and philosophers.[18] Unlike the philosophers, however, Propertius will countenance no personal responsibility for his suffering, but blames the gods for unreasonably frustrating his desires.[19]

/ *quae caput a caeli regionibus ostendebat / horribili super aspectu mortalibus instans, / primum Graius homo mortalis tollere contra / est oculos ausus primusque obsistere contra*). Cf. also Prop. 2. 30. 7-10 (trans. Lee) 'Always Love presses, presses on the lover's head / And settles heavily on the neck once free. / As a guard he keeps a strict watch and will never let you / Lift your eyes from the ground once they are caught' (*instat semper Amor supra caput, instat amanti, / et grauis ipse super libera colla sedet. / excubat ille acer custos et tollere numquam / te patietur humo lumina capta semel*).

[15] See further Allen (1950) 264-8, Hubbard (1974) 16-17, 20.

[16] So e.g. Sullivan (1976) 102-4, Lyne (1998b) 163-4. Possibly it is this loss of conventional respectability which makes Propertius call Love a 'villain' (*improbus* [6]), though such description of Eros/Cupid is also traditional.

[17] An alternative suggestion, based on the assumption that Cynthia herself could be called a 'chaste' (*casta*) girl when unobliging to Propertius or exclusively faithful to some other lover (cf. p. 31), is that Propertius is claiming here to resent her for making him suffer; so e.g. Allen (1950) 266-7, Ahl (1974) 84-5, Stahl (1985) 36-41. But such an interpretation would mean extracting from 'hate' (*odisse*) a sense at odds with all Propertius' other uses of the word. For distaste, and not resentment, is what it implies elsewhere in his work (i.e. at 2. 18. 19, 26. 25, 3. 8. 27); it refers always to things which the speaker wants nothing to do with because they are fundamentally unappealing – quite the reverse of Cynthia to Propertius.

[18] Cf. Prop. 3. 24. 17-20, with discussion on p. 75, Tib. 2. 4. 51-6, with discussion on p. 127, Ov. *Am.* 1. 2. 31-6, and see also Allen (1950) 261-4.

[19] Cf. Horace, *Odes* 1. 5. 6.

What has the story of Milanion and Atalanta to do with all this? The link with what has gone before is easily missed: Milanion was 'deranged' (*amens* [11]) just as Propertius is suffering from 'mania' (*furor* [7]). Love-*madness*, in short, is what the two of them have in common. Propertius intimates that Milanion at one stage attempted to comfort himself by withdrawing to the remote countryside and going hunting as a distraction. The first is a regular form of attempted consolation for unhappy love,[20] and interestingly both these 'treatments' are contemplated and then dismissed by Gallus[21] the rejected poet-lover in Virgil's tenth *Eclogue* (55-61):

> interea mixtis lustrabo Maenala Nymphis
> aut acris uenabor apros. non me ulla uetabunt
> frigora Parthenios canibus circumdare saltus.
> iam mihi per rupes uideor lucosque sonantis
> ire, libet Partho torquere Cydonia cornu
> spicula – tamquam haec sit nostri medicina furoris,
> aut deus ille malis hominum mitescere discat.

> But meanwhile with the Nymphs I'll range on Maenala
> Or hunt the savage boar. No frosts will hinder me
> From drawing coverts on Parthenius with hounds.
> Already I see myself explore the sounding rocks
> And groves, already long to shoot Cydonian darts
> From Parthian horn – as if this remedied our madness,
> Or that god learnt from human hardship to grow mild!

(trans. Lee)

Propertius, however, goes on to imply that Milanion's moaning aloud to the wilderness resulted less from the wounds of love than from a real wound inflicted by one of Atalanta's would-be ravishers. This converts Milanion from what appeared to be the familiar pathetic victim into a heroic adjutant and hints strongly that he saw at some point the possibility of using hunting to please or impress Atalanta[22] rather than just to solace himself. Not until lines 17-18 does the main point of the example – the contrast between Milanion's success and Propertius' failure – become clear. It is precisely because Cynthia is *not* like Atalanta – because what

---

[20] Memorably practised by Acontius, hungering for Cydippe, in Callimachus' account (*Aetia*, frags 72-3 Trypanis). See also the imitation by the late Greek erotic epistolographer Aristaenetus at 1. 10. 56-79 and Propertius' own exploration of the idea in 1. 17 and 18.

[21] See pp. xxvii-xxviii.

[22] Ovid explicitly claims this at *Ars Amatoria* 2. 189-90.

has to be conquered in her case is 'cruelty' (*saeuitiam* [10]) not out of high principle but out of plain cussedness – that Propertius cannot enjoy the same outcome as Milanion, whatever (un)heroic 'hardships' (*labores* [9]) of his own he may be prepared to undergo to impress *his* beloved. The implied comparison of the urban poet with the intrepid fighter of 'shaggy beasts' (*hirsutas...feras* [12]) is not without its humour!

The story that Propertius actually tells about Atalanta here is much less well-known than the version in which she, renowned for her running ability, declared that she would accept only a suitor who could beat her in a race, and Milanion (in some versions, Hippomenes) advised by Aphrodite (Venus), achieved this by throwing down three golden apples to distract her. This version of Atalanta's story, besides being arguably overworked, would not suit Propertius' purpose, for it depicts her as a shallow, materialistic woman, able to be won over by pretty, precious objects, rather than as a girl who in the end graciously responds to her lover's self-sacrifice on her behalf. But Propertius does bring in a reminder of it when he calls Atalanta a 'fleet-footed' (*uelocem* [15]) girl. This at first seems to be gratuitous, but in fact the epithet paves the way for the explicit contrasting of Propertius' situation with Milanion's. For the claim that Love is 'slow' (*tardus* [17]) neatly counterpoints the allusion to Atalanta's speed; it suggests that Cynthia remains out of Propertius' reach just as surely as if she were the swift Atalanta ahead of him in a race, because the god Love in his case (unlike Aphrodite in Milanion's) is not quick to help.[23] Propertius' general point is that love in real life is not like love in the fairy tales, and an inverted echo of Catullan sentiments in line 16 helps to bring this out: 'prayers' and 'kindnesses' may have won the day for Milanion,[24] but in the world of real human relationships, as Catullus had already painfully discovered,[25] these things sometimes achieve absolutely nothing.

The general sense of the aggressive challenge to witches in lines 19-24 is 'You who are supposed to be able to move heaven and earth, come on now, let me see you move Cynthia's feelings in my favour, and then I will *believe* that you can move heaven and earth'. The repeated notion of 'moving' things – clearer in the Latin (*deductae...conuertite...ducere*) – functions as a linking device. But instead of actually saying something

---

[23] The complaint of Love's inability to think of any 'devices' (*artis* [17]) is more suggestive of the apple-stratagem than the fighting of Centaurs.

[24] We could perhaps assume that the 'prayers' followed the 'kindnesses' and were answered specifically because the 'kindnesses' had been performed, but I suggest in a paper forthcoming in *Hermes* that 'prayers' to Venus, and not to Atalanta at all, are what Propertius had in mind here.

[25] See Catul. 76. 1-8 with discussion on pp. 26-8.

brief and simple like 'move heaven and earth' Propertius uses some specific examples of magical party-pieces: drawing down the moon (or stars) from the sky,[26] making propiatory sacrifices on 'magic altars' (*magicis... focis* [20]),[27] and changing the course of rivers.[28] The suggestion that influencing his beloved will be far more difficult than these traditional feats[29] is an attempt to show that he is trapped in a hopeless love-situation.[30]

Denied fulfilment, the only alternative means of alleviating his suffering he can envisage is release from love altogether, and this he calls upon his 'friends' to bring about. It has been suggested that friends of suitable status might in certain circumstances be made responsible for a man out of his mind,[31] as Propertius claims to be, but the appeal here need evoke only the upper-class social convention by which 'friends' were expected to offer support, practical or moral, in any time of need.[32] The sickness metaphor of the opening is explicitly resurrected in line 26,[33] and it leads to the idea of being healed by surgery and cautery (the alliterating English 'bravely...[suffer] blade' attempts to parallel a similar effect in the Latin *fortiter...ferrum* [27]); but the instruments of radical healing are the same as those of penal torture, and by line 28 Propertius' thoughts seem to have turned to the practice of applying a branding iron to make slaves under interrogation tell the truth. Propertius, apparently, *wants* to tell the truth about his 'anger' (*ira* [28]), i.e. to be allowed to get off his chest his indignation at the treatment he is receiving from Cynthia. Presumably he fears that a protest would make her more cruel still. The position of a slave under torture, therefore, horribly humiliating and painful though it may be, paradoxically seems to offer him, the free man, a type of 'freedom' (*libertas* [28]) of which he feels deprived.[34] His other notion of therapy for himself

---

[26] Cf. Tib. 1. 8. 21, Ov. *Am*. 2. 1. 23.

[27] Tibullus at 1. 2. 64 calls the gods of the Underworld the 'magic' gods (*magicos...deos*), and probably Propertius is here alluding to the alleged power of witches to mobilise the divinities of Hell.

[28] Cf. Tib. 1. 2. 46, Ov. *Am*. 2. 1. 26.

[29] The idea is perhaps helped by the associations of the very name Cynthia, through 'Cynthian' Apollo (see p. xxxvii), with (i) Apollo's sister, the notoriously unbending virgin deity Artemis (Diana), (ii) the moon itself, one of Artemis' manifestations (see O'Neill [1958]) and (iii) the formidable Hell-goddess Hecate, also sometimes identified with Artemis (see Papanghelis [1987] 37).

[30] Some, however, take it as an earnest appeal for a miracle; e.g. Allen (1950) 274.

[31] So Cairns (1974) 105.

[32] Cf. p. 25, with n. 14.

[33] Cf. Prop. 3. 24. 18.

[34] See further Lyne (1979) 129, and cf. Tib. 2. 3. 81-4, 4. 1-6, with discussion on pp. 120-21.

also involves reversal of a normal situation, but a literary rather than a social one. Instead of expressing the lover's usual willingness to follow a particular beloved to the ends of the earth,[35] Propertius sees a journey to the ends of the earth as an escape-route from all women, and instead of acknowledging the willingness of friends to accompany him anywhere,[36] he begs the friends to organise the curative expedition.

This extreme form of attempted cure through change of scenery (a philosophically approved remedy for all men tortured by love)[37] Propertius does not recommend in every case. Those who are happy in their love, he advises, should stay where they are and make the most of their successful pairing. The unusual image in line 31, which conflates the idea of a deity having 'nodded' (*annuit*) assent and having listened to prayers with a sympathetic 'ear' (*aure*), harks back to the thought of the gods being responsible for all amatory fortune. Propertius' own situation (33-4) is supposed to demonstrate the wisdom of his advice: Venus[38] puts him through some uncomfortable nights, and Love is always in attendance. Love (*Amor*) is at least semi-personified here as Venus' son and can be called 'empty' (*uacuus* [34]) in the sense of 'offering no fulfilment'.[39] This situation is the 'evil' (*malum* [35]) that the experienced Propertius warns other lovers not to let themselves in for by looking for a new and more challenging beloved (the foregoing theme of leaving and staying is sustained in lines 35-6).[40] The warning sounds altruistic, but it is worth observing that, if Propertius' fellow-lovers took his advice, he would himself conveniently be relieved of competition for the difficult Cynthia whose hard-to-getness is the source of all his anguish.

Propertius makes no explicit declaration of literary intent in his very first elegy. This is rather surprising, given that he provides very elaborate programmatic[41] statements in the opening poems of all his subsequent

---

[35] Cf. Prop. 2. 26, 29-34, Tib. 1. 4. 41-6, Plautus, *Mercator* 857-63.

[36] A cliché of friendship poetry; see e.g. Prop. 1. 6. 3-4, Horace, *Epode* 1, 11-14, and the semi-facetious versions at Catul. 11. 1-14 and Horace, *Odes* 2. 6. 1-4.

[37] See e.g. Cicero, *Tusculan Disputations* 4. 74, and cf. Allen (1950) 275.

[38] The Latin *nostra Venus* (33) is literally translated: 'our Venus'. This may mean 'the goddess of us lovers', i.e. both the unhappy, represented by Propertius himself, and the more fortunate, whom he now addresses, or it may mean no more than 'my (goddess) Venus', with *nostra* used as a poetic plural for *mea*. The point is contentious: see e.g. Heyworth (1984) 394-6.

[39] Some understand line 34 slightly differently as 'Love is never idle, never absent'.

[40] Literally 'Let each man's fancy detain him and not move on' (or 'flit' – the northern English word for moving house is exactly right here) 'when love has become familiar'.

[41] See p. xiv.

---

books and at various other points in his work.[42] All the more reason, there-
fore, to wonder whether poem 1. 1 could contain an indirect form of liter-
ary manifesto. It is certainly not difficult to read something of the kind into
it. Firstly, Propertius begins by saying that he was firmly put in his place,
when full of himself, both by a woman whose invented name has associa-
tions with Apollo, god of poetry, and by the personified Love: this could be
taken to hint at some sort of divine direction towards a career as an erotic
poet.[43] Secondly, although he does not specifically repudiate either ways of
life or forms of poetry considered more respectable than those he has cho-
sen for himself, he does address his claim to have 'gone off the rails' to
Tullus, a young man from an establishment family.[44] This arguably high-
lights his own resistance to both an establishment-approved career and
establishment-approved genres of poetry (especially epic).[45] Thirdly, the
striking difference between the Propertian Milanion and the superficially
similar Virgilian Gallus (the former working actively for success in love,
the latter passively accepting failure) perhaps implies Propertius' recogni-
tion of the real Gallus' poetic habit of identifying inappropriately with
mythological lovers.[46] If that is the case, the emphatic contrast between
Propertius' own amatory failure and Milanion's success (17), coupled with
the claim that Love in his case follows an unfamiliar course (18), could be
interpreted as an oblique declaration of his intent to use mythological ex-
amples in a novel and more fitting way in his own poetry.[47] He may mean
that he is going to use them to demonstrate how sadly *un*like, rather than
like, the lot of mythological lovers is his own everyday experience.[48] At
first sight, it seems that what he actually does in the poems which follow is
quite the opposite; but many of them, on scrutiny, do reveal a Propertius-
in-love who is ruefully aware of the chasm between himself and his
mythological role-models.

---

[42] See e.g. pp. 60-61, 69-70, 76-7.

[43] Cf. especially Ov. *Am.* 1. 1.

[44] See Lyne (1998b) 160-61.

[45] Interestingly, the Latin word *furor* which Propertius uses of his own 'madness' in line 7 is
the very one which is used of threat to the established Roman order at Virgil, *Aeneid* 1. 294;
see also p. 141.

[46] Ross (1975) 59-64 suggests that the real Gallus specifically used the Milanion example.

[47] This suggestion, based on suspicion of an intertextual dialogue with Gallus, is controversial; I
argue for it in more detail in a paper forthcoming in *Hermes*.

[48] The similarity of the expression to Callimachus' solemn commendation of 'unworn paths'
in poetry at *Aetia* frag. 1. 27-8 Trypanis (see p. xx) strengthens the case for an oblique
declaration of literary intent here.

Whether or not the poem does contain systematically hidden programmatic statements, however, it undeniably offers a foretaste of what is to come in the rest of Book 1. Apart from the general obsession with Cynthia, we can see here in embryonic form Propertius' preoccupation with the ideal and consequences of exclusive love,[49] the important theme of the mocker of love becoming a lover himself,[50] and the sustained tension between Propertius' pose on the one hand as the helpless victim of love and on the other as the expert adviser to fellow-sufferers.[51] Here too the reader can sample some of the characteristic features of Propertius' poetic technique: his love of erudition, particularly of a mythological kind; his challengingly abrupt but rarely inexplicable transitions; his complex obbligato of interrelated themes, images and allusions; his linguistic boldness (the mixed metaphor in line 31 is typical); and the hint of humour lurking beneath the passionate, romantic and often pessimistic surface.

It has sometimes been suggested that this poem is an elegiac expansion of Catullus' famous epigram 85, 'I hate and I love'.[52] But are the objects of the hate and the love and the reasons for those emotions in fact the same in the two poems? Do love, friendship and the gods mean the same thing to Propertius here as they do to Catullus? This poem has been called a piece of 'direct self-analysis' (Allen [1950] 265) and 'a clear-eyed recognition of Propertius' psychological orientation' (Sullivan [1976] 104), both of which judgements imply that Propertius' prime interest is in his emotion as emotion. But is it rather in his emotion as poetry? 'Strangely opaque' the poem has been labelled too, 'always hinting at a private dilemma which [Propertius] seems unable to talk about directly' (Hodge and Buttimore [1977] 63): does this kind of judgement tell us more about the critics than about the poet? As the very first poem of a book of love elegies, Propertius 1. 1 begs comparison especially with Tibullus 1. 1 and Ovid, *Amores* 1. 1.[53] Does Propertius present his love at the outset as anything more, or less, special than that of his fellow-elegists? Do we get to know anything more about Cynthia than about their respective beloveds? And what sort of a figure does Propertius cut here in comparison with Tibullus and Ovid? Any more or less of a suffering lover, and any less or more of a self-promoting poet?

---

[49] Cf. 1. 2. 25-6, 8A. 21-6, 10. 29-30, 11. 23-4, 12. 17-20, 13. 9-10 and 35-6, 15. 29-32.

[50] Cf. 1. 7 and 9.

[51] Cf. 1. 5, 9, 10. 11-30, 13, 15. 39-42, 20. 1-4.

[52] See pp. 32-3.

[53] See pp. 97-109 and 131-7.

Propertius 1. 3

As the girl from Knossos, while Theseus' keel receded,
  Lay limp on a deserted beach,
And as Cephéan Andromeda in first sleep rested,
  From hard rocks freed at last,
And as a Maenad, no less tired by the ceaseless dance,   5
  Swoons on grassy Apidanus,
So Cynthia seemed to me to breathe soft peace,
  Leaning her head on relaxed hands,
When I was dragging footsteps drunken with much Bacchus
  And the boys shook torches in the small hours.   10
Not yet bereft of all my senses I prepared
  To approach her, gently, pressing the couch.
But, though a prey to double passion, under orders
  (From Love on this flank, Bacchus on that, both ruthless Gods,)
To edge an arm beneath her, reconnoitring,   15
  And kiss, with hand at work, and stand to arms,
Still I dared not disturb my lady's peace,
  Fearing the fierce abuse I knew so well;
But there I stuck, staring intent, like Argus
  At Io's unfamiliar horns.   20
And now I loosed the garland from my forehead
  And placed it, Cynthia, on your temples,
Or pleased myself by re-arranging your stray hair,
  Or to cupped hands gave stolen fruit;
But all my gifts were lavished on ungrateful sleep,   25
  Gifts rolled from my pocket often as I leant.
Whenever, rarely moving, you drew a sigh,
  I froze in superstitious dread
That dreams were bringing you strange fears
  And some man forced you to be his –   30
Until the moon, passing the window opposite,
  The busy moon with lingering light
Opened those calm closed eyes with weightless beams.
  'So!' (and she dug an elbow into the couch)
'At last humiliation brings you back to our bed,   35
  Thrown out from another woman's door!
Where have you wasted the long hours of my night,
  Limp, alas, now the stars are set?

Villain, oh how I wish you could endure such nights
  As you always inflict on wretched me!   40
Sometimes I cheated sleep with crimson thread
  Or a tired tune on Orpheus' lyre;
Or I whispered complaints to my forsaken self
  At unmarried love's long absences –
Until I dropped off, stroked by Slumber's welcome wings,   45
  That thought, above all, made me weep.'

The sight of Cynthia asleep reminds Propertius of each of three sleeping
women of mythological fame (1-8). The first is the Cretan princess Ariadne
(Knossos was the chief city of Crete); after helping Theseus of Athens slay
her father's monstrous offspring, the Minotaur, she was abandoned by him
on the island of Naxos (1-2). The second is Andromeda, who was chained
to a rock on the shore by her father, the Ethiopian king Cepheus, to appease
a sea-monster sent to punish her mother for boasting that Andromeda was
more beautiful than the sea-nymphs; she was eventually rescued by Per-
seus, who fell in love with her and killed the monster (3-4). The third is a
Maenad, a female devotee of Bacchus (Dionysus); when possessed by the
god, the Maenads were thrown into destructive orgiastic frenzies before
collapsing in exhaustion (5-6). Thrace was the locality especially associ-
ated with the Maenads, and the 'grassy' (*herboso* [5]), i.e. 'grassy-banked',
R. Apidanus, here mentioned as the site of the collapse, belongs to that re-
gion. And Cynthia's likeness to all of these women occurred to Propertius
when he came to her drunk one night after a party (9-10)! Bacchus, god of
wine, here stands for wine itself, and 'boys' (*pueri* [10]), i.e. slaves, con-
ventionally escorted their masters back from convivial gatherings, lighting
their way through the often dangerous streets.

Propertius was not too drunk, though, to think of trying to kiss her –
and more (the general idea of sexual violation is clear) (11-16). He re-
frained, however, for fear of waking her and getting a tongue-lashing (17-
18), and instead just stood there gazing at her, as Argus gazed at Io (Argus
was the hundred-eyed guard appointed by Juno to watch Io, whom Jupiter
loved and turned into a cow in the attempt to protect her from his wife's
jealous anger) (19-20). Then Propertius began playing with her body and
hair and tried to put fruits into her hands.[54] It was a waste of time because
she slept on, oblivious to the repeated gifts (21-6). Whenever she sighed in
her sleep, Propertius fearfully imagined her having a nightmare in which
some unwanted lover was trying to rape her (27-30). Eventually, however,

---

[54] Apples were traditional love-gifts, and both these and the garland would have been
conventional 'take-homes' from the party.

she was roused by the light of the moon falling on her face and propped herself up on the couch (31-4). The tongue-lashing then materialised, and Cynthia's tirade is reported verbatim. 'Has she thrown you out, then – the other woman? Is that why you're here? Where were you, when you should have been with me? Yes, you, who come here now, all done in, just as it's getting light! I wish you could have a taste of your own medicine. I waited up for you for hours, keeping myself awake with fancy wool-working and wistful music' (the name of Orpheus instantly suggests love-anguish),[55] 'grieving because I knew you'd be dallying with another. Mercifully I dropped off to sleep in the end' (the idea is of being nudged over the borderline between wakefulness and sleep by a winged creature which, slightly illogically, is supposed to be Sleep itself)[56] 'but in tears, for that (unhappy) thought'[57] (i.e. of Propertius' betrayal of her) 'was the last thing on my mind' (35-46). So may one paraphrase the emotional outburst.

Of all Propertius' poems on Cynthia this has, at first sight, one of the most romantic of openings. It therefore comes as something of a shock to discover that the lover was drunk when the mythical quality of Cynthia's beauty struck him, and that he had only belatedly staggered into her presence after carousing the night away at a party (dalliance with another woman, of which he is eventually accused, is at no point positively excluded!). But he quickly re-establishes his pose of rapt tenderness with the claim that he 'gently' (*molliter* [12]) manoeuvred himself close to her – only to destroy it again immediately with the admission that, under the influence of both drink and libido, he was strongly tempted to rape her. Not that he puts it nearly so baldly. Indeed he does not say that he actually did anything at all, but only that he felt the urge to do it – first, tentatively to edge her into a promising position (the Latin *temptare* [15], translated 'reconnoitring', neatly suggests both exploration and sexual assault), then 'with hand applied' (*admota...manu* [16]), i.e. now quite confidently caressing either her breasts or, possibly, her genitals,[58] 'to take [up] kisses and [take up] arms'.[59] 'Take up/snatch kisses' (*oscula sumere*) is a standard Latin expression, and 'take up arms' (*arma sumere*) is a familiar metaphor for 'getting to work' at anything. 'Arms' (*arma*) in Latin, however, is also

---

[55] See p. 49 below, and cf. pp. 57 and 59.

[56] Cf. Virgil, *Aeneid* 5. 838-9, and for Sleep in art see p. 49 below.

[57] The Latin *cura* connotes both distress and love.

[58] For the breasts cf. Plautus, *Bacchides* 480; for the genitals see Kilmer (1993) fig. R 318 (a Greek vase-painting depicting a satyr approaching a sleeping woman).

[59] This is a literal translation of line 16, where some scholars, probably unnecessarily, doubt the correctness of the transmitted text.

a common euphemism for 'penis', and so Propertius' phraseology overall implies a specifically sexual kind of 'getting cracking'; he imagines progressing from caresses and kisses to full intercourse. There is an extra touch of audacity, too, in the military metaphor running through lines 13-16, which the English translation well conveys: 'approach' (*adire* [12]), 'under orders' ([*quamuis*] *iuberent*[60] [13]), 'on this flank' (*hac* [14]), 'reconnoitring' (*temptare* [15]), 'hand at work' (*admota...manu* [16], literally 'moved up', like troops), 'stand to arms' (*sumere...arma* [16]). Then, however, Propertius rehabilitates his image a little with the insistence that he restrained his lecherous urges (17) – only to tarnish it again immediately by revealing that he did so not out of consideration or respect for Cynthia but out of fear of her sharp tongue (18). Yet it is difficult to condemn him for anything worse than a clown when next he depicts himself doggedly making repeated attempts to place gifts in Cynthia's unconscious hands (21-6), too fuddled to see the futility of it, and blaming it all on 'ungrateful' (*ingrato* [25]) sleep. This almost endearing picture is itself soon undermined by his splendidly hypocritical fear that Cynthia's sigh (or sharp intake of breath) may mean that she is dreaming of 'some man' (*quis* [30]) trying to rape her (27-30).[61] Romance, however, briefly returns yet again with the description of her gentle awakening by the moon from the general serenity of her sleep (31-3), but there is nothing gentle and serene about her 'body language' on first waking (34) or the recriminations which follow (35-40).[62] Even this rough outburst, however, eventually gives way to a quieter complaint, full of pathos and melancholy (41-6).

We have in this poem, then, not just the one dramatic exploding of romantic illusion which occurs when 'the idyllic vision wakes, and not only wakes but talks, and not only talks but nags' (Hubbard [1974] 21), but also a seesawing throughout between tender romance and sharp worldliness.[63] On first reading, almost every undercutting of the romance is a surprise, but in restrospect there are various subtle pointers to what is to come. (i) The sexually inviting aspect of Cynthia's sleeping posture is hinted at through the 'soft peace ' (*mollem...quietem* [7]) of her breathing, since the Latin word for 'soft' (*mollis*) also connotes 'seductive'; and the cognate adverb

---

[60] Literally 'Although [*Amor* and *Liber*] issued orders'.

[61] The earlier reference to Io may suggest that Propertius remembered here Aeschylus' account of Io's dreaming of Zeus' desire for her at *Prometheus Bound* 645-54, but Calvus' *Io* could have been an even more direct source of inspiration; see n. 86 below.

[62] In the Latin Cynthia does not actually utter the aggressive 'So'. Propertius simply says 'Thus she spoke' (*sic ait* [34]), preserving for just a moment longer, with this epic phraseology, the illusion that a heroine or a goddess, and not a virago, is about to hold forth.

[63] See Curran (1966) 196-7.

molliter (translated 'gently') is used in line 12 of Propertius own libidinous approach to her couch.[64] (ii) The reader is forewarned (in passing) of Cynthia's capacity for verbal 'abuse' (*iurgia* [18]). (iii) The description of her hands as 'cupped' (*cauis* [24]) suggests not just their natural attitude in repose, but the grasping materialism of women of her kind.[65] (iv) The poem's mythological allusions are almost all obliquely subversive. The comparisons of Cynthia with Ariadne, Andromeda and the Maenad initially seem to be intended simply to depict her beauty in sleep, but all these mythological women in their own way suffered from male slight or exploitation, and two of them famously made men their victims in the end: Ariadne, after her desertion by Theseus, cursed his forgetfulness with lethal results,[66] and the Thracian Maenads were responsible for tearing to pieces the tragic poet-lover Orpheus for his alleged neglect of them in his grief over his dead wife Eurydice.[67] The more sinister roles of these fabled women thus foreshadow Cynthia's own subsequent retaliation against Propertius (who is himself, like Orpheus, both a poet and an errant lover and eventually emerges as more of a Theseus to Cynthia's Ariadne than the Bacchus – or the Perseus to her Andromeda – that his earlier posing might have suggested).[68] The comparison of himself with Argus, via which Propertius metamorphoses from active assailant into passive guardian, also darkly hints at things to come, for just as the 'unfamiliar horns' (*ignotis cornibus* [20]) of Io, whom Argus guarded, were in a sense not real, so the serene appearance of the woman Propertius gazes at is deceptive; and just as Argus came off the worse in the end (he was killed by Mercury after his hundred eyes had been lulled to sleep), so will Propertius himself eventually seem to suffer in his own way.

The mythological tableaux are also interesting in that all the individuals who feature in them were popular subjects of visual art, especially of the frescoes which decorated well-to-do private houses. The wall-paintings from dwellings in Pompeii include both a slumbering Ariadne (with a figure who is probably Sleep himself at her head) being discovered by

---

[64] This is itself called 'soft' (*molli*) in the Latin of line 34.

[65] Cf. Tib. 2. 4. 27-38, and see Lyne (1970) 64.

[66] See Catul. 64. 191-250.

[67] He very nearly retrieved her from the Underworld through the power of his poetry, but failed in the end through inability to control his passion; see Virgil, *Georgics* 4. 453-27, with the note of Thomas (1988) on 520-22.

[68] Bacchus, accompanied by a festive troop of attendants, which Propertius' escort of torch-bearing slaves (10) recalls, came upon Ariadne deserted on the shore of Naxos and made her his bride.

49

Bacchus and his attendants[69] and an exhausted Maenad, oblivious to the world.[70] Andromeda too – admittedly not asleep, but being liberated by Perseus – is pictured there.[71] The House of Livia on the Palatine contained a fresco of the vigil of Argus.[72] While pictures of this kind, however, almost certainly prompted Propertius' fancy,[73] he does not allow them, individually or collectively, to restrict it. His description of the sleeping Cynthia's posture in lines 7-8 suggests that he may have had two incompatible attitudes, both inspired by visual art, simultaneously in mind. For 'leaning her head on [her] hands' (*nixa caput manibus*) suggests something like the posture of the Pompeian Ariadne where the semi-prone, semi-naked sleeper's head is somehow pillowed not so much on her hands as her arms,[74] while '*relaxed* hands' (*non certis...manibus*) is more evocative of the attitude of the sleeping Pompeian Maenad, where she lies fully supine and again semi-naked with both hands limp and randomly outflung.[75] Though the artistic appeal of both postures is obvious, neither is a truly natural sleeping position, and neither would leave the subject's hands placed to receive the gifts Propertius attempted to bestow in lines 24-6. It therefore looks as if he has mentally set aside the pictures by this stage and is envisaging Cynthia in a much more normal attitude of rest, lying on her back with her hands loosely cupped on her chest (*sinu* [26]; this word, translated 'pocket' in the English version, can also refer to a woman's bosom, and an alternative – indeed, arguably preferable – interpretation of line 26 is 'Gifts kept on rolling down the slope of her bosom').[76] Still, the general suggestion of Cynthia's likeness to painted sleeping females well conveys the image of a creature *barely real*, which her slumbering figure

---

[69] See Brilliant (1984) 72, fig. 2. 8C.

[70] See Hubbard (1974), frontispiece.

[71] See Ling (1991) 131, figs 134 and 135.

[72] See Ling (1991) 37, fig. 35.

[73] The swift succession of evocative scenes from unrelated stories at the start is very reminiscent of the same sort of thing in successive painted room-panels; see Brilliant (1984) 71-2.

[74] This posture seems closer to what Propertius has in mind than that of the famous Vatican sculpture, which most critics mention, in which a fully clothed woman, conventionally assumed to be Ariadne (though the identification is disputed), sleeps with her face supported on the palm of her left hand only, while her right hand is artistically (but not comfortably!) positioned behind her head. A good photograph in *LIMC* III. 2, 733, fig. 118.

[75] See further Harmon (1974) 157, n. 24.

[76] It seems more likely that Propertius is to be imagined drunkenly replacing the same two apples in Cynthia's hands over and over again to no avail than that a never-ending supply cascaded from the pocket-like fold at the front of his toga.

presented to Propertius before his own rude awakening, when the picture, as it were, suddenly came to life.[77]

Interest in the visual arts has here in fact been most creatively combined with ideas drawn from the literary tradition. Almost all critics draw attention to a Greek epigram (*AP* 5. 275) by Paulus Silentiarius (sixth century AD), which has obvious features in common with Propertius' poem:

> Lovely Menecratis lay sunk deep in evening sleep,
> her arm curling round her head.
> Daringly I climbed up on to her bed, and when I had travelled
> pleasurably half-way along the path of love,
> the girl awoke from sleep and with her white hands
> tried to pull out all the hair from my head.
> In spite of her struggles we finished the rest of love's work,
> and, as her tears welled up and brimmed over, she said
> 'Scoundrel, you have now taken the pleasure for which
> I often refused your plentiful money.
> And you will go off and clasp another to your breast straight away;
> for you [men] are the workforce of insatiable Aphrodite'.

The crude and thoughtless lust of this highlights the romantic tenderness which is such an important element in Propertius' poem; and, as with most epigrams, its characters lack individuality and its action lacks setting. Even the second-rate Paulus could doubtless have done better than this if he had had Propertius as a model, and probably his poem imitates a now lost Hellenistic original. Possibly, though not inevitably, this was drawn on by Propertius too.[78] Admittedly, one way for him to have created an elegy out of the putative epigram would have been to engineer the gradual unfolding of the full situation which is such an effective feature of this poem; but, even if one particular epigram did suggest the main elements of the elegy, its influence was clearly not exclusive. A specimen by Philodemus (first century BC) seems to have prompted the detail of Cynthia being awakened by the moon shining on her face through the windows (*AP* 5. 123):

> Shine, Moon, lady of the night, two-horned one, friend of all-night partying,
> shine, falling through the latticed windows.
> Cast your light on golden Callistion; on the deeds of lovers

---

[77] Cf. Lyne (1970) 66, 75.

[78] There is a hint of the basic situation at Terence, *Eunuchus* 599-606, which suggests that it may have been a feature of Greek New Comedy; see further Yardley (1980) 241-3 and also p. xxii.

we do not mind an immortal spying.
You count both her and me as blessed, Moon, I know;
for Endymion set alight your own soul.

Here is a very good example of the creative use of intertextuality.[79] For a reader who knows of the moon's role as the lover's ally in Philodemus' poem Propertius' transformation of her into an interfering busybody[80] and a rival, almost, for Cynthia's attention will be all the more striking, For such a reader, too, mention of the moon's beams 'lingering' (*moraturis* [32]) cannot but recall her love-affair with the mortal Endymion, to which Philodemus alludes directly (the moon was allegedly reluctant to return to the sky after descending, during her periods of invisibility, to make love with Endymion while he slept).

There are also numerous reminiscences of Catullus in Propertius' poem. The idea of the Ariadne-like sleeping Cynthia eventually waking and berating her errant lover, wishing upon him the same suffering as he has inflicted upon her, owes something to Catullus' portrayal of Ariadne's predicament and distress in his poem 64.[81] At Catullus 64. 53 we hear of Theseus 'receding' (*cedentem*) just as his ship does in line 1 here (*cedente*). 'Forsaken' (*desertam*) is how Catullus describes Ariadne at 64. 57, and 'forsaken' is also how Cynthia feels here (*deserta* [44]). Both women abuse the deserter, calling for tit-for-tat revenge (in Latin their phraseology is similar),[82] and both accuse him of betraying a commitment to marriage (Cynthia in line 44[83] and Ariadne at Catullus 64. 141, 158). The mischievous line 11 has a faint resonance of the serious Catullus 51. 5-6, where Catullus (imitating Sappho) claims that the very sight of Lesbia 'robs him of all his senses' (*omnis / eripit sensus mihi*). Lines 24-5 contain verbal echoes of two other Catullan amatory passages: (i) 65. 19-24, where Catullus refers to the 'furtive gift' (*furtiuo munere*) of an apple rolling down from its hiding-place in a girl's bosom when she hurriedly jumps up at the

---

[79] See p. xiv. For the layout of this and the preceding non-metrical translation see p. ix.

[80] Such is the implication of *luna...sedula* (32), 'the officious moon'.

[81] At Catul. 64. 61 Ariadne is compared with a statue of a Maenad, and this, as well a picture, may have influenced Propertius in the choice of his third simile at the start.

[82] Compare Catul. 64. 200-201 *quali solam me Theseus mente reliquit, / tali mente...funestet seque suosque* with Prop. 1. 3. 39-40 (see p. 4).

[83] Cynthia's complaint of Propertius' dalliance *in externo...amore* (44), which may be literally translated 'external love', i.e. love outside the house, suggests that their relationship is as good as marriage in her eyes.

entry of her mother;[84] and (ii) 76. 9, where he complains that all his kind-nesses have been lavished on an 'ungrateful mind'.[85] The humorous petu-lance of Propertius' complaint here derives at least in part from this incongruous combination of Catullan echoes – of the mildly amusing with the deadly earnest.[86]

Some of the most significant intertextual messages for the interpreta-tion of the poem, however, are to be found in Cynthia's claim to have passed the time while waiting for Propertius in wool-working and music. Singing as she spins is what the hard-working farmer's wife does by her fireside on cold winter nights according to Virgil.[87] Spinning as she is told stories by an old duenna is how Tibullus likes to think his Delia will pass her evenings until he returns from overseas to claim her.[88] Weaving by day and unravelling her work by night was how the Homeric Penelope at-tempted to keep faith with the absent Odysseus, when beset by a houseful of suitors.[89] Weaving and singing was what Circe the witch was doing just before she turned Odysseus' companions into swine.[90] Weaving a crimson robe (its colour symbolising the bloody conflict so far) was what Helen was doing when she was told that her lover Paris and her husband Menelaus had agreed to fight a duel over her.[91] The two activities, then, separately and together, regularly connote female virtue and fidelity, particularly of a conjugal kind, though they also have a slightly sinister resonance as the oc-casional prelude to cruelty and suffering. When Propertius, therefore, has Cynthia make claim to such occupations, he is having her present herself as the equivalent of a faithful *wife*.[92] What is more, she is made to depict her-self as an essentially *powerless* wife – as helpless a victim as Orpheus, whose instrument she plays, or, indeed, as any of the storied women of the opening at their most vulnerable (there are numerous verbal echoes of lines 1-6). Not once in her tirade does Propertius have her threaten revenge by

---

[84] The closeness of the echo is obscured somewhat by the translation of *furtiuus* here as 'stolen' rather than 'furtive'.

[85] Cf. p. 28.

[86] There is a good chance, too, that Propertius' contemporary readers would have recognised in lines 19-20 reminiscences of the now lost narrative poem *Io* by Catullus' friend Licinius Calvus. See Lyne (1970) 71, n. 3, and cf. n. 61 above.

[87] *Georgics* 1. 293-4; cf. *Georgics* 1. 390.

[88] Tib. 1. 3. 85-8.

[89] Homer, *Odyssey* 2. 93-109, 19. 136-58.

[90] Homer, *Odyssey* 10. 221-3.

[91] Homer, *Iliad* 3. 125-8.

[92] See also n. 83 above.

terminating the relationship or seeking satisfaction in love elsewhere; for all her allegedly fierce temper, she apparently accepts that *he* has the upper hand. At the same time, however, his awareness that she is *not* a homely and submissive Roman matron, but a typically sophisticated and imperious elegiac mistress, shows through in what he has her say. Her witty pun on 'limp' (*languidus* [38]), which suggests Propertius' sexual as well as general exhaustion, sits ill with wifely modesty; her activities associate her with the cruel Circe as well as the faithful Penelope and others; the colour of the wool she spins is a flashy crimson, not a respectable white,[93] and connects her with the morally dubious Helen; and, in the way of sophisticated courtesans, she plays the lyre, rather than simply singing, as might a woman of *any* rank or character.

The awakened Cynthia who berates her lover in the final section, then, is an interesting mixture: in part the short-tempered, sophisticated and overbearing Cynthia that Propertius lets us see in many of the other poems, but in part Cynthia *as he would like to think she is* – the ideal creature who combines the delightful sophistication of the *demi-mondaine* with long-suffering wifely fidelity. A woman, too, whose shrewishness stems only from her jealous love of him and so makes her totally subject to his whim and control, without imposing on *him* the tiresome need to be the equivalent of the perfect husband.[94] After all, if Cynthia had really spent the night of his absence as he has her claim, and if his access to her had really been as unobstructed, and his status as privileged, as it would appear, his relationship with her would have been, from his point of view, on an exceedingly satisfactory footing. Can it be entirely right, therefore, to see this poem as an attempt to represent in a 'profound' and 'truthful' way (Hubbard [1974] 22) a (literally) sobering encounter with a sleeping beauty who turns out to be more of a battleaxe? A woman full of 'whining unjustified reproaches' and 'tenuous feminine logic' (Lyne [1970] 63, 76), 'like an only too real wife: complaining, suspicious, illogical, proprietorial' (Lyne [1980] 119)? Might it not be nearer the mark to see it as a new version of the inebriated lover's well-known return from his revels? A version immensely flattering to that lover's ego (and one born of wishful thinking), in which he finds the door to his beloved not locked as usual, but open,[95] and his beloved, rather than himself, keeping a lonely, faithful vigil through the

---

[93] Cf. Tib. 2. 4. 28, with discussion on p. 122.

[94] We may notice also the pleasurable irony (for him) of Cynthia's calling him 'limp', in the light of what he had just contemplated doing to her.

[95] He may even be envisaging it as the door of his own house which she has been prevailed upon to share; cf. Prop. 4. 7. 39-48, with discussion on p. 85 and n. 233.

night while he, not she, has been making love in the arms of another?[96] Is it perhaps the case that although Propertius in this poem may *appear* to be 'taking the woman's part'[97] by casting himself as the helpless victim, in fact he retains, or at the last reasserts, the control traditionally identified with the masculine role?

At all events, this poem is usually judged one of Propertius' best.[98] But what exactly is good about it? Does its quality lie in its originality of sentiment, structure and expression?[99] Or in its ability to surprise, subvert, entertain and even shock? Or in the altered slant it puts on the picture we are given of Propertius, Cynthia and the relationship between them in 1. 1?[100] And, in particular, is this a poem on whose merits male and female readers may well differ?

Propertius 2. 13

Fewer Achaemenid arrows defend Susa
  Than Cupid has shot darts into my heart.
He forbade me to deride Muses so slender
  And told me to dwell thus in Ascra's grove,
Not that Pierian oaks should follow my words   5
  Or that I draw beasts from Ismarus' vale,
But rather that my verse should dumbfound Cynthia:
  I'd then be an artist more famous than Argive Linus.
I am no mere admirer of distinguished looks
  Or of a woman's pedigree;   10
I'd like to read my work in the lap of a clever girl
  And have it approved by faultless ears.
Should I succeed, farewell to society's babble;
  A mistress's verdict acquits me.

---

[96] A different reading again is offered by Harrison (1994). He argues that the first and last of the opening mythological comparisons can be seen to reflect Propertius' own fear (drunken and perhaps irrational) that the sleeping Cynthia has in fact entertained a rival in his absence. He also suggests that her verbal attack on Propertius can be interpreted as a cover-up for her own guilt.

[97] The title of Wyke's article (1994) on the 'gender' role normally played by the male elegiac poet.

[98] See e.g. Hubbard (1974) 21.

[99] It is noticeable, for example, how little it relies on the conventional imagery of Latin love elegy; even the one sustained military metaphor lacks its usual polemical context.

[100] Cf. also Prop. 4. 7.

And if only she'd listen kindly to conciliation,   15
  Then I could bear the enmity of Jove.
Whenever therefore death shall close my eyelids
  Let this be the order of my funeral:
No long cortège bearing ancestral images,
  No trumpet vainly bewailing my fate,   20
No couch with ivory fittings to carry me,
  Spread for my death with cloth of gold,
No line of incense-bearing platters, but the small-scale
  Rites of a plebeian funeral.
Procession enough for me if I have three slim volumes   25
  To bring as my best gift to Persephone.
But you must follow, tearing your naked breasts,
  Tirelessly calling my name,
Pressing the last kisses on my frozen lips
  And pouring Syrian unguent from its onyx.   30
Then when the heat below has turned me into ashes
  Let a small clay pot receive my spirit,
And above it plant a bay-tree on the narrow grave
  To shade the site of my burnt-out pyre,
And write there these two lines: 'WHO NOW LIES HORRID DUST   35
WAS ONCE THE SLAVE OF BUT ONE LOVE'.
And this my tomb will grow to be as famous
  As the Pthian hero's bloody sepulchre.
You also, when white-haired you come to die, remember
  To come this way to the recording stone.   40
Meanwhile beware of slighting us the buried;
  Dust is conscious and can sense the truth.
If only one of the Sisters Three had decreed
  That I lay down my life in the cradle!
Why prolong breath for so uncertain an hour?   45
  Three generations passed before Nestor was ashes;
But had the doom of his long-lived old age been shortened
  By a soldier in the Trojan lines,
He had not seen the burial of Antilochus
  Or said 'O death, why come for me so late?'   50
Still you will weep at times for the friend whom you have lost;
  Always love is due to one's man who has passed away.
Witness a goddess, when the wild boar gored Adonis
  Hunting on the Idalian height;
He lay there, lovely, in the marshes, and you came   55

56

To him, Venus, with streaming hair.
But, Cynthia, you will call back my dumb spirit in vain,
   My bits of bones will have nothing to say.

Propertius is the victim of a heavy missile attack from the love god, his
heart shot with more arrows, he says, than the Persians use to defend their
capital, Susa[101] (1-2). This same love god – in other words, love itself –
dictates what sort of poetry Propertius is to write. His residence qualifica-
tion for 'Ascra's grove' (*Ascraeum...nemus* [4]), i.e. his right to a place in
the ranks of high-quality poets like Hesiod,[102] is to be won as a devotee of
'slender Muses' (*gracilis...Musas* [3]), i.e. of non-heroic, and especially
erotic, poetry (3-4). The aim of Propertius' poetry is not to charm nature, as
did the legendary lyric singer Orpheus (identified here only by references
to the location of his exploits),[103] but merely to enchant his own beloved
Cynthia. To succeed, however, would make him more famous than Linus
(another legendary singer, especially associated with elegy) (5-8). Provided
that a discriminating mistress approves of the poetry he recites in her arms,
the *hoi polloi* can go hang with their ignorant muttering (9-14). He can put
up with even 'the enmity of Jove' (*inimicitias...Iouis* [15]) – if only she will
'listen kindly to conciliation' (*bonas ad pacem uerterit auris* [16]) (15-16).
It would appear, then, there has been some sort of row, and Propertius'
potentially bewitching 'slender Muses' have so far failed to effect any
rapprochement.

   'Therefore' (*igitur* [17]; where, the reader will wonder, is the logic of
this?), when Propertius dies, he wants no elaborate funeral (line 19 alludes
to the carrying of wax busts or masks of ancestors in the funeral proces-
sions of those descended from praetors and consuls). He only wants to take
with him to the grave (Persephone is the goddess of death) 'three slim volumes'
(*tres...libelli* [25]) of his own poetry (17-26). Cynthia[104] is instructed to

---

[101] Susa was ruled by the Achaemenid dynasty up to 330 BC and is sometimes identified by
Roman writers with Parthia, which was renowned for the prowess of its archers. The Latin
text is corrupt here, and the version printed and translated rests on a plausible emendation. For
discussion and an alternative suggestion see Allen (1992).

[102] Ascra, near Mt Helicon in Boeotia, upon which the Muses reputedly lived in a grove, was
the birthplace of Hesiod (see p. xix). He claimed have been personally instructed by them
while tending his sheep on the mountain's slopes (*Theogony* 22-34). His name and experience
were often invoked by Callimachus and his successors to connote especially privileged or
respected poetic status.

[103] Ismarus was a mountain in Thrace, and Pieria, which has its own associations with the
Muses, a part of neighbouring Macedonia.

[104] Cynthia is the addressee from line 17 onwards, but not until line 57 is she addressed by
name.

display extreme grief and to follow the proper ritual of repeatedly calling his name and pouring libations at his funeral (27-30). Tearing the breast (or cheeks or loosened hair) was a conventional gesture of mourning, and fragrant ointment was poured over the corpse on the pyre. After his cremation she is to bury his ashes and see that his grave, shaded by a bay-tree, bears an inscription commemorating his enslavement to 'one love' (*VNIVS...AMORIS* [36]) (31-6). This lover's tomb Propertius is confident will be as famous as the 'bloody sepulchre' (*busta cruenta* [38]) of the heroic warrior Achilles. Pthia in Thessaly was Achilles' home, and his tomb was 'bloody' in that, according to post-Homeric legend, the Trojan king Priam's daughter Polyxena was sacrificed to Achilles' ghost there.[105] Into this same tomb Cynthia must be sure to come when she dies herself in old age (37-40), but in the meantime she should not slight him, for his mortal remains will 'sense the truth' (*non nihil ad uerum...sapit* [42]; perhaps he means 'the truth' about her infidelity after his death) (41-2).

It would have been best, he goes on, if he had died in infancy; the 'Sisters Three' are the Fates, who set the date of each person's death. It seems to him hardly worth living at all when life is such a mixed blessing – when, for example, one considers Nestor (the king of Pylos and an important elder statesman in the Homeric epics). His survival into extreme old age meant that he outlived his son Antilochus, killed at Troy, where, Propertius says, Nestor would have better been killed himself (43-50). Still, he reflects finally, Cynthia will be bound to mourn him, her lover, when his death does come. Indication enough of this is Venus' mourning for her beloved Adonis when the beautiful youth was killed by a wild boar on Mt Idalium (in Cyprus). But there will be no point in Cynthia trying to bring back *her* lover when he is dead, Propertius warns her (*frustra ...reuocabis,* 'in vain you will call back...' [57]):[106] dust and ashes can never respond (51-8).

What is Propertius most concerned about here? Success as a poet or success as a lover? And in life or in death? The reader will no doubt find it difficult to decide: so does Propertius, and that is the point! The poem[107] depicts his own mental wrestling with these questions, complete with 'ifs' and 'buts', partial changes of heart and brief, tangential fantasies. In adopting this technique of the 'shifting standpoint' (Lyne [1980] 131) Propertius

---

[105] See e.g. Euripides, *Hecuba* 188-90.

[106] Cynthia is by implication compared here not only with Venus but also with Laodamia, one of Propertius' favourite heroines; see p. 84 with n. 228.

[107] The sudden entry of the full-blown death theme with the apparently illogical 'therefore' in line 17 has made many suspect that it is in fact two poems accidentally conjoined in the MSS. Cf. p. xxxvi, with n. 101.

does not, however, articulate all the connections in his train of thought, or, like Tibullus, leave the general impression of a seamless piece of work, but invites the reader to intuit his thinking from subtle hints, especially those in the covert implications of his mythological allusions.

'I am in love', he begins, 'and therefore any poetry I write worthy of the name will have to be love poetry. Its aim, however, will be only practical success in love, not artistic renown. And yet might not the one lead to the other – eventually?' Here within lines 1-8 is the first statement of Propertius' basic viewpoint: poetic ambition, for all its merits, must be subordinated to ambition in love. But also the first vacillation: are the two necessarily mutually exclusive? In the allusions to Orpheus and Linus there is the first hint of concern with death and its possible compensations – or lack of them – for both poets and lovers. For Orpheus, despite all the spectacular skill of his poetry, met his violent end because of his love,[108] and Linus met his because of his poetry (he was allegedly killed by Apollo for boasting that he was a better singer than the god himself[109] or, in another version of his story, killed by Hercules with his own lyre while attempting to teach him to play).[110] Both Orpheus and Linus, however, enjoyed posthumous fame for their poetry,[111] and Propertius, in first rejecting the example of the one, then accepting the challenge of outshining the other, seems suddenly to see the possibility for himself of the same reward as theirs in death[112] – though he would obviously want to avoid the same mistakes and misfortunes in life. Also in these opening lines Propertius shows first signs of modifying the fashionable poetic principle of 'small is beautiful'[113] to suit his love-life. His claim of almost Hesiodic respectability,[114] and indeed divine mandate of a sort, for his 'slender Muses' initially suggests that he is about to justify his choice of poetic genre on the usual Callimachean stylistic grounds, but in the event he makes claims only for its practical usefulness, and not for its stylistic superiority. Such a line of defence is not in itself new,[115] but this version of it, which redeploys some

---

[108] See p. 49 with n. 67.

[109] Pausanias 9. 29. 6.

[110] Apollodorus, *Bibliotheca* 2. 63.

[111] They are often cited together as examples of supreme poetic expertise; see e.g. Virgil, *Eclogue* 4. 55-7.

[112] Cf. Prop. 3. 1. 33-8.

[113] See pp. xx-xxi and 70.

[114] See n. 102 above.

[115] Cf. Prop. 1. 7. 15-24, 9. 9-16, Tib. 2. 4. 15-20.

of Callimachus' own weapons, if not exactly against him, at least on an alternative front, *is* new.

The practical argument for devotion to love poetry seems to provide Propertius, as lover first and poet second, with the perfect reassurance for the order of priorities he is keen to settle on, and consequently he allows himself to elaborate on it in lines 9-16, this time translating the Callimachean ideal of modesty and discrimination rather than grandeur and conventionality into 'Give me a learned lady rather than a merely beautiful and well-born one, and her favour rather than popular poetic fame'. Then the moment of painful realism which neatly gives context to the whole poem, is allowed to intrude: 'Not even the displeasure of god almighty[116] would trouble me, *if* my poetry would bring her out of her huff' (15-16). Propertius does not then explicitly say 'As it is, though, she shows every sign of keeping it up till I die', but in view of the interest he has already shown in his prospects after death, this may well be the thought which brings him to his next reflection: '*Therefore*, whenever I do die, let me draw what satisfaction I can from sticking to my principles of unpretentiousness at that time' (17-26).[117] This prompts yet another reinterpretation of the Callimachean ideal: no 'long cortège' (*longa...pompa* [19]), 'trumpet' (*tuba* [20]), 'ivory fittings' (*fulcro...eburno* [21]), 'couch...spread... with cloth of gold' (*Attalico...toro*[118] [21]) or 'incense-bearing platters' (*odiferis...lancibus* [23]), but the '*small-scale* rites of a *plebeian* funeral' (*plebei paruae funeris exsequiae* [24]) and 'three *slim* volumes'.[119] We may notice how soon poetry comes back into the reckoning! The reference to 'three slim volumes' in a poem so obviously programmatic[120] (by virtue of its tendency to literary self-justification and resonances of famous programmatic passages in Hesiod and Callimachus)[121] has prompted the suggestion that it was the opener of Propertius' original Book 3.[122] But this is only one, and perhaps the least plausible, of several possible explanations of the wording of line 25. Alternatively it may signify that Propertius at this stage of Book 2 'felt he had at least another book in him' (Williams [1968]

---

[116] One wonders whether he could possibly be thinking of that 'Jupiter on earth' Caesar Augustus.

[117] Heyworth (1992) 45-7 posits a similar, but not identical, train of thought and suspects some loss of text between lines 16 and 17. He also claims that Propertius views his death here as imminent, but this assumption seems unwarranted.

[118] Attalus, king of Pergamum, reputedly invented the method of weaving with gold thread.

[119] The Latin *libellus* is a diminutive form of *liber*, the standard word for 'book'.

[120] See p. xiv.

[121] Possibly in Gallus (see pp. xxvii-xxviii) as well, to judge from Virgil, *Eclogue* 6. 64-73.

[122] So e.g. Heyworth (1992) 49-57, *id.* (1995) 167-8.

481) or – the most attractive idea – it may be that 'three' here means only an unspecified small number: 'a book or two', i.e. more than one, but not many.[123]

At all events, the dwelling on funerals makes Propertius think of mourners, and this makes him think again of Cynthia, whose present unresponsiveness is now forgotten, as he imagines her at least reconciled enough in the future to act as his chief mourner and executrix (29-36). The enticing thought of her personal attention seems to make him waver in his rejection of pomp and circumstance, for she is instructed to honour his pyre with exotic oriental perfume[124] from a precious onyx jar, even though the urn which is to hold his ashes is to be 'a small clay pot' (*paruula*[125] *testa* [32]) and the grave itself 'narrow' (*exiguo* [33]). Again Propertius flirts with the attractive idea of achieving a special status in and after death. The first hint of it within this section is barely perceptible, but a learned reader coming across the instruction to bestow loving 'last kisses' (*oscula...suprema* [29]) on a cold and lifeless body may well think of the *Lament* generally ascribed to the Hellenistic pastoral poet Bion, where Venus pays identical attention to the dead Adonis.[126] The 'intertextual message'[127] in this allusion seems to be that Propertius is hankering after the same status as a famous mythological figure (he is of course also flattering Cynthia by implicitly equating her at this point with a goddess). Next Propertius intimates that the narrow grave will be special for being a poet's grave – it would be recognisable as such by being planted with a bay (*laurus* [33]), ancient symbol of poets and poetry.[128] Then he requests that a two-line epitaph – the brevity would be in keeping with his small tomb – should commemorate him as an utterly faithful lover (35-6). What appeals to him most, it seems, has now been redefined: not success as a lover or fame as a poet, but fame for fidelity in love. 'That would be fame indeed', he reflects, 'and that tiny tomb of mine could equal in renown the biggest you can think of – the tomb of Achilles' (37-8). But Achilles' tomb was renowned for something else besides its size and magnificence: for the sacrifice of Polyxena. Legend had it, moreover,

---

[123] Cf. Ovid, *Ex Ponto* 4. 3. 26 'A page inscribed with three words' (*uerbis charta notata tribus*), i.e. 'a word or two'.

[124] 'Syrian' (*Syrio* [30]) is a conventional epithet of ointments, but it connotes luxury too.

[125] A diminutive of *paruus*.

[126] Bion 1. 42-53. It is possible that both Bion and Propertius were inspired by the same painting or sculpture; see Papanghelis (1987) 64-5. At any rate, the indirect allusion to the Venus and Adonis story here foreshadows the explicit one in lines 51-6.

[127] See p. xiv.

[128] Hesiod claims that a staff of it was given to him by the Muses at *Theogony* 30-32; cf. n. 102 above.

that Achilles in his lifetime had loved the girl who so gruesomely joined him in death,[129] and this is probably what prompts Propertius next to envisage (39-40) his beloved one day joining him in his grave and so bringing him success of a sort in love *after* he has died. Graciously he does not require that Cynthia be immolated to satisfy him,[130] but even allows her a generous natural life-span before expecting her company in the grave – she will be 'white-haired' (*cana* [40]) when she dies. At the same time, though, he is careful to imply that she owes him something, by reminding her that his tombstone will bear a record – a record, that is, of his exclusive love for her. But his subsequent warning to her against 'slighting' him in his grave (41-2) betrays his sudden realisation that she is quite capable of doing just that – of betraying his fidelity in death, as in life. This is doubtless what is supposed to provoke his descent into self-pitying despair (43-50).[131] 'If such pain is all that death can offer one who has loved, it would be better if I had never grown up to know love at all',[132] he cries. There is a splendid, almost Victorian, excess in the mythological parallel he cites – as if *he* were in danger of living anything like as long as the fabled years of Nestor or of suffering, in the (possible) infidelity of a mistress, a catastrophe anything like as grievous as outliving one's own child!

Then, however, as if acknowledging the irrelevance of his comparison, Propertius forces himself to take a supposedly more realistic view of things. 'At times' (i.e. even if not as constantly and perpetually as he would really like to think) Cynthia will mourn him after his death (51) – it's only natural (52). The example of Venus' mourning of Adonis, however, which he uses to support this view, is of a decidedly *un*natural love-relationship. The goddess' erotic interest in the adolescent mortal was in itself extraordinary, and unlike Cynthia, she was the instigator and not the object of the love. This is to say nothing, either, of the unlikelihood of Propertius' now much-anticipated death taking place in circumstances remotely comparable to Adonis'. An element in the Venus and Adonis story not explicitly mentioned here then leads to Propertius' final point: Venus was able to come to an arrangement with the gods of the Underworld to have Adonis restored to life – and hence to her love – on a half-time basis.[133] Once Propertius is dead, however, Cynthia will have lost her lover for good. The emphasis on his inability to communicate suggests in his case something more than the

---

[129] Hyginus, *Fabulae* 11.

[130] At 3. 13. 15-22, however, Propertius seems to admire suttees.

[131] A different interpretation at Papanghelis (1987) 77.

[132] An adaptation of a proverbial sentiment; cf. Posidippus, *AP* 9. 359.

[133] Laodamia's special arrangement (see p. 84) also comes to mind.

mere inertness of his physical state: it is a reminder that the dead cannot write conciliatory poetry (cf. line 15). This sobering thought, Propertius seems to hope, will persuade Cynthia to listen to what he is able to offer at the moment and return his love *now*.[134] The initial question of whether love or poetry, and in life or in death, counts for more is thus finally decided in favour of love, in life.[135] Propertius has also decided that poetry offers him his best chance of amatory success in life and some compensations after death, while death itself offers its own peculiar brand of erotic fulfilment.[136]

Death was one of the favourite literary subjects of classical antiquity, and many of the themes associated with it which Propertius handles here were conventional in poetic laments and epitaphs; e.g. description of the funeral, bidding to the mourners, praise of the deceased's achievements, description of the tomb and fitness of the sepulchral inscription.[137] Other conventional elements Propertius has inverted or modified in this poem; for example, instead of the usual protest against the prematurity of death Propertius offers one against its lateness, and in place of envisaging the after-life of the deceased he dwells on the nature of his physical remains after cremation[138] and speculates on their sentience. But this elegy's challenging form (an imaginative, if at times enigmatic, soliloquy?), unorthodox structure[139] and interleaving of the death theme with the themes of poetry and love ensure that 'conventional' is the last description that could be used of it as a whole.

The poem invites one direct comparison with Tibullus: how, if at all, does Propertius' attitude to the consequences of death here differ from Tibullus'? Is Propertius simply morbid about death in this poem? Or does he rather regard it positively, as a truly orgasmic kind of pleasure ('Propertius yearns for an erotic death, for death as love'; Papanghelis [1987] 64)? If so, it will remain to be seen whether he will ever stop 'looking forward to the sepulchral romance his eventual downfall will open the door to' (Papanghelis [1987] 74). This unusual poem prompts other interesting questions too. Is there evidence here of the purely self-indulgent Alexandrianism of which Propertius is often accused? Is the poem even 'cosmetically Callimachean'

---

[134] Again a different interpretation at Papanghelis (1987) 79.

[135] An identical decision at Prop. 1. 19. 25-6.

[136] An entirely different conclusion by Wyke (1987) 57-60.

[137] See further Booth (1991) 44.

[138] 'Ashes' (*cinerem* [31]), 'dust' (*terra* [42], literally 'earth'), 'bits of bones' (*ossa minuta* [58]); see further p. 95.

[139] More of 'a parabola rather than an ellipse, let alone a circle' (Wilkinson [1966] 141).

(Papanghelis [1987] 78), or does it rather justify the suspicion that Propertius had not even 'read very much of Callimachus' by this stage (Lyne [1980] 148)? And is there any indication at all here of external pressure upon him to write on any other subject or in any other way?

Propertius 3. 3

I had seen myself reclining in Helicon's soft shade
  Where runs the rill named for Bellérophon's horse,
And managing to mouth your kings and your kings' deeds,
  Alba, (such hard work for my powers!)
And I had just applied small lips to the great spring   5
  Whence thirsty father Ennius once drank
And sang of Curian brothers, Horatian javelins,
  Aemilian barges bearing royal trophies,
Fabius' invincible inaction, Cannae's
  Luckless field, Gods moved by duteous vows,   10
The Lares driving Hannibal in flight from Rome
  And Jupiter saved by cackling geese,
When Phoebus eyeing me from the Castalian tree and leaning
  On his gilded lyre near a cave spoke thus:
'Idiot, what right have you to such a stream? And who   15
  Told you to turn your hand to epic?
There's not a hope of fame, Propertius, for you here;
  Your little wheels must groove soft meadows.
Let your slim volume be displayed on bedside tables
  And read by lonely girls waiting for their lovers.   20
Why has your page diverged from its appointed round?
  You must not overload the rowboat of your wit.
With one oar feather water, with the other shore,
  And you'll be safe. Most flounder in mid-ocean.'
So saying, with ivory quill he points me to a seat   25
  To which on mossy ground a new path led.
Here was a grotto green embellished with mosaics
  And from its tufa vault hung tambourines,
The Muses' *orgia*, Father Silenus' effigy
  In clay, and your reed pipes, Tegéan Pan;   30
And Lady Venus' birds, my crowd of trouble, doves
  Dip red beaks in the Gorgonéan pool.
The several Maidens, allocated their nine duties,

Busy tender hands with special gifts.
This one picks ivy for a thyrsus; this one fits tunes   35
  To strings; that one plaits roses with both hands.
One Goddess of their number touched me (from her face
  I judge it was Calliopéa) saying:
'Content yourself to be conveyed by snow-white swans
  And ride no neighing charger into battle.   40
Not yours to blow the raucous laudatory trumpet
  Or sully the Aonian grove with Mars;
Or tell on what field Marian eagles fought
  And Rome repelled Teutonic power,
Or how the barbarous Rhine ran red with Swabian blood,   45
  Rolling maimed bodies down his grieving tide.
You'll sing of lovers garlanded at an alien door
  And drunken signs of nocturnal escapes,
So those who wish to steal a march on strict husbands
  May learn from you to charm girls from internment.'   50
Thus far Calliope. Then, drawing from the fountain,
  She wet my lips with water of Philitas.

Propertius had a dream, he says (*uisus eram* [1], literally 'I had seemed' or 'had been seen' – a standard formula for dreaming). In it he was pleasantly ensconced on Mt Helicon[140] by the spring Hippocrene (a favourite source of poetic inspiration reputedly created by a blow from the hoof of Pegasus, Bellerophon's fabled horse). He dreamed that he had the nerve to attempt poetry on the legends of early Rome ('Alba' is the pre-Roman settlement of Alba Longa)[141] (1-4). That was what Q. Ennius (239–c.169 BC) had done in his *Annals*, and had thereby earned himself the tag of 'father' (*pater* [6]) of Latin literature.[142] Propertius, in claiming to have dreamed that he had applied his 'small lips' (*parua...ora* [5]) to the same 'spring' (*fontibus* [5]) of inspiration, is saying that he saw himself as this famous epic poet's successor.[143] He then lists a number of topics he dreamed he was tackling, all supposedly treated by Ennius (5-12). The 'Curian brothers'[144] (*Curios*

---

[140] See p. 57, n. 102.

[141] Alba Longa was supposedly founded by Aeneas' son Ascanius-Iulus and had its own kings and stories of their exploits.

[142] The *Annals* was the first Latin epic poem in hexameters and covered the early history of Rome from its legendary beginnings up to Ennius' own day.

[143] Ennius himself reputedly dreamed that the soul of Homer had passed into him: see Rudd (1989) on Horace. *Epistles* 2. 1. 51-2. *iam* in line 5 is an old emendation for MS *tam*.

[144] Normally called the 'Curiatii'.

fratres [7]) were the three Albans who allegedly fought the three Roman Horatii, also brothers, in the war between Rome and Alba during the reign of the Roman king Tullus Hostilius. Only one of the Horatii survived, but he finally killed all three of his opponents and (according to some accounts) his spoils were set up as a memorial to his victory; these are apparently the 'javelins' (*pila* [7]) to which Propertius refers here.[145] The 'royal trophies' (*regia...tropaea*) which were especially noted for being borne on 'Aemilian barges' (*Aemilia...rate* [8]) were those taken from Perseus, king of Macedon, by L. Aemilius Paullus in 167 BC and carried to Rome on ships which sailed up the Tiber. But this event could not have been treated by Ennius, as it occurred after his death, and Propertius is probably transferring details of it to the victory of another L. Aemilius Paullus over King Antiochus of Syria in 190 BC, which doubtless *did* feature in the *Annals*. 'Fabius' invincible inaction' (*uictrices...moras Fabii* [9]) refers to Q. Fabius Maximus Cunctator's attrition of Hannibal's forces by the simple expedient of avoiding a direct engagement with him during his Italian campaign of 217–16 BC;[146] and 'Cannae's luckless field' (*pugnam... sinistram / Cannensem* [9-10]) was the scene of the battle in which Hannibal inflicted a massive defeat on the Romans in 216 BC after Fabius' strategy had been abandoned because of its unpopularity. The 'Lares', 'Gods moved by duteous vows' (*uersos ad pia uota deos* [10]), i.e. by the formal supplications after Cannae (10-11), would appear to be the *Lares Praestites*,[147] whose function was to watch over the city.[148] The saving of Jupiter by 'cackling geese' (*anseris...uoce* [12]) is a reference to the alarm being raised by the sacred geese kept in the temple of Capitoline Jupiter when the Gauls made a surprise attack on the Capitol in 390 BC.

As Propertius (in his dream) was dealing with all this, Phoebus Apollo, god of poetry, saw him, as he looked out from 'the Castalian tree' (*Castalia ...ex arbore* [13]). The spring Castalia, sacred to Apollo and the Muses and, like Hippocrene, associated with poetic inspiration, flowed on Mt Parnassus near Delphi. In Propertius' dream it is apparently located in a grove (one 'tree' here stands for many), another common setting for poetic inspiration.[149] 'Near a cave' (*ad antra* [14]) – yet another type of place with the same

---

[145] Cf. Livy 1. 26.

[146] Ennius' treatment of this episode produced what has become one of his best-known lines: 'One man by delaying saved the country for us' (*unus homo nobis cunctando restituit rem* [*Annals* 363 Skutsch]).

[147] These were quite separate from the hearth-gods of private homes, for which see Tib. 1. 1. 20, 2. 4. 54.

[148] Their role in forcing Hannibal to retreat from Rome in 211 BC is unattested elsewhere.

[149] Cf. Prop. 2. 13. 4, with n. 102 on p. 57.

inspirational associations[150] – with hand on lyre, Apollo reprimanded Propertius for taking on epic. The rebuke, quoted verbatim, is delivered on basically very simple grounds: Propertius is just not up to it. But this message is conveyed via an elaborate series of images (15-24). The first of them (15) again uses the idea of drinking from a particular source (cf. 5-6) to represent the poet's (wrong) choice of genre. All the others are travel metaphors, with Propertius' allegedly limited talent first represented as a chariot with 'little wheels' (*paruis...rotis* [18]) and then as a 'rowboat' (*cumba* [22]) – as opposed to a larger, sea-going vessel – and its proper milieu, i.e. non-epic, first represented as 'soft meadows' (*mollia...prata* [18]) – presumably as opposed to the paved main road – and then as inshore waters (23) as opposed to 'mid-ocean' (*medio...mari* [24]). His attempt to stray outside these bounds is represented by a metaphor from horse-training, the 'round' (*gyros* [21]) being the ring in which the animals were schooled. In the midst of all this imagery, however, is a completely metaphor-free statement from Apollo of what sort of verse Propertius *should* be writing (19-20): love poetry is his *métier*.

After this Apollo directed him (Propertius dreamed) by 'a new path' (*noua...semita* [26]) over 'mossy ground' (*muscoso...solo* [26]) to a seat in a 'grotto' (*spelunca* [27]), exquisitely decorated and full of numinous objects associated with poetry and music (25-32): 'tambourines' (*tympana* [28]), which accompanied ritualistic dancing; the Muses' *orgia* (a vague but evocative word for holy or mystical emblems of some kind [29]); and a statue of Silenus, traditionally a rustic satyr, mildly drunken and lecherous, but essentially benevolent and endowed with arcane wisdom and musical expertise. He is the figure who in Virgil's sixth *Eclogue* tells of the direct inspiration of Cornelius Gallus[151] by the Heliconian Muses and the legendary singer Linus.[152] Also in the grotto were the pipes of the pastoral musician god Pan ('Tegean', i.e. 'Arcadian', was one of his conventional titles)[153] and doves. These birds were sacred to the love goddess Venus[154] and hence are also claimed by Propertius the lover as his own. Birds in general are often portrayed as agents of poetic inspiration, and for good measure Venus' doves here sip the water of Hippocrene – not now running free as the powerfully gushing stream of epic, but tamed, as it were, for the lowlier elegist's consumption in a 'pool' (*lacu* [32]) – or 'basin' – at the foot of a

---

[150] Cf. Prop. 3. 1. 5, Horace, *Odes* 3. 4. 40.

[151] See pp. xvii-xviii.

[152] *Eclogue* 6. 64-73; cf. Prop. 2. 13. 8, with discussion on pp. 57 and 59.

[153] In some accounts he is the father of Silenus.

[154] Cf. Prop. 4. 5. 65, Ov. *Am.* 1. 2. 23.

fountain. The 'pool' is called 'Gorgonean' because Pegasus, the creator of Hippocrene, was supposed to have sprung from the blood of the Gorgon Medusa. The nine Muses ('Maidens' [*Puellae*, 33]) themselves were also present, each making her special contribution to the creation of poetry (33-6). Propertius gives just three examples[155] of the kind of things they were doing: (i) preparing the ivy-clad thyrsus (35), i.e. the frenzy-inducing wand of Bacchus (Dionysus), which was recognised as an instrument of poetic inspiration;[156] (ii) manipulating the 'strings' (*neruis* [35]) of the lyre, a reminder of the musical roots of classical poetry (35-6); and (iii) 'with both hands' (*manu...utraque* [36]) plaiting roses, presumably for the garland conventionally claimed by any self-respecting poet. Both the choice of vegetation[157] and the method of construction are doubtless symbolic here. Roses have sensuous and erotic connotations,[158] and they could appropriately represent the 'soft garlands' (*mollia serta*) of the love elegist which Propertius claims in an earlier poem in preference to the 'rough wreath' (*dura corona*) of the epic poet.[159] The pointed (and strictly speaking redundant) reference to the two-handed nature of the plaiting operation perhaps hints at the two-line character of the elegiac metre.[160]

Then one of the Muses, whom Propertius took 'from her face' (*a facie* [38]) to be Calliope(a),[161] in his dream ritually touched him and reinforced Apollo's message: for him, love poetry, not epic (37-50). Calliope's instructions, which are also quoted verbatim, are, rather like Apollo's, mostly expressed in a welter of richly allusive language. First, Propertius is ordered to travel only in a swan-drawn car (39); this was one of Venus' normal modes of conveyance,[162] and the idea thus symbolises the undertaking of love poetry.[163] Riding a 'neighing charger' into battle[164] on the other hand symbolises the foray into epic from which Propertius is debarred (40).

---

[155] Job-demarcation proper for the Muses does not appear in poetry before the imperial period.

[156] For the connection between Bacchus and the Muses see Prop. 2. 30. 33-40, and cf. Prop. 4. 1. 61-4.

[157] This varies among the poets according to taste and self-image at any given moment.

[158] Like the myrtle of Venus, used for the garlands favoured by Tibullus and Ovid.

[159] Prop. 3. 1. 19-20.

[160] See pp. xv-xvii.

[161] A showy piece of wit here: Calliope means in Greek 'beautiful of face'.

[162] Cf. Horace, *Odes* 3. 28. 15, Ov. *Ars Amatoria* 3. 809.

[163] In view of the subsequent association of strident noisiness with epic, the reader is perhaps expected to remember that swans, here associated with desirable love poetry, are conventionally (if erroneously) credited with a *sweet* song just before death.

[164] Line 40 more literally: 'nor shall the sound of a courageous horse carry you to arms'.

Forbidden epic is next represented by 'blowing the raucous laudatory trumpet' (*rauco praeconia classica cornu / flare* [41-2]), i.e. loudly singing the praises of men of war and their doings, and by 'sullying' (*tingere* [42]) the grove of the Muses (*Aonium...nemus* [42]) with 'Mars' (Aonia was the part of Boeotia containing Mt Helicon, and the god of war stands for war itself) (41-2). Two specific examples of prohibited subject-matter are then given: (i) the defeat of the Teutones at Aquae Sextiae in 102 BC by the Roman general Marius, who established the eagle as the legionary standard[165] (43-4), and (ii) the rout of the Suebi, another Germanic tribe (45-6). It is difficult to be certain whether Propertius is referring to the most recent defeat of the Suebi, by C. Carrinas, when they crossed the Rhine in 29 BC, or to the bloodiest, by Julius Caesar in 58 BC, which also took place in the Rhine valley. When Calliope reaches her positive instructions, like Apollo, she becomes relatively direct: 'You'll sing of...' (*canes* [48]), and as her example of proper subject-matter for Propertius she selects the locked-out lover theme[166] (47-50). Finally (Propertius dreamed), Calliope wet his lips with water 'from the fountain' (*a fonte* [51]) – water at this point in some way associated with the Alexandrian Greek poet Philitas.[167] Some see this as a kind of baptismal ritual, but it need be nothing more than a circumlocutory way of saying she gave him this water to drink; possibly we are supposed to understand that Philitas himself had drunk from the same inspirational fountain. At any rate, the general meaning is clear: Propertius received divine sanction for his writing of love poetry in the Alexandrian manner (51-2).

Propertius' initial announcement that he once dreamed of being on Mt Helicon beside the spring of Hippocrene prepares the reader sensitive to 'intertextuality'[168] for the type of programmatic poem which claims direct divine inspiration and sanction for its author's chosen type of writing. Helicon was where Hesiod had claimed that *he* was when he met the Muses,[169] and Hippocrene was where Callimachus had located Hesiod, when he dreamed of following in his poetic footsteps.[170] What is more, in the opening poem of Book 3 Propertius directly invokes Callimachus as a model, apparently embracing his stylistic principles and endorsing his rejection of traditional epic. Now, with the claim that he dreamed he was writing poetry on Roman

---

[165] The neighbouring Cimbri were also defeated by him on the Raudine plains in 101 BC.

[166] See p. xiii.

[167] See pp. xxi, xxiii.

[168] See p. xiv.

[169] See p. 57, n. 102.

[170] See *Aetia* frag. 2 Trypanis.

heroic themes (3-12) when Apollo intervened to veto the enterprise (13-16), he creates a scenario so similar to that in the celebrated preface to Callimachus' *Aetia*[171] that another polemic against epic from Apollo and another declaration from Propertius of commitment to non-epic on Callimachean aesthetic grounds must be anticipated. But these things do not materialise. Admittedly, Apollo's speech is full of distinctively Callimachean figures. As in the preface to the *Aetia*, general smallness, the untrodden path and driving off the highway represent the desirable sort of poetry, and loud noise, along with the places where 'most' (*maxima turba* [24]) go, the undesirable.[172] But *this* Apollo apparently does not disapprove of epic in principle, only of epic being attempted by Propertius, whose talent is inadequate for such a mighty undertaking. Indeed, Propertius himself has already intimated that this is the case: the attempt at epic was 'hard work' (*tantum operis* [4]) for him, and the lips he put to the 'great spring' (*magnis...fontibus*) were only 'small' (*parua* [5]). Furthermore, the position he started from was one of 'reclining in...soft shade' (*molli recubans...in umbra* [1]); this, as opposed to labouring under urban glare, symbolises the occupation of the poet of pastoral and erotic, rather than military or political, themes.[173] Propertius has thus taken from the *Aetia* the basic scenario of Apollo's advice to the aspiring poet and grafted on to it his own supposed insufficiency of talent to produce a *recusatio*, ('refusal').[174] The self-disparaging version of the Callimachean scenario here offers an excuse for declining to attempt epic rather than a positive reason for choosing elegy. Propertius and Horace[175] may well have developed it because of their unease about not writing the sort of poetry which they were aware would have most pleased Augustus, but it is worth noting that Propertius makes no claim here of establishment pressure upon him to attempt epic of any kind.[176]

---

[171] See p. xx.

[172] The great watercourse and the open sea stand for the undesirable also at Callimachus, *Hymn to Apollo* 105-12.

[173] See further Booth (1991) 183 on Ov. *Am.* 2. 18. 3.

[174] See further pp. xxxii-xxxiii.

[175] See Horace, *Odes* 4. 15. 1-4; cf. Ov. *Am.* 1. 1, with discussion on pp. 132-4.

[176] Some scholars determined to find an indication of it, however, have done so by guessing that the answer to Apollo's question in lines 15-16 is 'Maecenas' (so e.g. Luck [1969] 140), and some think we are meant to understand that the stories of the Alban kings, which Propertius was persuaded to abandon, potentially included Augustus, who claimed ultimate descent from them. But the closest Propertius comes to repudiating *contemporary* epic is when he has Calliope possibly allude to the relatively recent events of 29 BC (45-6) in her list of unsuitable subjects for him (for the date of Book 3 see p. xxxvi).

What is more, with the *recusatio* out of the way, Calliope's speech re-habilitates Propertius professionally. For, while she categorically states that war poetry is not for him to attempt, unlike Apollo, she does not accuse him of insufficiency of talent for martial epic, and indirectly she also suggests that war is not desirable subject-matter for poetry anyway. There is a condemnatory note in her talk of the 'raucous' trumpet and of 'sullying' the grove of the Muses with Mars, and she alludes to theoretically glorious Roman military achievements in line 46 in somewhat gruesome tones of disapprobation: 'maimed bodies' (*saucia...corpora*), 'grieving tide' (*maerenti...aqua*). So, in being debarred from martial epic and directed to-wards love elegy, Propertius thus suggests, he is not being demoted to an inferior type of art. Indeed, Calliope explicitly commends love poetry for its practical usefulness (47-50), and its parity with martial epic in artistic merit is perhaps hinted at by her description of it in terms which make love itself sound like a form of warfare: it involves siege or vigil ('at an alien door' [*alienum ad limen*, 47]), evasion ('nocturnal escapes' or, perhaps, 'routs' [*nocturnae...fugae*, 48][177]), clever offensives ('steal a march' [*arte ferire*, literally 'skilfully strike', 50]) and miraculous releasing of prisoners ('charm girls from internment' [*clausas...excantare puellas*, 49]). Proper-tius does not, however, have Calliope make any claim of *stylistic* superior-ity for love elegy. The nearest approach to anything of this kind in the poem comes in his final vague suggestion of his allegiance to the tradition represented by Philitas.

Propertius in fact seems less interested here in championing Alexan-drian, and specifically Callimachean, stylistics than in generally exploiting the Callimachean manner and using a conglomeration of miscellaneous echoes to create a sumptuous effect. Admittedly, he has learned from the *Aetia* preface how to pile up image on image and allusion on allusion to produce (twice) his own impressively dense sequence.[178] He has also in-corporated the two Callimachean motifs of the dream of direct inspiration by the Muses[179] and the location of Hippocrene as the setting for the en-counter; but he is not attempting to follow Callimachus or anyone else ex-clusively. He certainly glances at Hesiod, as already noted, and the idea of water from the same original source (here Hippocrene) being capable of in-spiring different sorts of poetry in different places may well have come

---

[177] The Latin text and its meaning are not certain here.

[178] Cf. Prop. 3. 24. 9-18, with discussion on p. 77.

[179] Propertius' singling out of Calliope may have been suggested by a conversation of Callimachus' with Erato, another Muse, later in the *Aetia*.

from Gallus.[180] His aim in this richly evocative rather than fully coherent scene of inspiration[181] seems to have been to present himself not so much as the 'Roman Callimachus' (as he calls himself at 4. 1. 64), but the Roman Callimachus, the Roman Hesiod, the Roman Philitas and the latter-day Gallus all rolled into one. The whole poem is crafted to give the impression that Propertius is destined to join the ranks of the foremost non-epic poets.[182] But he never explicitly makes that claim, nor does he specify the grounds on which he might do so.

For his generally 'impressionistic' picture Propertius has clearly drawn on visual art as well as literature. The notion of Apollo 'leaning on his gilded lyre' (*aurata nixus...lyra* [14]) comes straight from Roman painting, where this is one of the god's common poses.[183] The redness of the doves' beaks (32) is a detail which particularly suggests iconographic inspiration, and doves are depicted drinking from basins in many a mosaic.[184] The tessellated grotto (27) and clay images of Silenus' features (29) are exemplified in the gardens of Pompeii,[185] and in later art the Muses are pictured going about their separate tasks (33-6). The lavish visual detail in this poem contributes to the generally rich texture, which involves colour ('gilded' lyre, 'green' grotto, 'red' beaks, 'snow-white' swans),[186] sound ('cackling' geese, 'neighing' horse, 'raucous trumpet'; 'tambourines', 'reed-pipes', 'strings'),[187] material ('ivory' quill [with which Apollo plucks the lyre], 'mossy' ground, 'tufa' vault, 'clay' effigy, 'mosaics'),[188]

---

[180] See Coleman (1977) 194-6 on Virgil, *Eclogue* 6. 64.

[181] Propertius' selective drawing on the work of his famous predecessors for whatever inspirational detail took his fancy unsurprisingly results in some inconsistency: Apollo, for example, has to be credited with exceptionally long-range vision, even for a god, if he was able to see Propertius in the meadows of Helicon in Boeotia from a wooded grove near Delphi, and with unimaginable powers of communication, if he was able the next moment, apparently without moving, to address and guide the poet in person. Some would attribute this and other slight oddities, such as the disturbed chronological order and inaccurate detail in the topics supposedly handled by Ennius, to an attempt to represent realistically the illogicalities of a dream, but the attempt would have to be judged a poor one in comparison with Propertius' poem 4. 7 (see pp. 78-94).

[182] The reference to a special seat in the Muses' grotto suggests almost a throne of honour.

[183] See e.g. Ling (1991) 137, fig. 142, a Pompeian wall-painting now in the British Museum.

[184] Hubbard (1974) 165 cites the one from Hadrian's villa now in the Capitoline museum in Rome as 'the most exquisite example'.

[185] Hubbard, *ibid.*

[186] In Latin *aurata* (14), *uiridis* (27), *punica* (32), *niueis* (39).

[187] In Latin [*anseris*] *uoce* (12), [*equi*] *sonus* (40), *rauco...cornu* (41), *tympana* (28), *calami* (30), *neruis* (35).

[188] In Latin *eburno* (25), *muscoso* (26), *pumicibus* (28), *fictilis* (30), *affixis...lapillis* (27).

and sensation ('soft' shade, 'soft' meadows and 'tender' hands).[189] Added to this, a few deft and vivid brush-strokes produce the superb vignettes of (a) the potential reader of Propertius' poetry anxiously awaiting her admirer (19-20) and (b) the antics of the locked-out lover who is to be the subject of it (47-8).

In some respects this is one of Propertius' most disingenuous poems. He cultivates a Callimachean air without rigorously toeing Callimachus' line, and he strikes a self-disparaging and non-confrontational pose without sacrificing any dignity. Yet is he really any less wayward or self-promoting than Ovid in *Amores* 1. 1? As a programmatic piece[190] this elegy seems positively misleading, for it implies that Propertius will henceforth be devoting himself to love poetry, when in fact purely amatory themes feature less and less in his writing from this point on. The new technique he deploys here[191] arguably gives a foretaste of the paradoxically more ambitious direction in which his poetry is set to develop. Disingenuous, then, but also dazzling; for this is Propertius at his most sensuously baroque.

Propertius 3. 24

Woman, you're wrong to be so sure of your good looks;
   It's my eyes long since made you arrogant.
Such praises, Cynthia, my love accorded you
   That I'm ashamed my verses brought you fame.
I praised you as compounded of assorted beauty   5
   So that love thought you were what you were not;
Many's the time I compared your colour to rosy Dawn
   When in fact your cheeks were white with make-up –
A practice family friends could not dissuade me from
   Nor witchcraft wash away in the endless ocean.   10
I'll make this true confession, not forced by fire or steel
   Or even by shipwreck in the Aegean sea:
Carried away I was roasting in Venus' cruel bronze,
   A prisoner, hands tied behind my back.
But look, my ship has entered harbour, garlanded;   15
   I've passed the Syrtes and dropped anchor.
Now tired of the endless surge, I can at last think straight.

---

[189] In Latin *molli* (1), *mollia* (18), *teneras* (34).

[190] See p. xiv.

[191] See Hubbard (1974) 157-61.

That wound of mine has knit and healed.
Good Sense, if you're a Goddess, I dedicate myself
To your shrine. Jove was deaf to all my prayers.   20

Cynthia's beauty was in the eye of the beholder, and *he* was blinded by
love. This is what she, brusquely addressed as 'woman' (*mulier* [1]), is
now unceremoniously told by the beholder himself – Propertius. Regretta-
bly, he says now, he made her famous through his poetry and portrayed her
not as she really was, but as an amalgam of beautiful female types (or per-
haps beautiful individual features) (1-8). Nothing could dissuade him from
this course at the time (9-10), but now, without any coercion, he confesses
to the infatuation which proved so painful and degrading (11-14). He an-
nounces his survival and recovery by depicting himself as a ship coming
into port after safely negotiating the Syrtes (dangerous sandbanks off the
coast of N. Africa) and as one healed of mental disablement and physical
illness (15-18). Finally he dedicates himself to 'Good Sense' (*Mens Bona*
[19]), which saved him when God Almighty did not (19-20).

   This poem ostensibly marks the end of the affair between Propertius
and Cynthia which had its poetic beginnings in 1. 1, and pointedly it con-
tains frequent and multi-directional echoes of that poem. Propertius origi-
nally said that Cynthia captivated him with her eyes (1. 1. 1). Now he
maintains that his own eyes were at fault (2). Not because of that 'arro-
gance' of theirs, which he previously claimed Love quelled (1. 1. 3-4), but
because of their blindness, which he now says love induced (5-6), with the
result that Cynthia herself became 'arrogant' (*nimium...superba* [2]). At 1.
1. 19-24 he challenged witches to influence her in his favour and at 1. 1.
25-6 appealed to his friends, who were 'too late' to restrain him from in-
volvement altogether, to extricate him from the throes of love. Here he
intimates that 'family friends' (*patrii...amici* [9]), i.e. those of his own
social status who would doubtless have attempted to recall him to a con-
ventionally respectable way of life,[192] were not so much 'too late' as simply
ignored, and that witchcraft, whether or not able to make Cynthia love him,
could never have made him face the truth about her; the 'washing'
metaphor stems from the concept of love as a stain[193] (9-10). At 1. 1. 27-8
Propertius volunteered to be subjected to fire and steel, i.e. to the branding
iron used to extract the truth from slaves, if only he could, paradoxically,

---

[192] See Hubbard (1974) 18.

[193] Cf. Plautus, *Poenulus* 198 'This man's heart has the stain of love on it' (*inest amoris macula huic homini in pectore*).

have 'liberty' to articulate his 'anger'.[194] Here, apparently ready to embrace again the sober values of the conventionally free, he is willing tell the truth about his earlier love-induced condition without coercion by 'fire and steel' (*non ferro, non igne* [11]) or prompting to sudden honesty by imminent fear of drowning[195] (12). At 1. 1. 29-30 Propertius begged to be taken on a journey proper overseas, organised by his friends, to escape the consequences of love. Here his safe return from a metaphorical voyage (vessels were 'garlanded' [*coronatae*, 15] in thanks for their survival) represents his apparently unaided conquest of his dangerous infatuation (15-16). After complaining at 1. 1. 2 of being 'smitten', as if by physical disease, and at 1. 1. 7 of suffering from 'mania', he begged his friends to 'seek remedies' for his afflictions (1. 1. 26). Here he announces (17-18) that his wounds have 'knit' (*coiere* [18])[196] and that he is able to 'think straight' again (*resipiscimus* [18], literally 'I have recovered my senses'). Tacitly he appears to be conceding that the philosophers' prescription of self-help through right thinking is after all the one effective remedy for crippling love.[197] This is underlined by his final affirmation (19-20) of the quasi-divine status of 'Good Sense' (the 'if' clause implies acceptance, not doubt: 'seeing that you are a goddess');[198] and at the same time there is a barely concealed scoff at the idea of more conventional deities paying any attention at all to the fortunes of lovers (cf. 1. 1. 8, 31).

Intertextuality[199] in this poem, however, extends beyond its relationship with 1. 1 to another of Propertius' own earlier elegies: 2. 25. There he promised lifelong celebration of Cynthia's beauty in his poetry, whatever the cost in suffering might be. At 2. 25. 11-12 he asks himself 'Wouldn't it be preferable' (i.e. 'less painful') 'to be enslaved to a harsh tyrant / and groan inside your bull, cruel Perillus?'.[200] Perillus of Acragas in Sicily designed

---

[194] See further p. 41.

[195] This, at any rate, is what the version of the text translated here appears to mean, the Aegean being a proverbially stormy stretch of water. But the text of this couplet is much disputed, and a plausible alternative version (*hoc ego non ferro, non igne coactus, et ipsa / naufragus Aegaea – uera fatebor – aqua*) would require line 12 to be understood as a figurative reference to turbulent and ruinous love: 'after being shipwrecked – I will admit it – on a veritable Aegean Sea of passion'.

[196] Specific mention of 'wounds' (*uulnera* 18]) suggests a glancing back through Prop. 1. 1 to the epigram of Meleager which inspired lines 1-4 of that poem; see p. 37.

[197] See p. 37, n. 13 and p. 42 with n. 37; cf. also Posidippus, *AP* 12. 120. 4 (quoted on p. 139).

[198] A temple was dedicated to Good Sense after the Romans' defeat by Hannibal at L. Trasimene in 217 BC (cf. Ov. *Am.* 1. 2. 31).

[199] See p. xiv.

[200] *Nonne fuit satius duro seruire tyranno / et gemere in tauro, saeue Perille, tuo?*

for Phalaris, the notoriously cruel ruler of that city, a hollow bronze bull inside which those selected by Phalaris were cooked alive, their screams replacing a bull's bellows; Perillus himself became the first victim of the ghastly device he had invented. Propertius' implicit answer to his own question at 2. 25. 11-12 is 'Yes, even that would be less painful than persisting in my love for Cynthia and celebrating it in my poetry, but persist I shall, for there is something to be got out of it'. Here at 3. 24. 13-14 he seems to be alluding to the story of the cooking-pot bull again, substituting Venus for the tyrant, when he says 'I was roasting in Venus' cruel bronze, / A prisoner, hands tied behind my back'. He has now seen that there was to all intents and purposes no difference between the love he once celebrated and Phalaris' excruciating torture; it was not only just as painful, but also just as pointless. In a sense, like Perillus himself, he has had his own clever idea rebound on him.

Renunciation of love in general or of a particular beloved is a common enough theme in all Greek and Latin erotic poetry.[201] The lover sometimes gives way to a rival,[202] sometimes bows to advancing age,[203] and sometimes simply becomes sated[204] or, as here, disenchanted.[205] Much of Propertius' imagery is basically well-worn too: metaphors of sickness, madness and bondage regularly illustrate all manner of poetic love-situations, and sea-faring imagery is especially popular in references to recovery from love;[206] but Propertius' present poem is no routine or romantic lover's farewell. He shows neither the good-humoured detachment of Horace, Ovid and the Greek epigrammatists nor the emotional conflict of Catullus, but in 3. 24 arrives at a sharply objective view of his beloved, which is followed by a bitter, parting malediction in 3. 25.[207] What is more, this pair of dismissal pieces appears at the very end of Propertius' third book, in which poems about his love for Cynthia have become vastly outnumbered by those on other themes, including his expanding concept of his own role as a poet;[208] this change of direction is even more marked in the fourth book. By virtue, therefore, of its content, its tone and its typically programmatic

---

[201] See Cairns (1972) 79-82.

[202] E.g. Meleager, *AP* 5. 160, Horace, *Odes* 1. 5. 13-16.

[203] E.g. Philodemus, *AP* 5. 112, Horace, *Odes* 2. 4. 22-4.

[204] E.g. Horace, *Odes* 3. 26, Ovid, *Am.* 2. 9A, 3. 11A.

[205] Cf. Catullus 8 and 76.

[206] E.g. Meleager, *AP* 5. 190. 1-3, 12. 84, 85. 1-3, 167. 3-4, Ov. *Am.* 2. 9B. 31-2, *Remedia Amoris* 609-10; see further Papanghelis (1987) 98.

[207] Some scholars think this is not a separate poem, but merely a continuation of 3. 24.

[208] See pp. 71-3.

position[209] 3. 24 begs to be understood as a renunciation not just of
Cynthia but also of the personal love elegy which she has inspired (her
inspirational function is hinted at in 1. 1 and vigorously affirmed in 2. 25,
the two poems especially recalled in 3. 24). In addition, the metaphor of a
ship setting sail or coming into port and dropping anchor was generally
popular in Propertius' time as a method of announcing the start or comple-
tion of a poetic enterprise.[210] As if to reinforce the message that he has
reached an artistic watershed, Propertius alludes to his amatory-elegiac past
in the highly self-conscious style that has become the staple of the less
amatory Book 3. For example, in lines 5-8, where he admits that he once
praised Cynthia's complexion for its dawn-like *rosiness*, when its *white-
ness* was actually artificial, the Latin word he uses for 'rosy' (*roseo* [7])
connotes a whitish-pink, and (with reference to a woman's fair looks) the
one he uses for the 'white' effect (*candor* [8]) connotes a pinkish-white –
in other words, they both suggest the radiant clarity of a 'peaches and
cream' complexion, which Roman women, no less than their modern
counterparts, sought with the aid of make-up if necessary. There is, then,
no true contradiction in terms here, but providing the *appearance* of one is
Propertius' sophisticated way of underlining the extent of his mispercep-
tion of Cynthia. His newly objective view of his own situation he presents
through 'a series of startlingly diverse images' (Hubbard [1974] 92), un-
folding, one upon the other, with kaleidoscopic brilliance. The purificatory
power of magic is merged with that of the ocean (10); burning and bondage
are united[211] (13-14); recovery from physical injury follows hard on recovery
of the senses, which itself follows on survival of the perils of seafaring.
The relentless succession of striking images is especially reminiscent of
Callimachus, whom Propertius expressly invokes as a model at 3. 1. 1-2
and echoes on an impressive scale also in 3. 3.[212]

So, with this poem the moment of Propertius' final parting from
Cynthia, both emotion and poetic, has apparently come. How does it com-
pare, emotionally and poetically, with Catullus 76? And is there any reason
at all to suspect that this is not really the end?

---

[209] See p. xiv.

[210] See e.g. Virgil, *Georgics* 2. 41-5, 4. 116-17, Horace, *Odes* 4. 15. 3-4, Ov. *Ars Amatoria* 1.
772, 3. 99-100, 747-8, *Fasti* 1. 4.

[211] The oblique equation of Venus with the sadistic Phalaris, coupled with the metaphor of
confinement in line 14, may be a deliberate attempt to outdo the colourful imagery of Tibullus
1. 8. 5-8.

[212] See pp. 69-70. The Phalaris story, to which Propertius seems to be alluding in a
quintessentially oblique Callimachean manner in lines 13-14, was treated by Callimachus
himself at *Aetia*, frags 45-6 Trypanis.

Propertius 4. 7

A ghost is something. Death does *not* close all.
  A pale shade escapes, defeating the pyre.
For I have seen Cynthia leaning over my bed-head
  (Though lately buried by the busy road)
While sleep for me was hung up on love's funeral   5
  And I mourned my bed's cold kingdom.
She had the same hair as when borne to burial,
  The same eyes; but the dress she wore was charred
And the fire had eaten into that beryl on her finger
  And Lethe water had chafed her lips.   10
Anger and voice were those of the breathing woman
  As her brittle hands snapped their thumbs:
'Traitor, from whom no woman need expect good faith,
  Can you have fallen asleep so soon?
So soon forgotten stolen joys in the wakeful Subura?   15
  Those tricky nights and my worn windowsill
From which, time and again, I hung on a rope for you,
  Descending hand under hand to your embrace?
We often shared Venus at the crossroads breast to breast,
  Our cloaks warming the pavement.   20
Alas for that secret understanding whose specious words
  Deaf southern winds have blown away!
Yes, no one keened for me as my eyes closed. Had *you*
  Called *me* back I'd have gained another day.
No watchman rattled a split cane near me   25
  And the crock against my head hurt.
Besides, who saw you bowed in grief above my body
  Or in a black toga hot with tears?
If it bored you to go further you could at least have slowed
  The bearers' pace to the city gates.   30
Ingrate, why weren't you there to pray for wind for the pyre?
  Why were my flames not perfumed with nard?
Was it even too much trouble to strew cheap hyacinths
  And hallow my ashes from a broken wine-jar?
Put Lygdamus to torture! Hot irons for the home-bred slave!   35
  I knew, when I drank the poisoned wine that turned me pale.
Though artful Nomas hides away her secret juices
  The fiery potsherd will show whose hands are guilty.
Yesterday's prostitute parading for cheap nights

Now brushes the ground with gold-embroidered gown,   40
But hands out heavier stints in unfair basket-loads
   To any girl who gabs about my beauty.
For taking garlands to my tomb old Petale
   Must suffer chaining to a filthy clog,
And Lalage is hung up by the hair and flogged   45
   For daring to ask favours in my name.
You sit by while Madame melts down my golden bust
   To gain a dowry from my cremation.
But I'll not nag, Propertius, much as you deserve it;
   In your books my reign was long.   50
I swear by the Fates' irrevocable chant
   (So may the Triple Dog not snarl at me)
I have kept faith. If I speak false, may vipers
   Hiss in my grave and curl up on my bones.
For beyond the sullen flood two places are assigned   55
   And the whole crowd rows across on different courses.
One carries Clytemnestra's foulness and the Cretan
   Queen's who faked a monstrous wooden cow.
But see, the other group swept along in a flower-crowned boat
   To where blest airs caress Elysian roses,   60
Where numerous lutes and where Cybebe's brazen cymbals
   And Lydian plectra twang for turbaned dancers.
Andromeda and Hypermnestra, guileless wives,
   Tell of the well-known perils of their story.
The first complains her arms were bruised by mother's chains   65
   And her hands did not deserve cold rocks.
Hypermnestra tells how her sisters dared an outrage
   And how her own heart quailed at it.
So with death's tears we strive to heal life's loves,
   Though *I* hide all your criminal bad faith.   70
But now, if you have feelings and are not fast bound
   By Chloris' potions, here are my requests.
See that my nurse Parthenia in frail old age lacks nothing;
   Towards you she could have been but was not greedy.
Don't let my darling Latris, named for usefulness,   75
   Hold out the mirror for a new mistress.
And all those verses you made on my account,
   Please burn them. Cease your boasting about me.
Plant ivy on my grave and let abundant clusters
   Gently bind my bones with tangled tendrils   80

Where fruitful Anio descends on branchy fields
And ivory, thanks to Hercules, never yellows.
Here on a column write me a fit epitaph but brief
So travellers in haste from Rome may read it:
HERE IN TIBURTINE GROUND LIES GOLDEN   85
CYNTHIA, BRINGING GLORY TO YOUR BANKS, FATHER ANIO.
And pay good heed to dreams that come from the Gates of Duty;
When dreams of duty come they carry weight.
At night we roam around. Night frees imprisoned shades
And Cerberus too can range unchained.   90
At first light law demands return to Lethe lake;
We embark and the boatman counts his freight.
Others may own you now. Soon I alone shall hold you.
You'll be with me and bone on mingled bone I'll grind.'
Having thus dealt with me in bitter accusation   95
The shade from my embrace faded away.

Propertius had another dream (cf. Prop. 3. 3): the cremation-ravaged ghost
of Cynthia came and gave him a bedside lecture one night. After setting the
scene in his bedroom and describing the appearance of the ghost (1-12), he
fills the rest of the poem except the final couplet with her speech. Consider
first, though, *this* reflection:

'Ah me, there really is something in the halls of Hades – a soul,
but nothing of the human spirit in it at all. For tonight the soul of
hapless Patroclus stood over me, weeping and lamenting, and told
me each thing I should do and was wondrously like himself.'

Homer, *Iliad* 23. 103-7

This is the bereaved Achilles after being visited in his sleep by the ghost of
his beloved friend and comrade Patroclus, killed by the Trojan Hector,
while wearing Achilles' own armour. Achilles' words close rather than
open the account of the ghost's visitation. The scene is set at *Iliad* 23. 62-7:

As soon as sleep had overtaken him, releasing his heart from cares
and spreading sweetly around him (his glorious limbs were ex-
hausted after chasing wind-swift Hector to Troy), the ghost of
hapless Patroclus came up, absolutely true to life in every respect –
his stature, his lovely eyes and his voice, and wearing exactly the
clothes that he used to have.

The ghost, standing by Achilles' head, then addresses him thus (69-92):

'Asleep, Achilles! You have forgotten me. Certainly you never ne-
glected me in life, but in death you do. Bury me with all possible
speed; let me pass through the gates of Hades. The souls – the im-
ages of those who have died – are keeping me out and will not let
me mingle with them on the far side of the river. Instead I wander
around like this by the broad-gated house of Hades. Give me your
hand, I beseech you. For never again shall I return from Hades,
once you have granted me the rites of the funeral fire. Never again
shall we sit together alive, apart from our dear comrades, making
plans. For the fact is that hateful death has swallowed me up –
death which was my lot right from the day I was born. And your
fate too, Achilles, godlike as you are, is to die beneath the walls of
the wealthy Trojans. And there is another thing I ask and request
of you, if you will listen: do not put my bones apart from your
own, Achilles, but together with them, just as we grew up together
in your house, when Menoetius brought me to you from Opous as
a little boy because of the ghastly manslaughter on that day, when I
had killed the son of Amphidamas, without thinking, not meaning
to, in a moment of anger over the knucklebones. Then the horse-
man Peleus took me into his house, brought me up carefully and
called me your squire. So let a single, golden, two-handled urn –
the one your lady mother gave you – conceal the bones of both of us.'

Achilles subsequently reassures him (94-8):

'Why, dear heart,[213] have you come here, and why do you bid me
do all these things? Of course I shall do everything exactly as you
tell me. But stand closer to me. Let us have the pleasure of weep-
ing bitterly with our arms around each other for a moment.'

And in the same breath Achilles

...stretched out his own hands, but could not grasp him. The soul
departed like smoke, squeaking underground. (99-101)

Such are the events in Book 23 of the *Iliad* which prompt Achilles' com-
ment in lines 103-7 (quoted above) and which prove to be an intertextual

---

[213] Literally, 'dear head', a conventional salutation in both Greek and Latin.

presence[214] throughout Propertius 4. 7. In echoing Achilles' closing words so clearly in the opening couplet of his own poem Propertius instantaneously evokes a situation, a relationship and emotions which act as foils for what is to come. A difference in the situation is immediately apparent: the body of the ghost in Propertius' poem has already been cremated (2) and the ashes buried (4). So no pre-funeral reproach is going to be possible here, but a potentially similar relationship is suggested when the deceased is identified as Cynthia, to whom Propertius once liked to think himself bound in mutual affection as intense as that of Patroclus and Achilles. Gratitude, however, would seem more likely than reproach from Cynthia – if Propertius has done for her in death everything he earlier promised to do[215] and everything he envisaged her doing for him under the same circumstances.[216] And why doubt it, given his well-aired belief in death as the supreme opportunity for the expression and fulfilment of romantic love?[217] But then, why not, when at the end of Book 3 he declared his affair with Cynthia, both erotic and poetic, to be over,[218] and when Book 4 up to this point has been largely devoted to aetiological[219] and other non-personal themes? Reproach then – for something – *could* be coming after all, but Propertius sustains the suspense a little longer by focussing for a moment on himself, playing Achilles, as it were, to Cynthia's Patroclus.

His sleep, we learn, was not the heavy sleep of exhaustion which overtook Achilles, but an uneasy doze, in which the funeral of his one-time beloved preyed on his mind, as he brooded on the thought of that bed of his which she once ruled over now being bereft of her warmth.[220] So, grand manner, but incongruously unheroic subject. The ghost itself, even before it says anything, is a much more threatening bedside presence than Patroclus', for while *his* appearance was reassuringly unchanged by death, Cynthia's body bears the marks of both the funeral pyre and contact with the Underworld (Lethe [10] was one of its fabled waterways).[221] Yet at the same time she is recognisably the same Cynthia who once delighted in fine

---

[214] See p. xiv.

[215] See 2. 24. 51-2.

[216] See especially 2. 13. 27-30, and cf. 1. 17. 19-24, 3. 16. 21-4.

[217] Cf. 2. 13. 39-40, with discussion on p. 63.

[218] See pp. 73-7.

[219] See p. xix.

[220] This at least must be the general sense of the difficult Latin of lines 5-6, but its exact meaning is disputed.

[221] Lethe is also generally the river from which the ghosts of the dead drink to forget their past, but clearly it has not had this effect on Cynthia here.

dresses and jewels (her exotic beryl ring is a detail which makes this clear). Her eyes and (oddly?) her hair have been untouched by the fire, and her angry voice is unmistakable: a real horror-film figure, part skeleton, part corpse (7-12).

Reproach of some kind now seems inevitable, and indeed Cynthia's opening words are reminiscent of Patroclus' (*Iliad* 23. 81-2) in that she too chides the addressee for falling asleep and forgetting his obligations. But while Patroclus gently reminds Achilles of his duty ('my friend', he still calls him), Cynthia harshly condemns Propertius ('traitor' [*perfide*, 13]) for wilful disregard of his commitments ('southern winds' [*Noti*, 22], proverbially stormy, were conventionally alleged to dispose of dishonoured promises[222]). While Patroclus stresses the exclusiveness and dignity of his relationship with Achilles and bitterly laments never being able to be with him in the future, Cynthia harps on all the risks she took to get together with Propertius in the past (15-20). Their love-making was no tryst in comfortable seclusion, either, but a decidedly hole and corner affair[223] (the Subura [15] was a lively but disreputable district of Rome, and the 'crossroads' [*triuio*, 19] has connotations of the gutter).[224] Cynthia then comes to the point: it is the nature of the funeral accorded her – cheap and nasty – which is her chief cause of grievance (23-34). So it *is* the worst case: Propertius has, evidently, specifically failed to practise what he preached about death as an opportunity for the demonstration of love. The irony of his remissness is emphasised by extensive intertextuality with his own earlier poetry, especially, though not exclusively, 2. 13.[225] At 2. 13. 17-36, while deprecating pomp and circumstance for his own prospective funeral, Propertius nevertheless made it clear that he expected Cynthia, as his chief mourner and executrix, to do him more than the minimum honours. Here she contends that *her* funeral left in *his* hands fell short of common decency, let alone luxury. No question of 'ivory fittings' or 'cloth of gold' (2. 13. 21-2), but a mere 'crock' (*tegula curta* [26], literally 'broken tile') to rest her head against on the bier, and not even the most basic of offerings and flowers, never mind a 'line of incense-bearing platters' (2. 13. 23). There is a sharp contrast, too, between the 'Syrian unguent' from an 'onyx' flask, which, despite his supposedly simple tastes, Propertius did envisage

---

[222] Cf. Ov. *Am*. 2. 8. 20.

[223] Contrast the set-up sketched here with that in Prop. 1. 3 (see p. 54).

[224] See Papanghelis (1987) 154. Some, however, see 'romantic bravado' in this section; e.g. Warden (1980) 22.

[225] See pp. 55-64.

Cynthia bringing him at 2. 13. 30,[226] and the perfunctory libation from a 'broken wine jar' (*fracto...cado* [43]) and 'cheap hyacinths' (*nulla mercede hyacinthos* [33]) which she claims were denied *her*.[227] Not even the conventional watchman was arranged (to guard the body before cremation and rattle 'a split cane' [*fissa...harundine*, 25] to ward off evil spirits), let alone a lover's personal vigil (at 3. 16. 24 Cynthia is envisaged mounting one over Propertius' tomb). No more than the merest token of personal participation, in fact, was Propertius prepared to offer (29-30). Mourners normally followed the cortège to the burial grounds outside town or city gates, but Propertius, Cynthia claims, could not get it fast enough even as far the gates, which was the very furthest he was prepared to go! No normal signs of grief or mourning did he show (27-8), not to speak of the more extravagant gestures he had expected of her (2. 13. 27, 29). No ritual calling of her name did he venture (cf. 2. 13. 28), let alone try to emulate the mythological Laodamia, who was so distraught at the death of her husband, Protesilaus, that the gods allowed him leave of absence from the Underworld to be with her again for one day; at the end of this she killed herself so as to be able to remain with him.[228]

The circumstances mean that Propertius, unlike Achilles, cannot put right the neglect of which the ghost complains, and Cynthia is far from finished yet. Her menacingly controlled irony now gives way to an outburst of violently vindictive temper. For this she was always notorious,[229] but here in lines 35-48 it is overlaid with the paranoid exaggeration of the comic stage[230] as, again recalling the sentiments and incidents of earlier poems, she vents her anger. First (35-8) she calls for two slaves whom she suspects of having poisoned her to be tortured by burning.[231] One of them, Nomas, is a new character, but Lygdamus is familiar as the slave whom Propertius in 3. 6 promised to reward for acting as his go-between with Cynthia during a temporary rift when she accused him of having taken up

---

[226] At 3. 16. 23-4 he looks forward to flowers as well.

[227] The manner of her burial in fact sounds even worse than that Propertius wishes on the unscrupulous old brothel-mistress at 4. 5. 75-8.

[228] Cynthia's sarcasm in 23-4 may remind the reader of Propertius' hint at 2. 27. 15-16 that *he* would make a good Protesilaus, if *she* played Laodamia (cf. n. 247 below), and also of his sad intimation at 2. 13. 51-6 that, although he could well play Adonis, she would prove no Venus, when she tried – as *of course* she would – to 'call him back' back from the dead.

[229] Cf. Prop. 1. 3. 18.

[230] See Warden (1980) 33-5.

[231] To make them tell the truth; cf. Prop. 1. 1. 27, Tib. 2. 4. 6.

with another, unscrupulous woman.[232] Propertius denied it then, but Cynthia's ghost now implies that it was true, for she next (39-48) rails against 'yesterday's prostitute' (*modo...publica* [39], more literally 'recent street-girl') who currently queens it in Propertius' household.[233] The incomer wears a long, exotically gold-hemmed gown,[234] in a sense taking over the 'golden' image of the dead Cynthia (*aurea* [85]) and symbolically melting down her 'golden bust' (*imaginis aurum* [47]). She allegedly ill-treats Cynthia's former servants who still admire her by dishing out extra quotas of wool for them to work. She has Petale ('leaf' in Greek) chained to a 'filthy clog' (*codicis immundi* [44]), i.e. a block of wood to impede her movement, as punishment for bringing flowers to her grave, and Lalage ('chatterbox') hung up by the hair for invoking her dead mistress' name.

At this point Cynthia breaks off the attack. She concedes that she had a good innings in Propertius' books (49-50), and we may wonder whether now she is, like Patroclus after all, about to adopt a less aggressive approach and comfort Propertius with warm appreciation of his poetry about her. Not a bit of it! Rather (51-4), she fiercely asserts her own fidelity, swearing by the 'irrevocable chant' (*nulli reuolubile carmen* [51]) of the Fates[235] and the 'Triple Dog' (*tergeminus...canis* [52]), i.e. Cerberus, watchdog of the Underworld. She then goes on (55-68) to describe two categories of women allotted different dwelling-places in the world of the dead. Rowed off on one course across the 'sullen flood' (*turpem...amnem* [55]), i.e. the River Styx (border-control for entry to the Underworld), is the group which includes two infamous adulteresses: Clytemnestra[236] and Pasiphäe (the 'Cretan Queen' [*Cressae*, 57]).[237] The other group is rowed off across the Styx in a 'flower-crowned boat' (*coronato...phaselo* [59])[238]

---

[232] Nomas in Greek literally means 'nomad' or 'Numidian', and is perhaps meant to suggest a black woman with herbalist skill. Lygdamus' name, in witty contrast, is similar to the Greek word for a type of dazzling white marble. Some critics say it hints at the white-chalked feet of a slave bought in the market, but, if so, it produces one of the several – perhaps deliberate – oddities in the poem, for Lygdamus is supposed to be a more privileged 'home-bred' slave (*uernae* [35]), i.e. specifically *not* a bought-in one.

[233] Cynthia now appears to have shared Propertius' household at some time; progress indeed from the need to make love at the 'crossroads'.

[234] In contrast with the plain, short tunic, perhaps, of the slave she once was; cf. p. 144.

[235] See p. 58 on Prop. 2. 13. 43-4.

[236] With the assistance of her paramour Aegisthus she murdered her husband Agamemnon.

[237] She cuckolded her husband Minos with a bull (which the gods caused her to fall in love with) by concealing herself within a wooden cow specially constructed by the master-craftsman Daedalus.

[238] Cf. p. 75 on Prop. 3. 24. 15.

towards Elysium,[239] where Cybebe's 'brazen cymbals' (*aera rotunda* [61]) clash.[240] This group includes two women of legendary blamelessness: Andromeda[241] and Hypermnestra, the only one of the fifty daughters Danaus married to their cousins, the fifty sons of Aegyptus, who refused to murder her husband on her wedding night (Danaus' idea was that his daughters should settle an old score for him with his brother Aegyptus). With the latter company Cynthia herself identifies, claiming that she conceals Propertius' infidelities (69-70). Why should she do this? Perhaps because her fellow-passengers would shun her, if they discovered that her suffering was not in the least like theirs! Neither of those mentioned, after all, had been wronged in love, and Andromeda was not even renowned for her own wifely fidelity.[242] Cynthia's 'nagging', then, may cease, but only to be succeeded by cold dismissal.[243] In one respect, at least, Propertius does not now *need* to put things right for her. For, far from being excluded (like Patroclus) from the cohorts of the shades, she claims to have already found her rightful place among the ghosts of the virtuous, suffering and beautiful women of mythology, and in so doing she has achieved the heroic status which Propertius himself had coveted, not least in death.[244] In a sense she even seems to have been sanctified by death, as Propertius had promised her that she would be, when once she lay ill.[245] Infidelity, however, is the chief issue, and Cynthia's condemnation of Propertius for this evokes memories again of his earlier affirmations. At 2. 13. 25-6 he intimated that his faithfulness to her would be lifelong and exclusive, and in other poems he offered variations on this theme,[246] promising frequently to maintain his fidelity to her even after death,[247] despite his knowledge that she had been

---

[239] The idyllic part of the Underworld reserved for those who have lived virtuously on earth.

[240] The Anatolian cult of the mother-goddess Cybebe (or Cybele), much favoured by Roman women, was associated with joyous and exuberant music and dancing, and perhaps also with belief in a happy after-life, but the exact connection with the Underworld, if there was one, is obscure.

[241] See p. 46.

[242] Nor, of course, was Cynthia herself Propertius' wife, though this is not the first time she has been made to speak as if she were; see p. 53.

[243] Some critics, however, deny this; see e.g. Goold (1989) 117.

[244] See e.g. Prop. 2. 13. 29-30 with discussion on p. 61.

[245] Prop. 2. 28. 25-6.

[246] At his own funeral, he predicted, she would specifically commend him for his fidelity (2. 24. 35-8).

[247] E.g. Prop. 1. 19. 7-18 (where again Propertius hopelessly fancies himself as Protesilaus), 2. 15. 35-6, 2. 24. 33-4.

unfaithful to him in life[248] and fear that she might not measure up to his own standards of devotion if she outlived him.[249] In yet another variation he swore eternal fidelity by the bones of his dead parents, inviting them to come and haunt him if he failed to keep his word:[250] in our poem that invitation has been taken up – but by someone else!

Cynthia's ghost, however, like Patroclus' and most other literary ghosts, has primarily come to give instructions. Propertius must now hear what she wants him to do – if he has not been completely bewitched by the love-potions of Chloris (probably the ex-prostitute, whose name in Greek means 'green herb').[251] The first request (73-6) is that he look after her faithful old retainers: her nurse Parthenia (who evidently refrained from insisting on tips for arranging access to Cynthia) and her hairdresser Latris (witty Greek names again: Parthenia means 'virginal' – here almost 'old maid' – and Latris 'one who serves'). He is also *to burn his own poems about her* and stop basking in her reflected glory. She just wants ivy planted on her grave at Tibur on the banks of the R. Anio.[252] Tibur (modern Tivoli) was a hill resort 20 miles east of Rome with abundant orchards, where the air was supposed to keep ivory creamy white (here this is attributed to the favour of Hercules who had a cult there). She also wants a stone erected with a simple inscription to bestow on Tibur and the Anio[253] all the glory which 'golden Cynthia' (*AUREA CYNTHIA* [85]) can reflect (71-86). The adjective is generally honorific, putting the seal on her metamorphosis from the resident of the seedy Subura into the Elysian heroine, but perhaps it also suggests that the ex-prostitute's melting down of her 'golden bust' has failed to destroy her aura. All of this again pointedly recalls Propertius' own earlier utterances. At 2. 13. 31-6 he gave Cynthia instructions that his grave was to be planted with a bay-tree and marked with a brief but fitting inscription immortalising his love for her. The implication of that, of course, was that it would also immortalise Cynthia herself.[254] Here, after lulling him into a false sense of security with an innocuous first request, she brusquely disabuses him of the notion of his or his poetry's indispensability

---

248 Prop. 2. 9. 45-8.

249 Prop. 1. 19. 21-4.

250 Prop. 2. 20. 15-18.

251 At 3. 6. 25-30 Cynthia had insisted to Lygdamus that her rival had used love-magic on Propertius.

252 Cynthia addresses its eponymous spirit (85).

253 At Prop. 3. 16. 1-4 she is represented as having some sort of home or lodging in the area.

254 At 2. 11. 3-6 Propertius had warned Cynthia that she risked obscurity after death if she deserted him for an inferior poet or a non-poet.

to her reputation by telling him to burn his Cynthia-poems and claiming fame in her own right. What is more, it would even appear to be fame for her *own* poetic skill.[255] For the ivy which she wants on her grave[256] is just as symbolic of poetry[257] as the bay which Propertius wanted on his, and the notion of her literary prowess being able to reflect some glory on the locality of her residence parallels the male poets' habitual claims of the fame that their birthplaces will owe to them.[258] Her fame is to be recorded, like that which Propertius himself claimed, in a brief and fitting epitaph, but one with no mention at all of him, and (supposedly!) composed by Cynthia herself. Finally, whereas Propertius at 2. 13. 37-8 looked to his reputation as a poet and a lover to bring fame to his otherwise humble grave, Cynthia acknowledges the advantages of the location of hers in an already famous and well-frequented place (81-4). This location is also exactly the opposite of what Propertius asked Cynthia to arrange for him at 3. 16. 25-30 because of his general dislike of public thoroughfares and fear of lovers' tombs being desecrated in such places. Cynthia, seeking no commemoration as a lover and openly courting popular acclaim, is immune to similar anxieties.

These are last instructions devastatingly different from Patroclus' pathetic but tender final request for his bones to be consigned to the same burial urn as will hold Achilles' own; and Cynthia's ghost has still not quite finished. Her last word is a warning, whose validity she stresses (87-8) by explaining that dreams 'carry weight' (*pondus habent* [88]) when they come through the 'Gates of Duty' (*piis...portis* [87]). There is a touch of witty word-play here: the apparitions which manifest themselves in dreams are bodily weight*less*. Two Gates of Sleep, through one of which come false dreams and through the other true ones, first appear in Homer and are then relocated to the doorway of the Underworld by Virgil in an enigmatic passage at *Aeneid* 6. 893-9, where Aeneas, after visiting the dutiful dead and receiving a revelation of the future glory of Rome, unexpectedly leaves the Underworld through the gate of false dreams. Although Propertius obviously has these earlier passages in mind, he avoids Virgilian complications by making the gate of true dreams simply the passage-way of the dutiful and implying that Cynthia, because she uses it, is one of them. For good measure Cynthia also explains the eerie mechanism of her ghostly

---

[255] For Cynthia's ability in this sphere see Prop. 1. 2. 27, 2. 3. 19-20.

[256] The Latin text is in doubt here, but the version translated gives good sense. For an alternative see Papanghelis (1987) 186-8.

[257] Cf. p. 68 on Prop. 3. 3. 35.

[258] Cf. especially Prop. 4. 1. 62-4.

visitations (89-92); the 'boatman' (*nauta* [92]) is Charon, the ferryman who traditionally rowed the ghosts of the dead over the R. Styx. The actual warning she issues is this: whatever other women may possess Propertius now, after death he will be Cynthia's alone, as her skeleton grinds against his in grotesque embrace (93-4). There is a clear suggestion of sepulchral intercourse in the expression here, and the idea of togetherness in the grave, found comforting not only by Patroclus' ghost but also by Propertius himself at 2. 13. 39-40,[259] is thus given a horribly lively reinterpretation.[260] In her own way Cynthia is getting revenge for her discomfort at the 'crossroads' (19), and she makes it clear that, though she is dead, her ghostly presence can harass Propertius while he is still alive just as much as he had melodramatically anticipated that she would harass his spirit and mortal remains if she should outlive him (2. 8. 19-20).

At this point the ghost vanished as Propertius tried to embrace it, just as Patroclus' had eluded Achilles; and the menacing note on which Cynthia's ghost ends is highlighted by the contrast with the pathos and tenderness of Patroclus' closing appeal. But Propertius, quite unlike Achilles, has no further word for the deceased. In some respects the basic situation is a reversal of that in Poem 1. 3, where Cynthia, wronged and upset by Propertius, had her sleep in her own home disturbed by him and awoke to scold him, but did so in a way which showed that *he* actually held the upper hand.[261] Here *he* has *his* sleep in his own home disturbed by *her*, wronged and upset by him still, but now indisputably in control.

We imagine, of course, that at this juncture he woke up and made the opening observation which first reminded us of Achilles. Now, in spite of – and because of – all the expectations the reminiscence created, we can see that in Propertius' case it highlights an entirely different reaction to an entirely different experience. To Achilles the indication that 'death does not close all' was welcome: to Propertius, who had *liked* to believe that dumb and inert bones and ashes really were all that remained after death (cf. 2. 13. 57-8),[262] it has come as a nasty shock. While Achilles had the straightforward kind of admonitory dream common in the ancient literary tradition, Propertius had a psychologically realistic nightmare of the type in which one's worst fears are realised, one's secret shame laid bare, and one's fondest fantasies turned upside-down and inside-out – the kind of dream in

---

[259] A similar idea at Prop. 2. 26. 43-4.

[260] It more than matches Propertius' own macabre threat to murder Cynthia for company in death when he kills himself through grief at her infidelity (2. 8. 25-8).

[261] See pp. 54-5.

[262] See further Warden (1980) 62-9.

which a welter of images and experiences are fragmented and distorted into a queer jumble of patent illogicalities and potential truths. The illogicalities Propertius manages well enough (Cynthia's strangely unburnt hair, her sensational accusations, the slaves' improbably witty names,[263] and the odd company an elegiac mistress keeps in the Underworld). The potential truths, however, are his speciality. The two major preoccupations of his life as it is depicted in his work were his love-affair with Cynthia and his love-affair with himself – or at any rate with his poetic reputation – and both of them he was inclined to explore and link through the prospect of death. In his nightmare they are linked still, now by the *fact* of death,[264] and the frequent reminiscences of his own earlier poetry realistically point to suppressed guilt, jealousy and fear in relation to these matters. His guilt surfaces when Cynthia accuses him of failing her in death, and his jealousy when she implies that she has already achieved through death the truly heroic status he often seemed to crave fruitlessly for himself.[265] His secret fears, on the other hand, seem to be betrayed, when she (a) informs him that she has no need in death of the poetry he considered an invaluable asset to them both and (b) offers him, instead of the romantic notion of their inert dust and ashes being harmlessly mingled in the grave, the distinctly less enticing prospect of a larval embrace. If 1. 3 presented Cynthia's attitude to her lover's shortcomings as Propertius liked to imagine it was, 4. 7 shows it as he suspected it could be. There, to have a mistress laying claim to wifely fidelity was flattering: here, it is a severe embarrassment.

It is psychologically plausible that such a nightmare should be prompted by the death of one for whom a man had once felt intense romantic passion, even if that passion had now subsided, but what Propertius' readers long to know is how they are supposed to think he reacted to it. Though some of what the witness says must make her testimony suspect – the wayward Cynthia of the earlier poems is hardly entitled to claim an immaculate record of fidelity – the silence of the accused is deafening. In striking contrast with Achilles, Propertius within the dream neither protests innocence nor shows remorse, and outside it he gives no indication of how much the experience bothered him after the initial shock he felt on awakening. We can contrast the ending of 2. 26, where his amusing revelation that he woke up just as, in his dream, he was about to jump off a cliff to save Cynthia from drowning suggests that he subsequently dismissed the dream as

---

[263] See pp. 85 and 87 above with n. 232.

[264] At least, it is a fact as far as the poem is concerned; whether a real beloved had really died we cannot know.

[265] See pp. 61, 62.

nothing. There may, however, be some indication of Propertius' reaction to the dream of 4. 7 in the *next* poem of the book.

4. 8 has always caused a great deal of puzzlement because the woman who was presented as dead in the previous piece is there very much alive. The poem is Propertius' account of how a virago of a Cynthia, fresh from an outing to a religious shrine at Lanuvium for a tryst with a dandified gigolo, 'last night'[266] gate-crashed a party he was having with two prostitutes in an attempt to console himself for her infidelities (Lygdamus was there as the wine-waiter). She fought like an alley-cat, first with them and then with him, and finally, after laying down rules for his future behaviour and ritually decontaminating him, ordered him to bed – with her! 7 and 8 are the only Cynthia-poems in Book 4, and, despite their apparently unnatural sequence, it is hard to believe that they are entirely unrelated or that their order results from some accident of transmission. Admittedly, 4. 8's recalling of the final episode of the *Odyssey*[267] nicely complements 4. 7's reminiscence of an episode from the *Iliad*;[268] but by itself this does not satisfactorily explain the order of the two poems. The new suggestion here offered is that 4. 8 offers indirect comment on 4. 7, by juxtaposing relevant information from which readers can draw their own conclusions. This unromanticised memoir of Cynthia's actual behaviour in life perhaps represents Propertius' attempt to counteract the disturbing emotions raised by her accusations from beyond death in his dream. On the one hand there are some pointers to the essential truth of her charges: he was *not* above taking to prostitutes, and Lygdamus *was* an accomplice of sorts. On the other hand Cynthia's self-righteousness was clearly humbug. Even her apparently respectable association with Tibur now seems questionable, for her outing to Lanuvium prompts recall that Tibur was coupled with it at 2. 32. 1-6 as one of her suspected assignation spots. Craftily Propertius still does not say whether he was guilty or not of the cheap and nasty funeral she complained of, but rather implies that if he was, he could justify it, at least to himself. What is more, the whole tenor of the piece suggests that, guilty or not, he has now recovered his equilibrium after the initial shock and anxiety on awakening from his dream: a ghost may be 'something' (*aliquid* [1]), but, after cool consideration, it is nothing to worry about. In the end, the dream of 4. 7 has been shrugged off just as easily as that of 2. 26.

---

[266] This need not be taken any more literally than 'the other night' in English, which simply means 'on a night I recall not ever so long ago'.

[267] I.e. Odysseus' return to reclaim his wife from her suitors.

[268] See Evans (1971) 51-3; cf. Papanghelis (1987) 196-7.

At all events, both 4. 7 and 4. 8 clearly show that Propertius still finds his affair with Cynthia an attractive subject for poetry, but his interest in portraying the anguished intensity and shifting feelings of romantic love has given way to a taste for lively story-telling.[269] Furthermore, if the relationship of the two elegies is indeed as suggested above, Propertius would seem to be experimenting tentatively with a technique which may have a precedent in Tibullus 1. 8 and 9[270] and reaches its apotheosis in Ovid, *Amores* 2. 7 and 8.[271] This is the use of two consecutive poems to represent two stages in a single action or experience, with the second piece putting a different complexion on the first. With 4. 7 we have indeed 'come a long way since it made sense to do what we did at the beginning and analyse a poem of Propertius in relation to the elegancies of Meleager' (Hubbard [1974] 152); but this is not to say that Propertius no longer draws ideas from Hellenistic Greek poetry. The dream motif in general was exploited in this period in both serious[272] and comic[273] contexts. Cynthia's self-epitaph in particular smacks of Hellenistic sepulchral epigram,[274] and the scenes of nocturnal adventure in the Subura, together with the ructions in the household, perhaps owe something to New Comedy, literary mime[275] and other, 'subliterary' forms of entertainment known in the Hellenistic period.[276] The most important literary influence on the poem, however, is undoubtedly epic. Not only does it rely throughout on interaction with the tragic-pathetic dream of Achilles to point its direction and tone (always shifting and elusive) but it also recalls, particularly in respect of the ghost's ravaged appearance, other epic and especially Virgilian spectral manifestations.[277] The epic Underworld, too, has obviously given Propertius ideas.[278] Like

---

[269] Cf. Lyne (1980) 139.

[270] See pp. 118-19.

[271] See pp. 143-7.

[272] See pp. 69-70.

[273] In an anonymous epigram (*AP* 5. 2) of uncertain date but doubtless Hellenistic inspiration the writer claims to have dreamed that an expensive prostitute slept with him all night for nothing – which was just as good as the real thing, and a lot cheaper!

[274] See Yardley (1977) 83, who suggests this as the possible source of several other motifs in the poem too; cf. *id.* (1996).

[275] For New Comedy see p. xxii, and for mime, pp. xxiv-xxv.

[276] See Papanghelis (1987) 153-7, 163; cf. Muecke (1974) 128.

[277] E.g. Sychaeus, who warns Dido at *Aeneid* 1. 353-6, and Hector, who advises Aeneas at *Aeneid* 2. 270-79. Yardley (1977) 84-5 rightly observes, however, that various features of the Cynthia-wraith's behaviour are typical of all manner of ancient ghost stories.

[278] Already in the *Odyssey* (11. 235-327) and subsequently in the *Aeneid* (6. 440-76) it was populated in part by the heroines of mythological love stories.

Tibullus at 1. 3. 57-88, he is interested in applying the traditional separation of the virtuous from the wicked after death only to lovers, filling Elysium with the innocent and Hell with the guilty.[279] But Propertius' concentration on the actual moment of separation and his choice of mythological heroines to focus upon are clearly influenced by their potential for the richly evocative description in which he delights. In the case of the wicked he 'makes aesthetic capital out of moral lapse' (Papanghelis [1987] 172), and Cynthia weeps together with the innocent Andromeda and Hypermnestra over supposed amatory wrongs, not because it is appropriate,[280] but because it is picturesque – or even graphically grotesque, if all three of them are supposed to be in a cremation-ravaged state.[281] Propertius' achievement in this late poem is in having integrated what he has drawn from such a variety of sources into such a psychologically convincing episode.

The foregoing interpretation of 4. 7, 'a poem in which the reader cannot find a firm footing' (Warden [1980] 111), is only one of many, and in some respects it is very radical. The incongruous mixture of the down-to-earth – even sordid – with the tragic and heroic has been differently explained as an attempt to debunk the romantic picture of Cynthia-the-mythological-heroine often found in the earlier books by making her reveal her true self without apparently knowing it.[282] Others see the poem as essentially humorous – a satirical but tongue-in-cheek portrait of a Cynthia merely fallen from the pedestal on which Propertius once placed her.[283] Finally, here is yet another reading: 'Cynthia had died...from an illness whose origins were obscure,[284] leaving to Propertius the disposal of her effects and arrangements for her burial. In the prostration of his grief he seems not to have superintended the execution of his instructions for the funeral and to have allowed a certain Chloris, otherwise unknown, to usurp an unauthorised authority over the household. And this poem is an expression of

---

[279] In the *Aeneid* they are all together.

[280] See p. 86 above.

[281] The most appropriate dead beloved for Cynthia to have identified with in emotional terms would surely have been the Virgilian Dido, and indeed Cynthia's very first word to Propertius, 'traitor' (*perfide* [13]), is the word with which Dido, when still alive, memorably addresses Aeneas at *Aeneid* 4. 366. But Propertius sensibly does not attempt to improve on Virgil's own exquisite picture of Dido after death – though the idea of his virtuous heroines' mutual consolation may perhaps recall the reciprocity which Dido at last found in Sychaeus (*Aeneid* 6. 473-4).

[282] So Muecke (1974); cf. Hubbard (1974) 151-2.

[283] E.g. Lake (1937).

[284] This is offered as an explanation for Cynthia's claim to have been poisoned.

contrition and earnest reparation' (Postgate [1884] xxvii).[285] Is such a reading acceptable, or more persuasive, even, than some of the alternatives? Or is there reason to think that it has been unduly influenced by latter-day taboos, traditions and notions of taste surrounding the subject of death?

Propertius: Retrospect

Propertius' once entrenched reputation for writing poetry passionate and self-absorbed enough to make him 'an adolescent's day-dream' (Luck [1969] 144), yet too obscure and difficult in expression and general procedure for most to understand, has well-nigh evaporated under the scholarly scrutiny of the last twenty-five years.[286] Nor is it any longer generally agreed that the more he wrote, the more boring he became, going steadily downhill from the relatively straightforward Cynthia-poems of Book 1, through the opaquely structured personal love elegies of Book 2 and the experiments with non-personal themes in Book 3, to the full-blown aetiology[287] which dominates Book 4.

Obscure and difficult expression is admittedly to be found in Propertius, but there is good reason to believe that it results more often from the text's very poor state of preservation than from the linguistic perversity of the poet. This is not to say, of course, that Propertius' language is never adventurous (just the few poems included here provide plentiful examples of his liking for mixed metaphor and challengingly oblique expression). But his style has far more 'smoothness and elegance'[288] than the modern reader generally thinks.[289] The apparent disjointedness of Propertius' train of thought, along with – and sometimes because of – his frequent resort to mythological allusion and example, has also resulted in charges of obscurity and near-incompetence: 'his transitions are often harsh and forced...This may be partly the result of an inadequate application of Alexandrian technique' (Luck [1969] 120). Yet how many instances are there (within the present selection of his poems) of transitions which are not intelligible

---

[285] Warden (1980) 79 gives more examples of similar interpretations.

[286] Hubbard (1974) offers the most lucid, succinct and sympathetic of modern English studies. Papanghelis (1987) is more specialised and less immediately student-friendly, but acute and stimulating.

[287] See p. xix.

[288] The ancient critic Quintilian found these qualities supremely in Tibullus, but, by implication, also recognised them in Propertius; see p. xliv, and cf. Butrica (1997) 179-80.

[289] For a taste of it in English read again the translation of Prop. 3. 3. 1-12.

if Propertius is credited with a varied and imaginative structural technique and an insight into the workings of the human psyche?[290] How much of his mythology, ornamental and ostentatiously learned though it is at times,[291] is *mere* parade of precious Alexandrianism?

Many of Propertius' mythological tableaux are undoubtedly inspired by the visual arts,[292] and the visual arts in turn fuel his 'sensuous' imagination.[293] Propertius' liking for the pictorial and the aesthetic has an obvious bearing on his fascination with death and his manner of exploring it. This, in its preoccupation with dust, ashes and bones,[294] sometimes seems macabre or morbid to modern taste and is possibly responsible for creating the erroneous impression that Propertius is unheathily *obsessed* with death.[295] His predisposition to the lavish and the sensuous translated into words also explains at least in part the attraction for him of the Callimachean-Horatian manner; but the elegies selected here may give reason to believe that he found the substance of Callimachean principles less comprehensively seductive than is generally supposed. 'He was not in any real sense a Callimachean poet', opines one critic (Lyne [1980] 147), but 'was prepared to adopt Callimachus' mantle and invoke his authority' for the purpose of offering a diplomatic defence against the pressures of the Augustan establishment for morally and politically edifying poetry'. It seems debatable, however, whether this was *always* uppermost in his mind when he made 'Callimachean noises'. It seems debatable, too, whether he is truly any more concerned with his poetic image than Tibullus (or Ovid).

'Cynthia was the first' Propertius himself began (1. 1. 1), and at least in the present selection Cynthia is also the last,[296] which makes it appropriate for the final critical questions to focus on her and Propertius' love for her as it is depicted in his poetry. Is he really as subservient to and overawed by her as he would have us believe? Or is there reason to suspect that he is at times being as humorously ironic and chauvinistic as Ovid? And does Propertius' depiction of his affair with Cynthia in fact chart his development as a poet just as well as, if not better than, his more direct claims of

---

[290] Paradoxically, critics are only too ready to take refuge in the possibility of textual corruption when these apparently 'harsh' transitions present themselves.

[291] The demand on the reader, especially for knowledge of alternative versions of well-known stories, is considerable.

[292] See Hubbard (1974) 164-8, with useful bibliography listing sources of photographs at 173 (though many are now also available in *LIMC*); also Lyne (1980) 83-6.

[293] 'Sensuous' is probably the epithet Papanghelis (1987) most frequently uses of him.

[294] See Hubbard (1974) 35-6.

[295] A balanced discussion of this issue at Michels (1955) 171-9.

[296] Cf. Prop. 1. 12. 20 *Cynthia prima fuit, Cynthia finis erit.*

altered direction and identity? Is it true that 'unlike Catullus' poems, those of Propertius are not really poems of love, but poems about love' (Luck [1969] 120), and, if so, should he be rated more or less highly than his predecessor? There were some in the ancient world, Quintilian tells us,[297] who preferred Propertius to Tibullus: is it understandable that, for all his alleged obscurity, the modern world as a whole has always been inclined to prefer him to Tibullus (and to Ovid as well)?

---

[297] See p. xliv.

TIBULLUS
(translations by Joan Booth)

Tibullus 1. 1

Let others heap up riches for themselves in tawny gold
  And possess great acreage of cultivated ground,
Scared by constant struggle at close quarters with the enemy,
  Their slumbers put to rout by the martial trumpet's blast.
But let my poverty post me to a life of inactivity,   5
  As long as I've a hearth which glows with constant fire.
I would myself plant out the tender vines in season
  And the tall-grown fruit trees with my own deft peasant's hand.
Hope would never fail me but always pile up produce
  And a brimming pool of full-bodied must.   10
For the fields' lone tree-stump and the crossroads' ancient stone
  Garlanded with flowers receive my veneration,
And whatever first-fruits each year produces for me
  Are given as an offering to the farmer-god.
In your honour, golden Ceres, there would be from my own furrows   15
  A spiky circlet which would hang upon your temple door,
And a red guardian Priapus would be stationed in the orchard
  To frighten off the birds with his fearsome sickle.
And you too, O Lares, guardians of a holding
  Once prosperous, now poor, carry off your gifts.   20
Then a slaughtered heifer purified unnumbered cattle:
  Now there is a ewe-lamb as the tiny croft's small victim.
For you shall fall the ewe-lamb with the peasants standing round
  And shouting '*Io*! *Io*! Grant good harvest and good wine'.
If now, if only now, I could live content with little   25
  And not be committed to endlessly long travels,
But avoid the Dog-star's summer rising, shaded
  'Neath a tree, by streams of running water!
Yet I wouldn't be ashamed to hold a mattock sometimes
  Or to reprove the laggard oxen with a goad.   30
Nor would it be beneath me to carry home a lamb or kid
  Unmindfully abandoned by its mother.
But you, O thieves and wolves, spare my tiny herd;
  From a large-sized flock you should seek your prey.
Here it is my wont to purify my shepherd   35
  And sprinkle gracious Pales every year with milk.

97

Lend your presence, gods, and do not show disdain
  For gifts from a poor table or from clean earthenware.
The countryman of old first invented earthenware
  And fashioned his own cups from malleable clay.   40
I do not miss the riches of my father or the profit
  Stored-up harvests brought my grandfather of old.
A small crop is enough; enough is rest in bed
  And lightening one's limbs on a familiar couch.
How pleasant 'tis to lie a-listening to the wild winds   45
  And to clasp a mistress in affectionate embrace!
Or pursue safe slumber with the comfort of a fire
  When the wintry South Wind pours down freezing squalls!
Let this be *my* good fortune: rightly rich be he who'll suffer
  The madness of the sea and the miserable rain.   50
O let all gold and emerald in existence perish
  Before our travels cause any girl to weep!
It is right that you, Messalla, wage war by land and sea
  To put up enemy spoils in your house's hall.
But I'm kept back in bondage by a pretty girl with chains 55
  And mine's the porter's post before her cruel door.
I do not care, my Delia, for glory; just as long as
  I can be with you, let them call me idle slacker.
Let me gaze on you when my final hour approaches,
  And with my weakening hand let me hold you as I die.   60
Delia, you will weep when I'm laid on the couch for burning
  And you'll give me kisses mixed with tears of grief.
You will weep; not bound with rigid iron is your heart
  Nor does your tender breast hold flint.
From that funeral 'twill be impossible for any youth   65
  Or girl to go back home dry-eyed.
Hurt not my spirit, Delia; but spare your loosened hair
  And spare your tender cheeks.
Meantime, while Fate allows, let us unite in love.
  Shortly Death will come, head covered, in the dark;   70
Shortly there'll creep on inactive age, and it won't be fitting
  For a grey head to make love or winsome talk.
Now's the time for merry Venus, while there is no shame
  In forcing doors and brawling is a pleasure.
In this field I do well, as general and as ranker; standards and trumpets 75
  Be off; bring wounds to greedy men.
And bring them riches too: let *me* live secure in what I have in store,
  Looking down on wealth and looking down on want.

Is Tibullus supposed to be a love poet? A fair question at the start of this very first elegy of his, where no lover is anywhere in sight. Tibullus introduces himself only as a character who rejects the idea of winning material wealth by military activity in favour of 'poverty' (the Latin *paupertas* [5] does not imply dire deprivation, but rather contentment with a simple way of life) (1-6). He then elaborates on the kind of life he has in mind (7-40) – that of a farmer of emphatically modest means (19-20 and 34-40) and homely, rustic piety (11-16, 19-24, 35-40[1]). It is the life of one who can enjoy the Mediterranean equivalent of leaning over a gate, chewing a bit of grass (27-8), but also carry out the unglamorous, day-to-day tasks of the Italian countryman: planting vines and young trees (7-8); setting up scarecrows (conventionally effigies of the lecher god Priapus)[2] (17-18); hoeing the land (29); herding cattle (30); and caring for stray lambs and kids (31-2). Wealth is something Tibullus can do without, even though his forbears had it. His needs are completely satisfied[3] by a 'small crop' (*parua seges* [43]) and a good sleep in a 'familiar' (*solito* [44]) bed (41-4). What a letdown after Catullus or Propertius!

Not the full story, however: that 'familiar' bed ideally sleeps two! In lines 45-6 Tibullus reveals that his idea of absolute contentment includes having a mistress in his arms, snug and warm in that simple home of his, while a winter storm rages outside.[4] Suddenly, with this apparently casual remark, he begins to intimate that love plays a significant part in his preferred alternative to the life of soldiering. Braving the elements and going away from home (which is what soldiering involves) he will leave to others – not for him to upset 'any girl' (*ulla puella* [52]) (49-52).

Soldiering is all right for some, though, Tibullus concedes – for Messalla, his supporter and benefactor,[5] to be precise, because the purpose of Messalla's campaigning is the pursuit of glory. In the entrance hall of his house he can conventionally display 'enemy spoils' (*hostiles...exuuias* [54])[6] to advertise his prowess and standing (53-4). But for himself Tibullus rejects the idea of soldiering even for glory's sake in favour of a life of devotion to his beloved (55-8), whom he proceeds to address directly. She

---

[1] The 'table' (*mensa*) in line 37 is one at which sacrifices are performed.

[2] These effigies were equipped with a huge phallus, which is perhaps hinted at here by both Priapus' sickle and his redness – though statues of the gods were regularly painted red for festivals.

[3] This is stressed by the emotive repetition 'enough', 'enough' (*satis...satis*) in line 43.

[4] The picture of simple rustic security seems to be modelled on Virgil, *Eclogue* 7. 49-52. Cf. also Virgil, *Georgics* 2. 513-26.

[5] Messalla is conventionally described as Tibullus' 'patron', but see pp. xxxix-xl.

[6] Much as the old colonial or aristocrat might display his tiger-skin.

is now named as Delia,[7] and in fact, far from detaining Tibullus for their mutual pleasure, she is difficult and unresponsive to him, as witness her 'cruel door' (*duras...fores* [56]). In her company it is, though, that he declares he wants to die. He envisages her at his deathbed and funeral pouring out to the point of excess all the affection and devotion which we gather she withholds from him in life (59-68).[8]

Although Tibullus can envisage compensations in death itself, the very thought of its grim approach and, still more, that of pathetic old age, apparently prompts him to pursue his love for Delia with all the greater urgency in life and to reaffirm his rejection of commitment to soldiering proper in favour of the battles of love (69-75). Once he has reintroduced the possibility of amatory fulfilment in non-military life rather than in non-military death, he re-links it with the simple existence free of both want and wealth within which he first envisaged it, and which he first presented as a complete alternative in itself to soldiering for riches. The military life, as at the start, he consigns to other people (76-8).

This elegy is about what Tibullus wants but cannot have; why he wants it and why he cannot have it; and what he proposes to do about it all. But he does not convey any of this in a straightforward way, and the reader is left wondering how the whole poem hangs together. Is it the free-ranging meditation on loosely related desires and deprivations that it appears to be at first sight? Or is it in fact as artfully engineered as the neat return at the end to the theme of the beginning would suggest?

A simple life on a country estate is presented as the first (and therefore ostensibly the most important) of Tibullus' desires. The reader is clearly supposed to believe that he possesses such an estate already.[9] Does he actually live on it at all, though, and do there any of the things he talks about? It is usually assumed not, but rather that the picture he paints of his life, work and love on the farm is wholly a day-dream. The indicative verbs (i.e. those saying what *does* happen or *will* happen) which puzzlingly take over from the subjunctives (i.e. those saying what *would* happen)

---

[7] See pp. xl-xli.

[8] Emotive repetition again: 'Delia...Delia' (*mea Delia* [57]...*Delia* [61]); 'let me gaze on you...let me hold you' (*te spectem* [59]...*te teneam* [60]); 'you will weep...you will weep' (*flebis* [61]...*flebis* [63]); 'spare your...hair...spare your...cheeks' (*parce...crinibus* [67-8]...*parce genis* [68]).

[9] If ownership of the place had been no more than part of a pleasant fantasy, it would have been ludicrous for Tibullus to give it the unhappy history that he does. Probably he is hinting in 19-22 and 41-2 at reduced circumstances resulting from confiscations of land to compensate war veterans; see also p. xxxviii.

three times within lines 7-48[10] are generally explained as attempts to represent intensely vivid phases of the day-dream.[11] It seems possible, however, that the indicatives express what the Tibullus who appears in this poem actually does do on his farm (mainly the more gentlemanly things, which a 'weekend' farmer could well do), while the subjunctives express what he *would* do (mainly the more mundane, 'sleeves up' things), and what *would* happen, if he were to become, as he wishes, a *full-time* farmer.[12] This explanation of the changes in the verb-forms makes the logic of lines 7-14 clearer: Tibullus' hope of a good vintage *would* never be disappointed if he were personally to take over care of the vines (7-10), because he *is* pious enough already to deserve divine favour (11-14). But how about the sleeping with a mistress on a stormy night? This too, according to the interpretation suggested, should be what Tibullus actually does do, for the controlling verb in line 45 (*iuuat*) is indicative ('How pleasant it *is*'). The sort of woman denoted by the Latin word used for 'mistress' (*domina*) is not normally to be found living on a country farm.[13] Yet in the world of Latin love elegy urban mistresses do go on *visits* to the country which have amatory potential,[14] and Tibullus could well be casting himself as one who has experienced the benefits of this. At all events, what he wants now begins to look rather different. It is a 'package': not *just* the hard-working rustic life, but the hard-working rustic life *with love* and on a permanent basis.[15]

The picture of what motivates Tibullus towards an 'alternative' way of life also changes over the first two thirds of the poem. One of the accepted ways for a young middle- or upper-class Roman to 'get on' was by collecting from a stint of military service the sort of pickings which would finance a sophisticated city lifestyle.[16] But all activity aimed purely at the

---

[10] Subjunctive main verbs *seram, destituat* and *praebeat* in lines 7-10 give way to indicatives *ueneror* and *ponitur* in lines 11-14, subjunctives *sit* and *ponatur* in lines 15-18 to indicatives *fertis, est* and *cadet* in lines 19-24, and subjunctives *pudeat* and *pigeat* in lines 25-32 to indicatives *soleo, requiro, est* and *iuuat* in lines 33-48.

[11] See e.g. Putnam (1973) on lines 11-12.

[12] Line 5 ,'Let my poverty post me to a *life* (*uitae*) of inactivity', and line 25 ,'Now, if only now, I could *live* (*uiuere*) content with little', both suggest that full-time rural residence is indeed what Tibullus has in mind.

[13] *domina*, as well as meaning 'mistress' in the amatory sense, is etymologically connected with *domus*, 'town-house', and so properly denotes the resident 'mistress' of such an establishment.

[14] See e.g. Tib. 2. 3, Prop. 2. 19, and cf. Ov. *Am.* 2. 16.

[15] See further Lyne (1980) 152-7, Murgatroyd (1980) on 11-44 (with some differences in detail).

[16] See Lee (1974) 98-9, Lyne (1980) 72.

acquisition of wealth was regularly condemned by traditional moralists, while the hard-working rural existence of primitive simplicity (37-40) and 'contentment with little' (25, 41-3) was commended as spiritually healthier than the urban one of ambition and opulence.[17] The natural assumption is therefore that Tibullus wants the rustic life because it is morally better – until he suggests that the moral life might in his case accommodate a cosy love-life too. *Then* the opening starts to look like humbug! Honesty begins when he admits that he really wants that 'package' of his purely because it is pleasant and it is safe (45-8). He implies, through his rejection of the sort of hardships the soldier has to face (49-50), that it is specifically safer than soldiering, and, by saying how enjoyable it is as a countryman to sleep comfortably with his mistress in his own bed, he also suggests how *unen-joyable* it is as a soldier to sleep rough and alone on a foreign campaign.

Why can Tibullus not enjoy his 'package' on a full-time basis? In line 26 he intimates that it is because he does indeed sometimes have to sol-dier.[18] The real evil of soldiering is that it comes between him and his lady-love (51-2). He then goes on, however, to make it clear that there is nothing immoral about *Messalla*'s soldiering, because he, properly, sol-diers for glory, not riches. Initially it appears that the only purpose of lines 53-4 is to cover Tibullus against giving offence and to offer a graceful compliment to his distinguished friend,[19] but in fact Messalla is the means by which Tibullus is able to pass from depicting his true ideal – the 'pack-age' – to revealing obliquely the true reason why he cannot have it. The mention of Messalla's glorious display of military trophies at the front of his (town-)house[20] allows a smooth transition to Tibullus' own inglorious stationing of himself in front of the cruel Delia's (town-)house[21] in pursuit of his love for her. Far from protesting at his departure on active service (52), it seems, she keeps him at arm's length whenever she pleases (55-6). Clearly he will never be able to install this woman permanently in the

---

[17] Cf. Virgil, *Georgics* 2. 458-74, 495-540, and see further Lee (1974) 99-100, Cairns (1979) 14-15, Booth (1991) 140.

[18] This is consistent with what Tibullus says about himself in 1. 3 and 1. 10, and some even claim that he is to be understood to be actually on a tour of duty as he writes; see Lee (1974) 114. But hardly, if the activities which he refers to in lines 55-6 are supposed to be more or less current. There is nothing to stop us imagining, though, if we like, that he has just received an unwelcome invitation – from Messalla perhaps – to join an expedition. Cf. p. xxxix.

[19] The direct address to him in this opening poem effectively makes him the dedicatee of the book.

[20] The Latin *domus* makes it clear that the house is an urban one. Cf. n. 13 above.

[21] The very situation sketched here confirms the urban setting. Cf. previous n.

country as a sort of perfect farmer's wife,[22] but must continue to woo her at her own urban front-door. This, and not pressure to be a soldier, for *whatever* end, is really why he cannot have a full-time life in the country with his beloved. When that beloved is not just 'any girl' (52), but Delia, the two things are incompatible.

Happiness in love has finally emerged as much the more important of the two things Tibullus professes to want. Now also his initially implied objection to the military life on moral grounds looks even more like humbug, as he declares that he has no more interest in (honourable) soldiering for glory than in (dishonourable) soldiering for wealth, but on the contrary will be perfectly content with a life of disreputable idleness, provided that his all-important love for Delia is requited (57-8). Given Delia's character, of course, that possibility must indeed be remote. For one thing, as a citified sophisticate, she is likely to have expensive tastes which a 'poor' poet will find beyond his means.[23] Tibullus does, however, find a context, suggested to him by the unwanted life of soldiering, within which he can safely envisage amatory fulfilment. Though he does not explicitly say so, the thought of the horror of dying a soldier's painful death away on one of those long journeys he has mentioned must be what leads him to the thought of the pleasure of dying in Delia's company (59-60).[24] What is more, his pleasant fantasy of having her mourning at his funeral (61-8) is one which can never be destroyed, for he will never actually know whether his dream is fulfilled or not: in death at least there is protection from her cruelty.[25]

The very thought of this extreme solution, however, turns Tibullus' attention to the alarming shortness of life and to what he might do about his yearnings *now* (69-78). His solution is to compromise. To settle for as much as he can get of what he wants: love – with all its tribulations – in preference to soldiering whenever possible, and a modified version of the moral life which does not demand a full-time rural existence, but just contentment with a modest yet adequate livelihood.[26]

---

[22] Tibullus does not use the *language* of marriage, but it is obvious enough that a rural version of this relationship is what he hankers after. Echoes here, then, of Catullus', and perhaps even Propertius', amatory ideal? See pp. 23-4 and 53-4, and cf. Tib. 1. 5. 21-34.

[23] This a practicality which Tibullus naively seems not to have considered in his enthusiastic denial of his need for wealth; cf. Tib. 2. 4. 21ff., with discussion on pp. 121-2, 125-6.

[24] Cf. Prop. 1. 17. 19-24.

[25] See Bright (1978) 129-30.

[26] What Tibullus has 'in store' (*composito...aceruo* [77]) could represent sufficient means of any kind rather than specifically what has been harvested from the land. The final line of the Latin is heavily alliterative, as Tibullus signs off with an emphatic flourish.

Clearly, then, this is no unstructured ramble, but a carefully orchestrated progress from deception, through revelation, to resolution. Linguistic devices subtly reinforce the poem's unity. One of them is the recurrent use of military imagery to describe the non-military, and sometimes specifically the amatory, life.[27] In line 5 poverty seems to promise to 'post' (*traducat*) Tibullus to a more agreeable demobilised existence. In 17-18 the scarecrow is to be 'stationed' (*ponatur*) in the orchard like a soldier on guard (*custos*) and the same word in the Latin also describes the function of the 'guardian' (*custodes*) Lares.[28] In line 48 Tibullus speaks of 'pursuing' (*sequi*) only sleep,[29] which the war trumpets in line 4 'put to rout' (*fugent*) for the hapless soldier. In line 55 he is 'kept...in bondage' (*uinctum*) and 'chains' (*uincla*) by a woman instead of a victorious foe, and he 'takes his post' (*sedeo*, literally 'I sit'), sentry-like himself, at her door (56). When he says in line 58 that he is happy to be labelled an 'idle slacker', we can take it that he means as a soldier proper, for the Latin terms (*segnis* and *iners*) are regularly used of specifically military inadequacy. Finally in 75-6, neatly following on from his contemplation of getting involved in various sorts of amatory fracas (73-4), he makes a more or less explicit statement of what has been hinted at all along: love itself is the battlefield on which he can perform well 'as general and as ranker' (*dux milesque* [75]). The other notable unifying device is a more wideranging sort of echo or counterbalance. The contrast in lines 1-6 between the acquisitive soldier's lot and the simple countryman's is underlined by the one's 'constant' (*assiduus* [3]) struggle in military action with the other's desire only for a 'constant' (*assiduo* [6]) fire in a life of inactivity (a mischievously relative term, for farming is in fact no life for idlers).[30] 'Golden' (*flaua* [15]) Ceres, the corn-goddess, keeps the 'tawny gold' (*fuluo...auro* [1]) of the opening in mind and her 'door' (*fores* [16]) later finds an echo in the 'door' (*fores* [56]) of Delia's house. The enemy 'scares' (*terreat* [3]) the soldier, and the effigy of Priapus 'frightens' (*terreat* [18]) the birds. The comforting fire of the rustic hearth, beside which Tibullus the part-time countryman has known love fulfilled (48), is poignantly recalled by the fire of the funeral pyre (61), in which Tibullus the troubled urban lover can envisage some amatory consolation. The poet

---

[27] See Fisher (1970) 768-9, Lee (1974) 106-9.

[28] See p. 106.

[29] There is arguably another military metaphor (hidden in the translation) in line 46 where Tibullus uses for 'clasp' *continere*; this means both 'embrace' and, in a military context, 'contain'.

[30] Though there is no *verbal* echo, the implied gleam of the desired gold in line 1 is arguably counterbalanced by the 'glow' of the desired fire in line 6.

'kept...in bondage' (*uinctum* [55]) by Delia wishfully believes that Delia's own heart is not 'bound' (*uincta* [64]) with iron. Nevertheless he begs her to 'spare' (*parce* [67, 68]) herself in grieving for her lover, just as he entreated wolves and thieves to 'spare' (*parcite* [34]) his modest farmstead. His 'carrying home' (*referre domum* [32]) of stray animals to his farm (32) is echoed in the mourners' imagined inability to 'take back home dry eyes' (*lumina...sicca referre domum* [66]) from his funeral. The sort of inactivity which Tibullus eventually commends, i.e. not farming, but love, itself becomes impossible with 'inactive' old age (the same Latin word *iners* is used of age in line 71 and of the 'slacker' in line 58), and there is no more 'shame' (*non pudet* [74]) in indulging in love while he is young (74) than there would be 'shame' in getting down to proper work on the farm (*nec...pudeat* [29]). The overall effect produced by the combination of structure and language is that of a superbly crafted piece of woodwork, with a smooth, polished – even slippery – surface, almost invisible joints and a certain amount of secret nailing.

How original, though, is Tibullus' poem? Its penultimate theme of the need to make love before old age and death supervene is ancient and universal,[31] and a number of its other motifs are already to be found in the first book of Propertius and, at least in embryonic form, earlier still in Hellenistic epigram[32] and/or New Comedy:[33] for example, the ideas of the lover being his beloved's slave, of his being locked-out of his beloved's house, and of love being a form of soldiering. Tibullus' intricate conflation, however, of all three of these common motifs in lines 55-6 is a good example of how creative he can be. The initial connotation of his claim to be 'kept...in bondage...with chains' is military – he cannot soldier like Messalla because he is a captive (in love's war). Then the prisoner of war metamorphoses into a more of a slave when we are told that his post is that of porter, which was conventionally the job of a slave, possibly kept on a chain, just inside the house. Finally, the slave becomes recognisable as the familiar locked-out lover, when we discover that this porter is stationed outside, not inside, the mistress' door.[34] Individual expressions, too, are memorably inventive: for example, in the description of death in line 70 the Latin construction can be understood in two ways (either 'Death will

---

[31] Cf. 'Theognis' 973-8 West, Catul. 5. 1-6.

[32] See pp. xviii-xix.

[33] See p. xxii.

[34] There is a neat implied contrast here, too, with Tibullus' earlier picture of himself comfortably ensconced in bed within, listening to the wild weather (45-8), for this is exactly the kind of weather which traditionally afflicts the excluded lover on the doorstep.

come in the dark with head covered' [*tenebris* going with *ueniet*] or 'Death will come with head covered in darkness' [*tenebris* going with *adoperta*]); this is powerfully suggestive of both death's unseen approach and the eternal night it brings.[35] At the end of the poem comes a fine stroke of wit. Tibullus uses for 'greedy men' (76) a Latin expression (*cupidis...uiris*) which can also mean 'sex-hungry husbands': to have *these* out of the way on a campaign would clearly be just as advantageous to him as leaving soldiering to the morally suspect!

Tibullus' intertextual[36] manipulation of themes also found in Propertius' first book is especially interesting. Propertius' simple statement at 1. 6. 25-6, 'I was not cut out at birth for glory or for arms; this' (i.e. love) 'is the soldiering to which fate wants me to submit',[37] is probably what prompted the lengthier and more sophisticated Tibullan exploration of the idea of love as a kind of *substitute* soldiering. But Tibullus also appears to react against some of Propertius' more exaggerated attitudes. Instead of emitting howls of anguish at his state of enslavement,[38] Tibullus just accepts it (55-6). The idea of his mistress grieving at his funeral (61-8) appeals to him as much as it does to Propertius,[39] but the ghoulish element in his case is tempered by concern for Delia (67-8), and he shows no neurotic anxiety about how she will behave after his death.[40] Instead of visualising the mourners at his own funeral bewailing the loss of a 'great poet',[41] Tibullus imagines plain tears from the mourners at his (65-6). He seems to challenge Propertian practice too in his own consistently striking avoidance of bookish Greek mythology to illustrate his unrealisable amatory ideal. What he uses instead is the setting of the Italian countryside. All the named deities he venerates are native: Ceres, the Italian equivalent of the Greek corn-goddess Demeter (13-14); the Lares, ancient guardian spirits of the home and possibly also in origin fertility gods (19-24); and Pales, goddess of flocks and herds, whose traditional festival, the Palilia (or Parilia), was celebrated on Rome's own birthday, 21 April (35-6). Two other indigenous rustic deities, Terminus, god of boundaries, and Silvanus,

---

[35] Tibullus may have been thinking of the cap of Hades (see e.g. Homer, *Iliad* 5. 884-5).

[36] See p. xiv.

[37] *non ego sum laudi, non natus idoneus armis: / hanc me militiam fata subire uolunt.*

[38] Cf. Prop. 1. 1. 1-4, 27-8 and see p. 41.

[39] Cf. Prop. 1. 17. 19-24, 2. 13. 27-8.

[40] Cf. Prop. 1. 19. 21-4, 2. 13. 41-2. Tibullus' final pragmatic solution to his immediate problem, however, is not dissimilar to Propertius' at 1. 19. 25-6.

[41] Prop. 1. 7. 23-4 *nec poterunt iuuenes nostro reticere sepulcro / 'Ardoris nostri magne poeta, iaces'*. Some scholars doubt the authenticity of this couplet.

who is named as one of the 'rustic deities' at Virgil, *Georgics* 2. 494 and is a receiver of the season's first fruits at Horace, *Epode* 2. 19-22, may be in Tibullus' mind at 11-12 and 13-14.[42]

His use of the Italian countryside as the setting for an ideal inevitably brings to mind Virgil's similar use of it in the *Eclogues*, but Tibullus seems to adopt a technique which is almost the mirror image of Virgil's. While Virgil's rural backcloth is illuminated by individual shafts of Italian local colour, but dissolves into a hazily impressionistic and geographically chaotic picture when viewed as a whole, Tibullus' remains stable and has an overall veneer of authenticity, but on closer scrutiny lacks specifically localising detail.[43] Arguably there is more of Horace than of Virgil in this first poem. In general the moralising flavour of the *Satires* is strong in Tibullus' commendation of rustic 'poverty' and contentment with little,[44] and in particular he seems to have drawn on Horace's *Epode* 2. Line 25 ('If now, if only now, I could live content with little', i.e. 'if only this could be the moment when it came about') clearly recalls *Epode* 2. 68. Praise of the rustic life very much like Tibullus' occupies lines 1-65 of Horace's poem, but in lines 66-7 it is unexpectedly revealed that the speaker is one Alfius, a money-lender, and in line 68 that he is 'now, now going to become a countryman' (*iam iam futurus rusticus*) – in other words, always going to, but never quite able to bring himself to give up his disreputable business and actually do so. It is difficult to know quite how to take Tibullus' echo. Most scholars see it as a poignantly serious re-working of the savagely ironic original, but Tibullus could be counting on its ironic associations to introduce a subtle note of irony into his own portrait of himself as an apparently gentle, wistful and ill-used character. He could be hinting at his own awareness of being just as laughably lacking in will-power as Alfius is – though in his case it will emerge that love of a woman rather than love of money is what undermines his dreams. Furthermore, in his insistence on his willingness to 'muck in' (7-8, 29-32) there is perhaps also a touch of irony: he is no peasant, and he knows it. Intertextuality with the Horatian *Epode*, then, may be an important pointer to underlying humour in the first half of Tibullus' poem.[45]

---

[42] Murgatroyd (1980) has useful notes on these lines. For the 'literariness' of Tibullus' choice of deities see Luck (1969) 77-8.

[43] Cf. Elder (1962) 82-3.

[44] See e.g. *Satires* 1. 1. 73-9, 2. 2. 1-7.

[45] Compare also *Epode* 2. 5 and 19-22 with Tib. 1. 1. 2-3 and 27-8, and *Epode* 2. 23-8 with Tib. 1. 1. 11-14 .

The first poem of a collection is one of the places in which an Augustan poet can particularly be expected to make some kind of 'programmatic' statement,[46] but overt political and literary polemic are no more to be found in 1. 1 than they are in the rest of Tibullus' work. He respectfully acknowledges the military achievements of Messalla (and only Messalla), while disclaiming any such aspirations for himself. There is nothing apologetic, however, in his distancing of himself from his supporter's military lifestyle, no attempted excuse for his rejection of military (i.e. epic) poetry in favour of love poetry, and indeed no mention of his choice of poetic subject-matter at all. If there was any political pressure upon him, his way of dealing with it was evidently to ignore it. Nor does he make any explicit declaration of artistic allegiance or policy. It has been alleged that the poem is shot through with oblique statements of commitment to Callimachean principles,[47] and certainly Tibullus does commend what is small, pure and unpretentious (see especially lines 33-44), all of which convinced Alexandrians adulated in poetry.[48] But no symbolic interpretation of what Tibullus says is essential to the understanding of the poem; and appreciation of smallness, naturalness and plainness has as much to do with the nostalgic primitivism of traditional Roman morality, which he is trying to evoke in the first part of this elegy, as it has with the aesthetic doctrines of Alexandria. In practice, however, this poem *is* Alexandrian: elaborately learned mythological allusion is admittedly avoided, but Callimachus himself would have found it hard to fault it in polish, finesse and attention to detail. Conceivably Tibullus thought it so self-evident to anyone of taste that this was now the only way for decent poets to write that theorising itself struck him as unsophisticated and superfluous. Paradoxically, through his silence on two issues on which his peers seem to feel obliged to speak, Tibullus perhaps demonstrates a 'gently tough independence' (Elder [1962] 78).

1. 1 can, however, paradoxically again, possibly seem 'programmatic' in retrospect, for it touches upon many of the themes of Tibullus' later pieces (in both Books 1 and 2). As well as those which appear in most poems and dominate some – distaste for soldiering and travelling abroad, preference for the simple and pious rural life, affectionate respect for Messalla and commitment to love – there are a few which are individually explored in particular elegies. These include the sufferings of the locked-out lover (1. 2, 1. 5), the prospect of death (1. 3), the figure of the scare-

---

[46] See p. xiv.

[47] So Cairns (1979) 11-35.

[48] See pp. xx-xxi.

crow god Priapus (into whose mouth is put the lecture on how to conduct a love-affair with a boy which occupies almost the whole of 1. 4) and the power of Hope (2. 6).[49] What is more, the very multiplicity of theme in this first poem is characteristic of much of his *oeuvre,* even if not particularly of the other two poems chosen to represent Tibullan elegy in the present selection.[50]

Tibullus, then, has apparently not crept into this volume under false pretences after all: love of a woman is the fundamental concern of his first poem. But is it the same sort of love as Catullus' and Propertius', and does it occupy the same position in Tibullus' life and scale of priorities? Is his different poetic presentation of it – the discursive manner and the muted and elusive tone – a bonus or a drawback? And what sort of character do we see in this poem? A simple, sentimental dreamer? Or at the very least a person of 'some complexity, not to say contradiction' (Lee [1974] 110)?

Tibullus 1. 8

You cannot hide from me what a lover's nods convey
   Or what blandishments there are in softly whispered words;
The secrets of the gods neither lots nor entrails tell me
   Nor do I rely on prophetic song of birds.
My knowledge comes from Venus and my suffering of her floggings,   5
   My hands so often bound in magic knot behind my back.
Stop trying to dissemble; the god scorches more cruelly
   Those he finds unwilling to submit to him.
What good does it now do you to tease out flowing tresses
   And endlessly experiment with style after style?   10
What good to paint your cheeks with brightening dab of rouge
   And bring the artist's touch to filing down your nails?
In vain you change your clothes now, in vain you change your cloak
   And let a tight-laced sandal squeeze your constricted feet.
That girl's attractive, though she come with face unpainted   15
   And glossy head unmarked by styling's tedious art.
Can it be an old crone's chants or her blanching herbs

---

[49] Tibullus' resurrection of this, a transient theme of the first poem, in the very last one of the surviving corpus is an argument for believing that Book 2 is complete as it stands, and not broken off at the poet's death, as is often thought (see p. xxxix).

[50] A more elaborate (and contrived) case for the programmatic function of Poem 1 within Tibullus' first book is made by Lee-Stecum (1998) 27-71.

That have utterly bewitched you in the silence of the night?
Spells move crops from neighbours' fields,
   Spells stop an angry snake in its tracks,   20
Spells try to drag the Moon down from her chariot, too –
   And would do it, were not brazen cymbals clashed.
Ah, why complain that spells and herbs have hurt the suffering lad?
   Beauty has no need of help from magic;
Touching flesh does all the damage, kissing long and hard   25
   And closely joining thigh to thigh.
But you now, don't be awkward with the boy;
   Venus pursues ungraciousness with pain.
Don't ask for gifts; let your grey-haired lover give
   To warm his cold old limbs in your bosom's softness.   30
Dearer than gold's the youth whose face is shiny-smooth
   With no bristly beard to scratch in close embrace.
You, put your fair arms beneath his shoulders
   And you can look down on the wealth of kings.
Ah, but Venus has found how to lie with a boy in secret,   35
   While he's afraid and burrows ever deeper into your tender lap,
How to plant moist kisses on his panting mouth with tongues a-wrestle
   And leave your toothmark's imprint on his neck.
Neither precious stones nor jewels please her who sleeps alone,
   Cold and undesired by any man at all.   40
Too late, alas, too late to wish back love and youth
   When age has left its greying mark on your old woman's head.
Then beauty needs attention; then hair needs the years disguised
   With dye from a nut's green shell.
Then white hairs are carefully rooted out   45
   And loose skin removed to lift the face again.
You, then, while the bloom of youth is yours,
   Use it: it soon marches past for good.
And do not torture Marathus. No kudos in conquering a boy;
   To your aged veterans, girl, be hard.   50
I beg you, spare one young and soft; he can't plead genuine sickness
   But an overdose of love has turned his flesh pale yellow.
How often the poor wretch upbraids you in your absence,
   Bitterly complaining and drenching all with tears.
'Why do you reject me? The guard could be defeated;   55
   God himself gives leave to lovers to deceive.
Furtive love's well known to me – how to draw a silent breath
   And snatch a kiss without a sound.

I too can creep about to order in the middle of the night
   And stealthily unbolt the door with not a hint of squeak.   60
What's the good of know-how if a girl rejects her suffering lover
   And cruelly takes flight from the very couch itself?
Or, when she makes a promise, suddenly turns treacherous
   And keeps me all night long in wakeful misery,
While I fancy she will come to me and at every movement   65
   I think I hear the sound of her approaching feet?'
Stop your crying, lad; she does not crack,
   And now your tired eyes are swollen up with weeping.
The gods, I warn you, Pholoe, detest aloofness
   And incense on their holy altars does not make amends.   70
Marathus here once led his poor lovers a merry dance,
   Oblivious of the vengeful god at his back.
Often he even laughed, they say, at their anguished tears
   And kept desire going with disingenuous delay.
Now he hates all pride, now he disapproves of   75
   The obstructing bolt of every cruel door.
And you too will suffer, unless you drop your arrogance.
   How you'll wish your prayers could bring back this day!

Tibullus, expert that he is – not from resort to quackery but from personal experience[51] – has recognised the tell-tale signs of love (1-8). But in whom? Man or woman? Friend or foe? In someone, at any rate, who fruitlessly goes to enormous lengths with hair, make-up and clothes to be seductive (9-14). Unlike 'that girl' (*illa* [15]), who 'is attractive' (*placet* [15]) without such elaborate toilette (15-16); Tibullus need not mean that she *never* dolls herself up, but just that *if* she does not, she is still fetching. But 'attractive' to whom? Admirers in general? Or specifically the natty dresser? If the second, can this person be male? Tibullus is not yet ready to tell, teasingly musing instead with portentous gravity on whether his addressee could have been affected by love-magic (17-22).[52] Then the revelation: the love-stricken character *is* male (23),[53] and not magic but personal experience in the form of some sort of sexual contact with the attractive girl is responsible for his condition (23-6). It is not clear whether

---

[51] The metaphor in lines 5-6 is most convincingly explained as one of painful and humiliating initiation into a cult; see Cairns (1979) 138.

[52] Cf. Tib. 2. 4. 55-60, Prop. 1. 1. 19-24, with discussion on pp. 36, 40-41.

[53] In the Latin there is no word for 'lad', but just a masculine form (*misero*) of the adjective meaning 'miserable'.

he and the girl have actually made love or not, since 'closely joining thigh to thigh' (*femori conseruisse femur* [26]) suggests activity associated with intercourse but not necessarily its completion. There are more surprises to come, however. Tibullus next turns to address the girl (she must be there, then?) and reveals that the love-smitten male is only a 'boy' (*puer* [27]). Does he just mean a 'youngster'? Or a 'pretty boy' (*puer delicatus*) – the object of a man's paederastic love and, in Roman society, normally a figure of contempt and ridicule?[54] The effeminate behaviour already described strongly points to the latter.[55] What is more, in an earlier poem in the book (1. 4) Tibullus himself eventually emerged as the lover of a boy called Marathus:[56] could this boy by any chance be the same? Again Tibullus does not immediately relieve the suspense, merely warning the girl to treat the boy well and not demand of him the presents which her 'grey-haired lover' (*canus amator* [29]) can give (27-30). So, she must have a silly old man in tow too?[57] The description of the youth's smooth-cheeked beauty (31-2) then more or less confirms his passive homosexual status,[58] and Tibullus' commendation of his amatory potential (33-4) in words which echo his own valuation of his love for Delia[59] keeps open the suspicion that he has some personal interest in the situation.[60] Then, as if to forestall a protest from the girl on grounds of practical difficulties,[61] he goes on to reassure her that 'Venus has found' (*Venus inuenit* [35]) how to carry on an affair surreptitiously with a boy who is timid (35-8). Tibullus himself has claimed to be one of Venus' initiates (5-6), and he may be hinting that he knows all about these things and even that he personally can give – or has already given – some assistance in this situation. What would the boy have to fear? Detection, no doubt, by the girl's husband or keeper,[62] if the encounter had taken place on *her* premises – yet there is no clear indication here that it had. Again we have to wait for the situation to

---

[54] See p. xxx.

[55] Elaborate attention to appearance was frowned on in men; see Murgatroyd (1980) on lines 9-14.

[56] See p. xl.

[57] For the silliness cf. Tib.1. 1. 71-2.

[58] Cf. Strato, *AP* 12. 10, Statilius Flaccus, *AP* 12. 27.

[59] The echo is clearer in Latin: cf. line 34 here, *regum magnae despiciantur opes*, with Tib. 1. 1. 78, *dites despiciam despiciamque famem*.

[60] We may notice incidentally the pun on 'dearer' (*carior*) in line 31: both 'more valuable' and 'more expensive'.

[61] The Latin *at*, which introduces lines 35-8 often has this countering function.

[62] The boy's inexperience would be reason enough for him not to find the risk part of the fun, as does, for example, Ovid the lover at *Am.* 2. 19. 53-6.

be clarified. Meanwhile Tibullus warns the girl that, as her sexual attractiveness is but ephemeral and the loss of it is not to be restored by cosmetics or compensated by riches (39-46), she had better make the most of it (47-8) and not 'torture *Marathus*' (*neu Marathum torque* [49])! So it *is* as suspected: her conquest is none other than Tibullus' own boy-friend.[63]

Still, Tibullus appears to be going to make nothing more of it than a neat variation (49-51) on the old adage 'No kudos in winning an unequal fight',[64] for the girl is advised to be 'hard' (*dura* [50]) to old campaigners,[65] who can cope, but spare 'one young and soft' (*tenero* [51]). The meaning of the next line and a half (51-2) is debatable. The literal translation of the Latin *non illi sontica causa est / sed nimius luto corpora tingit amor* is: 'he does not have a legitimate excuse' (or 'case'), 'but (it is) excessive love (which) gives his flesh a yellow' (i.e. pallid) 'tinge'.[66] To have 'a legitimate excuse' (*sontica causa*) is an expression which has a technical ring in Latin, with both legal and medical associations. It suggests almost the ancient equivalent of being able to present an official 'sick note' – having some incapacity formally recognised as serious enough to bring dispensation from the need to perform a given duty. Marathus, in other words, may not be genuinely sick, but his overdose of love is making him *look* rather off-colour and should at least win him some consideration from the girl.[67]

Tibullus then proceeds (55-66) to exemplify the distress caused by the girl's behaviour through an extended complaint put into the mouth of the 'poor wretch' (*miser* [53]). It will be essentially familiar to anyone who has already heard Tibullus' own complaints of Delia's behaviour towards him: she too is criticised for excessive respect for guards and locked doors, for unwillingness to resort to stealth and subterfuge, and for haughtiness and betrayal.[68] But it is not just a case of Marathus as a locked-out lover[69]

---

[63] Cf. Tib. 1. 4. 82, 'Alas, how Marathus tortures me in unrelenting love!' (*eheu, quam Marathus lento me torquet amore!*).

[64] Cf. Alcaeus, *AP* 5. 10. 3-4, Tib. 1. 6. 3-4, Ov. *Am.* 1. 2. 22, 2. 9A. 6.

[65] The favourite military metaphor of the elegists is hinted at here; see p. xv.

[66] Paleness makes a dark complexion look yellow, not white; for the pallor of love see p. 36, n. 7.

[67] Alternatively lines 51-2 are taken to mean that the girl has no need to keep away from Marathus for fear of catching a real illness (so Lee [1990] in his translation). It seems hard, however, to understand 'Spare him' to mean 'Don't keep away from him', and the indications from the rest of the poem are that it is not the girl's complete aloofness anyway, but her cat-and-mouse game, which troubles Marathus.

[68] See Tib. 1. 6. 5-14; cf. Tib. 1. 2. 15-24.

[69] See p. xiii.

now getting from his own beloved what Delia used to give Tibullus. Rather his words strongly suggest that *he* is the one under guard or surveillance in his own house, and that he was willing to do for his girl everything that Delia was not willing to do for Tibullus; but in his case the girl – herself the one on the outside – was unwilling to take advantage of it.[70] Marathus is told to save his tears (so he is actually standing there crying – like a woman?); they cut no ice with the girl, and they give him swollen eyes[71] (67-8). Finally Tibullus turns back to the girl, naming her at last as 'Pholoe'.[72] Her name is that of a rugged mountain in northern Greece and is not attested as a personal name outside poetry;[73] perhaps it is meant to be generic – 'hard' or 'hard-faced one'. Tibullus tells her to learn her lesson from what has happened to Marathus. She should stop playing awkward, as Marathus himself used to do with *his* lovers.[74] Tibullus never mentions that *he* was once the victim of this uppity behaviour from Marathus[75] and even archly intimates that it was no more than hearsay to him (69-74). Now Marathus dislikes all stand-offishness and every bolted door (75-6); his own suffering has apparently turned him against these things in principle[76] (Tibullus' snigger is practically audible!). Pholoe too will suffer, Tibullus warns, if she remains haughty (77). 'Too' (*et*[77]) is important, for it implies that Marathus is *already suffering* (his change of attitude having come too late to help him) for his own past haughtiness – to Tibullus! Pholoe will give anything to have again (when in old age she is

---

[70] Most scholars prefer to assume that Marathus is the locked-out lover and the girl, as usual in love elegy, is the one immured in the house.

[71] Cf. the description of Lesbia on the death of her pet sparrow at Catul. 3. 17-18.

[72] This kills the possibility of the ultimate irony which the reader may by now almost have expected – that she is Delia.

[73] Cf. Horace *Odes* 1. 33. 7; see also p. xxxviii, n. 113.

[74] There is an amusing stroke of wit in line 74, where the Latin verb *detinere*, which normally means 'keep from leaving', is used in the context of 'keeping (someone) waiting' – in hope but not satisfaction. Lee's translation (1990) 'kept desire on edge' conveys this well.

[75] Cf. Tib. 1. 4. 81-4.

[76] The 'pride' (*fastus* [75]) and the 'obstructing bolt' (*opposita...sera* [76]) at first sight look like references to the cruel treatment meted out by Pholoe in particular and so undermine the assumption that Marathus is supposed to be the one under guard in lines 55-66. But in fact it makes little sense to relate the bolted door mentioned here to that in line 60, irrespective of whose it should be there, since Marathus has said that he can deal with a bolted door anyway. More probably the 'pride' and the 'obstructing bolt' are cited simply as examples of the means by which lovers can be impeded, *all* of which Marathus now disapproves of. The emphatic generality of the expression ('*all* [*omnes*] pride'...'*every* [*quaecumque*] cruel door') supports this.

[77] *et* is an old conjecture for redundant *at* transmitted by the MSS.

unattractive and rejected) the chance that she has now, i.e. she will rue the day that she rebuffed a lover (78). By analogy, the implication of this must be that Marathus, with his boyish beauty already on the wane, is currently regretting the chance he missed – with Tibullus!

This most startling and inventive of Tibullus' poems contains several common amatory themes, but Tibullus presents them in novel combination and in a novel form and context. He also constantly plays intertextually on the reader's expectations which arise from familiarity not only with his own preceding poems but also, especially, with those of Propertius' first book. For in that collection a recurrent motif is Propertius' observation of the signs of love in another person, invariably a man and a friend (or a friendly rival), and sometimes a fellow-poet.[78] Propertius offers his comments directly to the sufferer in what can be thought of as a speech, a letter, or even a soliloquy, and his attitude is a mixture of *Schadenfreude* and sympathy, know-it-all advice and rueful admission of his own inadequacy. In his opening lines Tibullus allows the reader to think that he is going down a similar path; he dismisses the need for divinatory skill with much the same mock-solemnity as Propertius does at 1. 9. 5-8. Very gradually, however, he reveals that the 'friend fallen in love' is not a comrade in adversity or a rival for his mistress' affections but his own one-time boy-friend, and the only rival around is not a man at all but a woman. The theme of an unobliging boy-beloved becoming in his turn a frustrated lover is not new,[79] nor is even the idea of the boy-beloved falling in love with a girl;[80] but Tibullus' exploration of the concept is in form and detail unique. So is the intricate way in which he uses the common motif of the inevitable decline of a woman's looks and sexual desirability with the passage of time[81] to suggest the equally well-worn one of the even greater transience of paederastic beauty.[82] In the earlier part of the poem the futility of the boy's self-titivation in youth is simply mirrored by the woman's in old age, when she will herself be as 'grey' (*cana* [42] as her despised 'grey-haired' (*canus* [29]) lover is now. The message in this seems to be that the boy runs just as much risk as she does of not using his looks at the right time for the right purpose and will be just as unable to restore them by the use

---

[78] See especially Prop. 1. 7 and 1. 9, and cf. Catul. 6 and 55. In essence the motif dates back at least to Hellenistic epigram (see pp. xviii-xix); cf. Callimachus *AP* 12. 71. For 'intertextuality' see p. xiv.

[79] Cf. 'Theognis' 1305-10 West, Theocritus, *Idyll* 7. 118, Statilius Flaccus, *AP* 12. 12.

[80] Cf. Meleager, *AP* 12. 109.

[81] Cf. Prop. 3. 25. 11-16, Horace, *Odes* 4. 13. 1-12, Ov. *Ars Amatoria* 3. 73-6.

[82] See e.g. Alcaeus, *AP* 12. 29, 30, Meleager, *AP* 12. 33, Tib. 1. 4. 29-38.

of hair-dye and some kind of do-it-yourself facelift or exfoliation once they have gone. By the end of the poem, however, the intimation is that the threat has become a reality: he has missed his chance, and now faces a lifetime of misery.[83]

It also emerges gradually in the course of the poem that both the boy and the girl are actually supposed to be present throughout as Tibullus harangues them alternately, and, though they never speak themselves, their reactions to his lecture and to each other can to some extent be imagined from what he says (e.g. at 35-8[84] and 67-8).[85] Although Hellenistic poetry does offer some examples of lively personal monologues,[86] presentation so nearly, yet not fully, dramatic occurs here for the first time in the surviving corpus of Latin love elegy. Callimachus' third *Iambus*, however, in which the beautiful boy Euthydemos was apparently chastised for being lured away (from Callimachus?) by a rich rival, may well have been particularly in Tibullus' mind in this poem and in the following one, 1. 9. Stage dramatics could have influenced him too. The mime[87] regularly featured a confrontation scene arising from a triangular situation involving man, wife and paramour, or lover, beloved, and rival of one or the other; and New Comedy[88] often contained instruction (usually given by an experienced madam or prostitute) on how to handle a love-affair. Tibullus here uniquely combines the two motifs, posing as the apparently detached professional counsellor to the lovelorn youth and his haughty girl, while in fact being part of the amatory triangle himself as the duped lover – and of the boy, not the girl.

Tibullus' own involvement in the situation makes his attitude somewhat puzzling to the reader. Is the poem essentially 'a fable which externalises his own experiences with Delia' (Bright [1978] 245)? Are we really supposed to see Tibullus as a kindly, if humorously patronising, figure trying to do his former boy-friend a favour – to ease his transition into the grown-up role of the active heterosexual lover by asking for consideration

---

[83] The motif of retribution eventually coming to the unobliging beloved is also basically common; cf. Callimachus, *AP* 5. 23. 5-6, Horace, *Odes* 1. 25, Tib. 1. 6. 75-84.

[84] See p. 112 with n. 61 above.

[85] Admittedly some suspension of disbelief is required in respect of the lengthy quotation of Marathus' complaint in Marathus' presence, for it seems unlikely that anyone would listen without protest while being made to look such a fool. But this is far easier than taking the poem, as one German scholar has done, to be a soliloquy, with the whole episode played out only in Tibullus' own mind.

[86] See Cairns (1979) 134-7.

[87] See pp. xxiv-xxv.

[88] See p. xxii.

for his naivety and inexperience? Most scholars think so: 'Tibullus [is] the interested onlooker who places his expertise at the disposal of his heartsore young friend' (Bright [1978] 247); 'Tibullus rises above his own past disappointments over Marathus' (Cairns [1979] 149); '[Tibullus'] attitude seems to be that this attachment is a harmless diversion' (Murgatroyd [1980] 234). At first sight all this certainly seems likely; for Tibullus poses as the champion of Marathus, while depicting Pholoe unflatteringly as the typically demanding and disdainful elegiac mistress, involved with an old man when she could have the beautiful youth. But on closer scrutiny the portrayal of Marathus himself is no less damning. As well as openly characterising him as a fop and describing his good looks in terms which emphasise their paederastic appeal, Tibullus suggests with more malicious subtlety that, despite his aspirations to the active adult masculine role, his circumstances and sexual instincts remain those of the effeminate juvenile passive. Not only does his domestic situation appear to be that of the woman in the usual elegiac love-relationship, but he is also represented as accusing his beloved of being an insufficiently enterprising locked-out lover – as if she were the type of male suitor he was used to dealing with.[89] What is more, when Tibullus asks the girl to spare 'one young and soft' (51), the Latin adjective he uses for 'soft' is *tener*, which certainly can mean 'tender' simply in the sense of 'young and fragile', but in conjunction with 'boy' (*puero* [49]) has exactly the connotations of 'pretty boy' (*puer delicatus*).[90] So Tibullus' variation on the old adage in 49-51 is capable of a less benign secondary meaning: 'A "pretty boy" is no great conquest...go easy on one who is in a "delicate" state. He may not be really sick, but love which is too much (for him)' (i.e. love of a woman) 'is taking its toll on his looks.' In other words, Tibullus insinuates here that Pholoe and Marathus are ill-matched in more than mere age and worldly wisdom, and, while apparently putting pressure on the girl to accept Marathus, he actually suggests that she would have good reason to drop him altogether.

A less benevolent Tibullus (as far as the character in the poem goes) now seems to be discernible: a character out to blight the embryonic heterosexual relationship of Marathus and Pholoe by typecasting him as the effeminate passive and her as the predatory female. Why should he want to do this? Could it be that, crossed in love by both sexes, he sees a

---

[89] Euthydemos, the pretty boy in Callimachus' third *Iambus*, was apparently introduced to his rich lover by his mother. A mother or mother-figure similarly 'running' Marathus could well be imagined to be one who is now responsible for maintaining the guard on him. Cf. also Dioscorides, *AP* 12. 14.

[90] Cf. Tib. 1. 4. 9, 58.

form of revenge in playing them off against each other? Or is there something even more cruelly manipulative behind it? Is he aiming to *get Marathus back*?[91] Not so much by heading off Pholoe (who is clearly the type to please herself anyway) as by panicking Marathus into resuming the role of *puer delicatus* with the suggestion on the one hand that it is all he is fit for and on the other that he is already past it? In short, are all the warnings addressed to Pholoe about the transience of sexual desirability and the sureness of retribution for unobliging behaviour really designed to frighten Marathus? Could Tibullus' hope be that Marathus will immediately feel the need to prove his continued paederastic viability and will put his fine new principles (75-6) into practice to his own, Tibullus', advantage? If so, his logic might be thought shaky in that he has conceded the classic paederastic beauty of Marathus' *current* looks. But although he mostly calls him a 'boy' (*puer*), in line 31 he uses a Latin word for 'youth' (*iuuenis*) which denotes one well past puberty (at least sixteen), and this could be meant to hint cruelly at his increasingly borderline status.[92]

At all events, the rhetoric is impressive? Indeed, but, apparently, not impressive enough – if the very next poem, 1. 9, is understood as a sequel to this one.[93] For Marathus there (he is not named, but there is no mistaking his identity) is certainly back in the role of the boy-beloved – but not with Tibullus. Rather, to the open outrage and disgust of his former lover, who has now cast off all pretence to amused detachment, he is being kept in comfort by another man, a repulsive old codger. And, to cap it all, he has the girl-friend *as well*! This girl-friend, we discover, is one who has allowed Tibullus in the past to help her sneak an assignation with Marathus (1. 9. 41-4). Apparently there *was* a stage, then, when he did consider such a liaison to be no more than a 'harmless diversion', best encouraged to get it over with. Moreover, she is the wife of the disgusting elderly paederast. She is, it must almost certainly be concluded, none other than the Pholoe of 1. 8 ('hard-faced one' indeed!), with her true relationship to the 'grey-haired lover' now revealed. She does apparently often enough doll herself up for her beau (1. 9. 67-72), and we can now surmise that the intimation at 1. 8. 15-16 that she *need* not do so to be attractive was designed only to remind Marathus of the attractiveness of his own youthful beauty unadorned. The old man has indeed had to stump up love-gifts, but, ironically, to

---

[91] So Bulloch (1973) 89.

[92] For recognition of the attractiveness of this threatening transitional period cf. Strato, *AP* 12. 4. 5-8 'The sixteenth year is that of the gods, and the seventeenth / is for Zeus to seek, not me. / But if anyone has a desire for those who are older [he will find that] the youth no longer plays, / but is already on the hunt.'

[93] Generally it is not; see e.g. Bright (1978) 231-2.

bring Marathus, rather than the woman, to his bed. Tibullus can now only vow to replace Marathus with another. His gamble with the oblique approach would appear to have spectacularly misfired.[94] If this interpretation of the relationship between 1. 8 and 1. 9 is tenable,[95] it seems that Tibullus may have been inspired to two separate semi-dramatic scenes by the monologue of Callimachus' third *Iambus*, mischievously replacing the rich rival paederast with a woman in 1. 8, only to bring him unexpectedly back into the picture in 1. 9. Although it could not be said that the relationship between the two pieces is anything like as clear or as devastating as in the case of Ovid, *Amores* 2. 7 and 8, the conception of a linked, semi-dramatic pair perhaps constitutes a precedent of some importance for the Ovidian diptych.

Tibullus 2. 4

So, slavery and a mistress stare me in the face;
  Now it is goodbye for me to the freedom of my fathers.
The slavery is grim, and I am held in chains
  And never does Love relax his wretched victim's fetters.
He burns me irrespective of my blamelessness or guilt;   5
  Burning am I now; cruel girl, ee-ow, remove the brand!
Oh, that I were able to avoid such grievous suffering,
  I would choose to be a frozen mountain stone
Or as a rock stand open to the madness of the winds
  And the wrecking force of the mighty ocean's wave!   10
But now the day is bitter, night's shadows bitterer still;
  Now every conscious moment is steeped in ghastly gall.
And elegy's no help, nor Apollo, poetry's prompter:
  Madame with hand cupped keeps on demanding money.
Muses, be off with you, if you can't help a lover: 15
  I do not look to you to enable songs of war
Nor do I record the journeys of the Sun or how the Moon runs home
  After turning back her horses on finishing her cycle.
Easy access to a mistress is what I seek from poetry:
  Muses, be off with you, if that's beyond your powers.   20
Gifts I must obtain, then, by recourse to crime and slaughter
  To avoid the tearful vigils outside a locked-up house;

---

[94] Cairns (1979) 152-3 identifies the characters in 1. 9 with those in the previous poem but does not argue for any close sequential connection between the two.

[95] For an expanded version of the critical analysis offered here see Booth (1996).

Or the hung-up emblems from sacred shrines I'll pillage,
  With Venus first in line for my acts of violation.
She prompts me to wrongdoing, gives me a grasping mistress: 25
  Let her feel the touch of sacrilegious hands.
Oh, perish every man who gathers up green emeralds
  And dyes the snowy fleece with murex-shell from Tyre!
They engender girlish greed, as do Coan silks
  And the gleaming nacre derived from the Red Sea.   30
They're what make girls wicked, they're why doors have keys
  And why a dog patrols as guardian of the threshold.
But if you bring a big fat sum, the guard gives way,
  Keys do not exclude and the dog itself keeps mum.
Alas, whichever god it was gave a greedy woman beauty,   35
  What a boon he added to a heap of ills!
This is what starts loud tears and brawls, this the basic reason
  For the god of love's bad name today.
But you who shut out lovers defeated by your price,
  May you have wind and fire deprive you of your pile.   40
Yes, may young men then rejoice to see your conflagration
  And no one bustle in with water for the flames.
Alas, when death shall come to you, there will be none to mourn
  Nor pay his last respects at your sad funeral rites.
But one who was not greedy, but was kind, may live a hundred years   45
  And yet be tearfully lamented beside her burning pyre;
And some ageing man, his old-time love revering,
  Will bring a yearly gift of flowers to her tomb
And as he leaves will say 'Rest surely and in peace
  And may the earth lie lightly upon your bones serene.'   50
True indeed's my warning. But what use to me's the truth?
  On *her* terms it has to be that I will worship Love.
Yes, should she even bid me sell my ancestral home,
  Lares, off you'll go for auction at her nod.
All the potions of a Circe, all those of a Medea,   55
  Along with every herb grown on Thessalian soil,
And horse-madness dripping from groin of mare on heat
  When Venus' breath brings love to the untamed herds,
And a thousand other brews mixed by my Nemesis I'd drink,
  If only she would look on me with favouring countenance.   60

With the following fantasy of working as a real slave in the countryside for the mistress who is detained there Tibullus has ended the previous poem in his collection (2.3):

nunc, si clausa mea est, si copia rara uidendi,
heu miserum laxam quid iuuat esse togam?
ducite. ad imperium dominae sulcabimus agros:
non ego me uinclis uerberibusque nego.

Tibullus 2. 3. 81-4

But if my girl's immured now and to catch a glimpse is rare,
what good to one so wretched's a toga freely draped?
Lead on. I'll plough the fields at a mistress' command
and I'll not refuse the fetters and the lash.

Now, in 2. 4, he turns to face facts: he is already subject to slavery of the worst kind – the metaphorical slavery of love. No longer does he joke about the connotations of the toga: it symbolised freedom in that only a Roman citizen could wear it, but when worn 'freely draped' (*laxam* [2.3.82]), it was the mark of a dandy.[96] Instead, more simply, and apparently seriously, he speaks (2-4) of losing his precious ancestral 'freedom' (*libertas* [2]) and of 'chains' (*catenis* [3]) and 'fetters' (*uincla* [4]) already in place (3-4). He is not being beaten[97] but burned by Love (the Latin *Amor* implies both the god and the emotion) and by the 'cruel girl' (*saeua puella* [6]) herself (5-6). He is obviously drawing on the age-old imagery of love as a fire,[98] but he suggests at the same time the penal branding of real slaves;[99] and he is aggrieved about it all, claiming that he would rather be a rock than live in such all-consuming misery (7-12).

This evidently is his lot because the one thing his mistress wants is money. Money spent or to spend on herself, and he has got nowhere with her through his elegy, the one thing he relied upon to win him the *entreé* (13-20) – literally to her house as well as metaphorically to her affections.[100] If Tibullus has to write off poetry as a means of saving him from the perpetual role of the locked-out lover,[101] he will, he says, be forced to take up a life of crime and violence in order to meet the mercenary demands of his 'grasping mistress' (*dominam...rapacem* [25]). He will not

---

[96] Cf. Tib. 1. 6. 37-40.

[97] Cf. Tib. 2. 3. 84.

[98] See pp. xiv, xviii-xix.

[99] Cf. Prop. 1. 1. 27, 4. 7. 35, with discussion on p. 41 and 84.

[100] The incantation-like verbal repetition (*ite procul, Musae*) at the beginning of lines 15 and 20, together with, in line 19, a Latin word for 'poetry' (*carmina*) which also means 'spells', could perhaps evoke an 'open sesame' kind of door-charm; cf. Plautus, *Curculio* 147-54.

[101] See p. xiii.

even stop at sacrilege – and Venus, goddess of love, will be the first victim of it (21-6). He curses the providers of luxury goods, such as jewels, purple-dyed wool and sheer fabrics (27-30). Much-prized pearls, emeralds and other gems were often believed to be conveniently washed up on the shores of what the Romans called the Red Sea, i.e. the modern Persian Gulf;[102] the famous 'Tyrian' dye was extracted from the murex shell found off the shores of Carthage, whose inhabitants originally came from Tyre; and the Greek island of Cos produced a particularly exquisite type of fine material. All of these luxuries, in suggesting ostentatiously bright display, adulteration of what is natural, and immodestly diaphanous dress, charac-terise as vulgar and immoral the sort of women who crave them. What is more, Tibullus claims, such women are made greedy by the availability of these things. This greed is the cause of the lover's exclusion by locks, guards and dogs, to all of which he will find that money talks (31-4). Unfortunately these grasping bitches are beautiful too, and that in turn is the cause of all the trouble which gets Love a bad name (35-8)! Then, addressing a nameless representative of the type, he wishes disaster on the greedy mistress who locks out lovers when they cannot meet her price and warns that at her funeral no one will be paying his last respects (39-44), whereas the 'kind' (*bona* [45]) girl *will* be mourned and honoured (45-50).

Still, Tibullus acknowledges (51-2), the fact that he speaks the truth on these points is no solution to his own immediate problem: the tyranny of his love for his mistress (hers are the 'terms' [*lege*] in line 52). He ends with two illustrations of the extent of his infatuation. First, to finance his love-life he would even at her bidding put up for sale his 'ancestral home' (*sedes...auitas* [53]) and 'Lares'[103] (53-4). Second, all manner of formid-able magic draughts – those patented by Circe and Medea, the two arche-typally powerful and dangerous witches of Greek mythology,[104] tisanes from Thessaly, notorious home of every kind of sorcery, and 'horse-madness' (*hippomanes*), the discharge of a mare on heat[105] – all of these, if only Nemesis (named at long last) would but look kindly upon him (i.e. find him acceptable as a lover and oblige him), he would drink, together with whatever other such concoctions she might mix (55-60). In the Latin the climactic verb 'I would drink' (*bibam*) is the very last word of the poem.

---

102 See e.g. Quintus Curtius 8. 9. 19.

103 I.e. guardian gods; cf. p. 106.

104 Cf. Prop. 2. 1. 53-4, Ov. *Ars Amatoria* 2. 101-4.

105 A standard ingredient of magic potions; see e.g. Aristotle, *Historia Animalium* 6. 18. 4, Virgil, *Georgics* 3. 280-83, Prop. 4. 5. 17-18, Ov. *Am.* 1. 8. 8.

Familiar motifs abound here. A couple are characteristically Tibullan: religious awareness and attachment to an ancient family home.[106] More belong to the stock-in-trade of Latin (and sometimes also earlier Greek) erotic poetry: for example, the lover as slave, the mercenary, luxury-seeking beloved, the locked-out lover, the anticipation of old-age and death, the amatory application of magic, and the practical usefulness of elegiac verse.[107] But Tibullus' poem is not a bland synthesis of traditional material. We may have heard before of the lover being excluded and the beloved being greedy, but the idea of the lover being excluded because – and solely because – of the beloved being greedy, with no suggestion of fear or even simple cussedness playing any part in her disinclination to admit him,[108] is first developed fully here.[109] The guard on the door, far from being imposed by the mistress' husband or keeper to preserve her fidelity,[110] is imposed by the mistress herself to preserve her profits (the bribes apparently go straight to her and not to the guards[111]). These she needs to finance her expensive tastes for the luxury goods whose purveyors Tibullus curses.[112] Growing old and dying are portrayed unusually positively in the touching picture of the kind mistress still being affectionately honoured at and after her death in extreme old age (i.e. when her physical beauty has long since gone) by her one-time lover now grown old himself. Smaller details, too, suggest a thoughtful interplay with ideas in earlier poetry. For example, whereas Callimachus' Acontius, Virgil's Gallus, and Propertius himself seek to assuage love's pain by taking to the open sea or the lonely mountains,[113] Tibullus longs for the total immunity from feeling that *being* a mountain stone or wave-lashed rock would offer.[114] He complains not just routinely of the lover's bitter daily – or nightly – disappointments,[115]

---

[106] See Tib. 1. 1. 7-40.

[107] For the usefulness of elegy, see pp. 59-60 and 71.

[108] Cf. Tib. 1. 2. 15-16, 6. 5-14.

[109] There is just a fleeting glimpse of it already at Tib. 1. 6. 67-8.

[110] Cf. Tib. 1. 6. 15-16.

[111] Cf. Ov. *Am.* 2. 2. 39-40.

[112] A variation on the stock motif of cursing of the inventors or discoverers of various things, such as travel, commerce or implements of war; cf. Tib. 1. 10. 1-2, and see further Booth (1991) 112.

[113] See p. 39, and for intertextual play in general, p. xiv.

[114] Cf. Horace, *Epode* 17. 54-5, 'Not deafer to exposed sailors [than I am to you] / are the rocks that wintry Neptune pounds in the briny deep (*non saxa nudis surdior nauitis / Neptunus alto tundit hibernus salo*)'; the speaker is the witch Canidia.

[115] Cf. Tib. 1. 2. 77-80, Prop. 1. 1. 33, 11. 5, 2. 7. 11, 4. 3. 29, Ov. *Am.* 1. 2. 1.

but more strikingly of 'every moment (*omnia tempora*) soaked in gall'. The Latin *tempora* also means the 'temples' of the head, which are often said to be 'soaked' or 'dripping' with wine in the case of somebody drunk, and Tibullus has therefore also wittily suggested excessive consumption of the lover's conventional cup of gall.[116]

Most notable of all, however, is the fact that Tibullus' procedure and attitude here are untypical of *him*. He develops his opening theme in a relatively straightforward linear way, with none of the excursions into wishful thinking which characterise the majority of his heterosexual love elegies. Even the unexpected picture of the kindly mistress' long-term fate[117] is carefully integrated into the whole through very precise contrast with what awaits her grasping counterpart. An *elderly* man who once loved her will *grieve* for the kindly one at her funeral, *bring flowers* to her grave and *wish her well in death*,[118] while the other will have no mourners, and Tibullus *wishes ill* on her *in her lifetime*, hoping that *young* men badly treated by her will *laugh*, and none will even *bring water* if her house is on fire.[119] The reader may notice also how the house-fire of the greedy one is mirrored in the funeral pyre of the kind. Along with the tighter structure comes an openly less romantic and naive outlook. The willing slave-prisoner of earlier poems[120] who positively relished servile punishment[121] seems now more resentful of his amatory servitude – more Propertian, at least superficially, in his reaction to the tyranny of love.[122] Tibullus it was who trusted in his own religious piety[123] when suffering a setback in his love-affair with Delia:

---

[116] For this see Plautus, *Cistellaria* 69.

[117] This is, perhaps significantly, reminiscent of Tibullus' picture of his own decline and death at 1. 1. 57-68. See Bright (1978) 213-14.

[118] The words he is given in lines 59-50 are the formulaic Roman equivalent of R.I.P.; cf. Prop. 1. 17. 23-4.

[119] A similarly comfortless future is envisaged for the mistress who is unfaithful at Tib. 1. 6. 77-84.

[120] See Tib. 1. 1. 55-6, 1. 6. 37-8, 2. 3. 83-4.

[121] See Tib. 1. 6. 5-6, 9. 21-2.

[122] It may well be a half-developed thought at Propertius 1. 1. 27-8 (see p. 41) which prompted Tibullus to bring a new dimension to the old imagery of both the fire and the slavery of love through the idea of his subjection to the servile punishment of branding at the hands of the beloved herself (line 6).

[123] This is amply demonstrated at Tib. 1. 1. 11-24 and 35-40.

num Veneris magnae uiolaui numina uerbo
  et mea nunc poenas impia lingua luit?
num feror incestus sedes adiisse deorum
  sertaque de sanctis deripuisse focis?
non ego, si merui, dubitem procumbere templis
  et dare sacratis oscula liminibus;
non ego tellurem genibus perrepere supplex
  et miserum sancto tundere poste caput.

Tibullus 1. 2. 81-8

Surely I've not violated great Venus by some word
  And find my impious tongue now paying for its guilt?
Surely in profanity I've breached no sacred shrine
  Nor torn away the garlands from any holy altars?
Were I guilty, I'd not hestitate to fall down in the temple
  And bestow my kisses on the blessed thresholds,
Nor to crawl along the ground, a suppliant on my knees,
  And beat my wretched head upon the holy door.

He it was who dreamed of a perfect future with Delia on that modest family estate in the country[124] which meant so much to him:[125] he it is here who is prepared to sacrifice both his principles and his property to keep his chances with Nemesis alive apparently on no more than a day-to-day basis. Such reckless behaviour the philosophers tended to regard as characteristic of any lover,[126] but its contrast with Tibullus' conduct as portrayed in other poems gives it special point in his case.[127] Here there is no more romantic fantasy of simply lavishing upon Nemesis everything she wants,[128] but instead a grim awareness of what will be the cost. There is some attempt to blame the greed of women of her kind (she is not thought of as unique in any way) on the commercialism of the age,[129] but the pithy summary of the effects of money 'talking' in lines 33-4 strikes a

---

[124] Tib. 1. 5. 19-34.

[125] See pp. 100-101.

[126] See e.g. Plato, *Republic* 574D, Lucretius 4. 1121-40.

[127] Soldiering to raise money, something equally against his normal inclinations, he does not contemplate – presumably because it would inconveniently take him away from the scene of the amatory action.

[128] Cf. Tib. 2. 3. 53-62.

[129] Cf. Tib. 2. 3. 39-50. The motif was apparently prominent in Callimachus' third *Iambus*; see p. xxiv.

new note of unmistakable cynicism.[130] The man who is elsewhere either naively fearful of magic being used against him in love,[131] or keen to exploit it in his favour,[132] here declares his willingness to submit to Nemesis' use of it on him, if so doing would neutralise her amatory hostility.[133] He would know, of course, that in all probability it would not. Though magic potions could reputedly cure as well as induce love,[134] those mentioned here are all by implication and association aphrodisiac, and in the hands of a Nemesis would inevitably be used only for intensification of her lover's passion – she would have too much to lose from healing his infatuation. The witch-procuress figure whom Tibullus once accused of corrupting Delia into using her evil magic for material gain at her lover's expense[135] is now redundant: Nemesis has become the witch in her own right. By depicting her thus Tibullus highlights her implacability, for as a witch-like figure dabbling in aphrodisiacs she cannot but recall Horace's ghastly Canidia, exposed in *Epode* 5 as one who will even kill a young boy to use his liver and marrow as ingredients in her potions, and in *Epode* 17 as one who is moved only to viciously retaliative anger by a gently mocking plea for release from her power. Nemesis' sinister name ('Retribution'), so long delayed, also points the futility of Tibullus' hope, coming as it does hard on the heels of the Latin *placido* (59), 'favourable'. For the adjective *placidus* stems from the same ultimate root as Latin words meaning 'appease', or 'placate'; and there is, of course, no 'placating Nemesis'. Tibullus' grasping mistress is just as unpleasable and unrelenting as the Daughter of Night after whom she is named.[136] If Nemesis does to some extent symbolise the darker side of love,[137] the more general message here would seem to be that, despite every effort, once in love's clutches, there is no escaping the grimmer aspects of it.

---

[130] A Greek epigram by Antipater of Thessalonica (*AP* 5. 30. 3-4) includes much the same sentiment: 'Yet if you bring the cash, friend, there's no door-keeper / in your path, no dog chained by the entrance'. But Tibullus' poem probably antedates this as well as two other variations on the theme at Prop. 4. 5. 47-8 and Ov. *Am.* 3. 8. 63-4. See Bright (1978) 211-12.

[131] Tib. 1. 5. 41-2.

[132] Tib. 1. 2. 43-66.

[133] Tibullus skilfully manipulates his structure and word-order (55-60) to keep us guessing for a few moments about who will use magic on whom – the expectation is that it will be Tibullus himself on Nemesis.

[134] Cf. Horace, *Epode* 5. 71-2.

[135] Tib. 1. 5. 47-8, 59-60.

[136] See pp. xl-xli. For a similar play on words cf. Tib. 2. 6. 27 'Hope promises me a favourable Nemesis, but she herself negates it' (*Spes facilem Nemesim spondet mihi, sed negat illa*).

[137] See Bright (1978) 202-3.

Along with Tibullus' sharper perception of both his mistress' true nature and his own degradation comes a revelation of what is in fact the cause of his undoing: perennial weakness of the will when sexual desire conflicts with moral outrage (35-8), personal sentiment (53-4) and common sense (55-60). The underlying tone of Tibullus' appraisal of his situation is debatable. Is it a cry of genuine anguish, shame and despair from 'a used up man who has no hope and has ceased to struggle' (Smith [1913] 55)? Does Tibullus wallow masochistically in these emotions?[138] Or is there a humorous edge to the poem – a hint of rueful self-ridicule? How seriously can we take a man's claim to be on the verge of criminality, when he is smart enough to draw up an order of merit for his sacrilegious attentions?[139] And how seriously can we take his claim to be prepared to sacrifice his precious inheritance, when he can talk so wittily about the sale of his estate ('Off you go, Lares, under her thumb and under the hammer')?[140] What, too, are we to make of that startling declaration of willingness to imbibe whatever magic brews Nemesis may offer him on the off-chance of this winning her compliance? Could Tibullus be using this implausible scenario to articulate in an ironically detached and un-Catullan way the perennial conflict between the lover's heart and his head? Could he be wanting the very implausibility to demonstrate that he has become totally irrational in his infatuation[141] – and, somewhat to his own amusement, knows it? Or is the whole idea just an ill-judged inclusion which 'strains belief' (Maltby [1990] 152)?

Whatever questions the poem raises about Tibullus' attitude to his love, however, it also has something to say about his attitude to writing poetry. Like Propertius (and later Ovid), he claims (15-20) to favour elegy over the grander genres of epic (represented here by war) and didactic (represented by astronomy[142]) on grounds of its greater potential for winning over a beloved. Tibullus' admission that in practice it does not always do the trick serves as a wry corrective to Propertius' unrestrained confidence in the power of elegiac verse – *all* elegiac verse, but especially

---

[138] So Elder (1962) 94.

[139] There is just a suggestion of sexual *double entendre* about this, too, in that the Latin word Tibullus uses to convey his envisaged 'violation' of Venus (*uiolanda* [24]) is one which can also signify rape.

[140] This free translation perhaps captures something of the flavour of the Latin in line 54. See further Bright (1978) 214, n. 69.

[141] Cf. Prop. 1. 1. 7.

[142] This was the subject of Aratus' third-century BC Alexandrian poem *Phaenomena*.

his own.[143] At the same time Tibullus' admission allows him to affect very limited poetic ambition on his own part: all he wants from his elegy is practical assistance in love, and if it fails him in that, he has no use for it. Interestingly he does not follow what was evidently Callimachus' example in *Iambus* 3 and simply complain about the inadequacy of the Muses, i.e. poetry, in an age of materialism, but spiritedly he treats the Muses as his minions rather than his mentors: if their product does not get results, they can have the sack! For accolade as a poet he apparently cares nothing. Yet consider the learning and artistry of, for example, lines 57-60. The allusion to the magical properties of *hippomanes* in line 58 closely echoes in phraseology Virgil, *Georgics* 3. 280-1: 'horse-madness...drips as a sticky secretion from the [mare's] groin' (*hippomanes.../...lentum distillat ab inguine uirus*); but the reference to 'herbs' in line 60 suggests that Tibullus recognised and is also echoing Virgil's own oblique allusion at *Georgics* 3. 282-3 ('horse-madness, which wicked stepmothers often pick / and mix with herbs' [*hippomanes, quod saepe malae legere nouercae / miscueruntque herbas*]) to the Hellenistic pastoral poet Theocritus' claim that *hippomanes* is an Arcadian plant for which mares and fillies go crazy (*Idyll* 2. 48-9). Is such richly intertextual writing[144] the work of a poet who is truly indifferent to his literary reputation?

Tibullus: Retrospect

Quintilian[145] famously judged Tibullus the most 'polished and elegant' (*tersus atque elegans*) of the Augustan elegists; Ovid called him 'cultivated' (*culte Tibulle*)[146] and his talent 'refined' (*ingenium come*).[147] Quintilian certainly, and Ovid probably, made these judgements on grounds of style, and even in a translated medium it is perhaps possible to appreciate something of the understated sophistication and graceful lucidity which result from a generally restricted range of vocabulary, straightforward sentence-structure and unpretentious imagery. Yet if ever a Roman poet

---

[143] See Prop. 1. 7. 21-2 (addressed to the epic poet Ponticus): 'Then', i.e. 'when you have fallen in love', 'you will often admire me as no mean poet; / then I shall have preference among the talents of Rome' (*tum me non humilem mirabere saepe poetam, / tunc ego Romanis praeferar ingeniis*). Cf. Prop. 1. 9. 11.

[144] See p. xiv.

[145] See p. xliv.

[146] Ov. *Am.* 1. 15. 28, 3. 9. 66.

[147] Ov. *Tristia* 5. 1. 18.

has been damned by the faint praise of modern scholars, it is Tibullus. 'This is not great poetry, because it lacks originality of language or thought, but it is poetry in which style, form and expression harmonise most successfully. Tibullus has no real powers of invention nor the ability to shape traditional material to new ends.' 'A severely limited range of themes...find unity in an adaptation of the biographical approach.' 'The most rigorous technical requirement was to create transitions from one theme to another...and Tibullus' most original contribution to Roman poetic composition lies here.' (Williams [1968] 499-500) The message in this one substantial example is clearly that many things have been looked for in Tibullus and found wanting. But are they really wanting, or is it just necessary to *look harder* for the desired coherence, the ingenuity, the individuality, the spark, and the light and shade? If 'Tibullus is a better poet than he seems on first reading' (Lee [1974] 110), is this a strength or a weakness of his writing? Some have at least perceived an interesting 'tension' between the image of himself which Tibullus mostly presents – pious and gentle, wistful, passive and naive – and the stylistic finesse with which he presents it.[148] Do the three elegies in the present selection suggest that there is also another kind of deliberately created 'tension' – one between the milk-and-water personality which overlays the poems and a sharply ironic, self-mocking and even maliciously scheming character to be glimpsed through the smokescreen from time to time? Is it, too, an unworldly and introverted writer, or an almost perversely independent and self-assured one, who, despite plenty of evidence that he knew and inter-acted with the work of Callimachus and Theocritus, Virgil, Horace and Propertius,[149] pays no homage to any other poet or poetic principles, and makes no excuse or apology to anyone for not engaging with the concerns of the Augustan establishment (Augustus is never even mentioned by him)? These questions are all well-worn. A few less familiar ones about the positives in Tibullus' work (besides his famously understated style) should also be asked. Does the fact that he has not one but three named beloveds – two different women and a boy – allow him to say anything about love that the other poets do not say? Does the greater length of Tibullus' elegies give him any advantages over, say, Catullus? And are the techniques which are distinctively his ever taken up by his successors?

Tibullus' 'polish' is as much a general as a stylistic trait, and this all-pervading quality handicaps him in the modern world, where 'smoothness' can be synonymous with empty and slightly repellent charm. He has

---

[148] E.g. Elder (1962) 85; Lyne (1980) 189.
[149] 'The names alone are lacking' (Leach [1980] 79).

acquired through his cultivated simplicity the reputation of being unde-
manding, and even his defenders are inclined to saddle his poetry with all
the derogatory connotations of 'easy listening' music: 'It is a pleasure to
read a Roman poet who does not for one moment assume the strained
posture of a bard in full attire' (Luck [1969] 81).[150] But simplicity can
deceive. An attractive (though apocryphal) story has it that the learned
Fellows of Queens' College, Cambridge, once took it upon themselves to
dismantle their college's wooden 'mathematical' bridge over the River
Cam to see how it was made and in full confidence of being able to
reassemble it, as it was originally constructed, without nuts and bolts –
only to find this in the event utterly beyond them. The reader who tries to
demonstrate the simplicity of Tibullus' love elegies by taking them to
pieces may well only then make a similar discovery of interdependent
component parts which none but the original designer could put together
into a sound, complete and aesthetically pleasing construction, with noth-
ing superfluous and everything in its place.

---

[150] Neither the sympathetic studies of Bright (1978) and Cairns (1979) nor similarly positive
treatments in German by F. Mutschler, *Die poetische Kunst Tibulls* ['*The Poetic Art of
Tibullus*'] (1985), and C. Neumeister, *Tibull: Einführung in seine Werk* ['*Tibullus:
Introduction to his Work*'] (1986) have succeeded in eradicating the traditional view. Lee-
Stecum (1998) is the latest to take on the task.

OVID

(translations by Guy Lee)

Amores **1. 1**

My epic was under construction – wars and armed violence
  In the grand manner, with metre matching theme.
I had written the second hexameter when Cupid grinned
  And calmly removed one of the feet.
'You young savage' I protested 'poetry's none of your business.   5
  We poets are committed to the Muses.
ImagineVenus grabbing Minerva's armour
  And Minerva brandishing love's torch!
Imagine Ceres queen of the mountain forests
  And Diana the huntress running a farm!   10
Or longhaired Phoebus doing pike drill
  And Mars strumming the seven-stringed lyre!
You've a large empire, my boy – too much power already:
  Why so eager for extra work?
Or is the whole world yours – the glens of Helicon included?   15
  Can't Phoebus call his lyre his own these days?
Page one line one of my epic rises to noble heights
  But line two lowers the tone
And I haven't the right subject for light verse –
  A pretty boy or a girl with swept-up hair.'   20
In reply the god undid his quiver and pulled out
  An arrow with my name on it.
'Poet' he said, flexing the bow against his knee,
  'I'll give you something to sing about – take that!'
Alas his arrows never miss. My blood's on fire.   25
  Love has moved in as master of my heart.
I choose the couplet – rising six feet, falling five.
  Farewell, hexameters and iron wars.
Garland your golden hair with myrtle from the seaside,
  Hendecametric Muse, my Elegia.   30

Ovid had just written the first two lines of a grand martial epic in the appropriate metre, the six-footed 'hexameter'[1] (1-2), when Cupid spoilt the second one by filching one of the feet, leaving him with a hexameter plus a pentameter – in other words, an elegiac couplet, the appropriate metre of love poetry (3-4). 'How dare you meddle with things which don't concern you?',[2] Ovid had rebuked him, attempting to demonstrate the preposterousness of his interference in poetry by hypothesising ludicrous invasions of each other's territory by three pairs of incompatible deities – (i) Venus, goddess of love, and Minerva, the warrior; (ii) Ceres, the mother corn-goddess, and Diana, the virgin huntress; and (iii) Phoebus Apollo, patron of music and poetry, and Mars, lord of war (5-12). Huffing and puffing still more, he had accused Cupid of assuming global power – making a take-over bid for Mt Helicon[3] and putting Apollo out of a job (13-16).[4] Finally, outraged at the threat of his own demotion from epic to love elegy, he had claimed that having no beloved in his life ('a pretty boy or a girl with swept-up hair' [20][5]) meant that he lacked the appropriate subject-matter for down-market elegiacs (17-20). Cupid, he says, soon remedied that by shooting him with one of his notorious arrows to produce the requisite passion in him at a stroke (21-6). 'And there's my reason for shelving epic', he concludes. 'Hendecametric Muse' (literally 'Muse to be set to rhythm in eleven feet'[6] [30]), – in other words 'Elegy' – 'don your myrtle ready for an airing'. The myrtle, being sacred to Venus, connotes love, and the sea-side habitat with which it is credited also evokes Venus' fabled birth from the surf[7] (27-30).

'I was just embarking on a martial epic, when divine intervention forced me to go in for love elegy instead'. Unmistakable in Ovid's poem are these essential elements of the scenario in the preface to Callimachus' *Aetia*[8] which was developed by Propertius and Horace into the so-called 'refusal' (*recusatio*) and used by them as a jocular but tactful excuse for not producing an epic flattering to Augustus.[9] But Ovid here gives the Callimachean tune

---

[1] See pp. xv-xvii.

[2] Line 5 more literally: 'Who gave you, cruel boy, this jurisdiction over poetry?'

[3] The home of the Muses; cf. p. 57, n. 102.

[4] He was on amusingly shaky ground here, for Love's universal influence was a common-place; cf. *Am.* 1. 2. 37, and see Kenney (1990) 175-6.

[5] Line 20 more literally: 'Either a boy or a girl with coiffed long hair'.

[6] Six of the eleven feet coming from the hexameter and five from the pentameter.

[7] Myrtle is not in fact found only, or even mostly, in coastal regions.

[8] See p. xx.

[9] See pp. xxxii-xxxiii, and pp. 69-71 on Prop. 3. 3.

a sparkling new libretto and a more uncompromisingly major key. In place of Apollo, god of poetry, with his riddlingly expressed admonition (cf. Prop. 3. 3. 15-24) there is Cupid, god of love, with his childish prank. In place of the writer who meekly allows himself to be taken in hand (cf. Prop. 3. 3. 25-6) there is one who, unprecedentedly, ventures to protest, playing the superior, finger-wagging adult to Cupid's naughty child ('You young savage' [*saeue puer*, 5], 'my boy' [*puer*, 13]) and bursting with self-importance ('We *poets*'[10] [6]). In place of the absolute earnestness of Callimachus and the muted humour of Propertius there is the exuberantly playful spirit of Hellenistic epigram.[11] The figure of the impish love god owed much of its development to this genre, which features both Love's prompt bringing to heel of any who has ideas of defiance or escape[12] and his laughter at his victim's predicament[13] or in the face of his reproaches.[14] Here Ovid has replaced the reluctant epigrammatic lover usually brought into line by Cupid with a reluctant love *poet*. In this way the epigrammatic motif is made to fit the 'refusal' scenario, and the scenario in turn provides the degree of context which is typical of elegy but generally lacking in epigram. In identifying Cupid's arrows with poetic subject-matter and making Cupid personally responsible for his change of poetic direction Ovid may be taking yet another cue from Hellenistic epigram, where Love is shown putting a stop to poetic production in general.[15] Propertius, however, had already asserted its deleterious effect on the writing of epic in particular[16] and claimed to have been compelled by Love to seek fame as an erotic poet.[17]

Ovid's deviations from the standard pattern of the Augustan 'refusal' carry some of the poem's most significant messages as well as providing much of its humour. For, far from acceding to any suggestion that he is not up to epic,[18] Ovid gives every indication that he *is* up to it. No claim of

---

[10] Ovid uses for 'poets' a Latin word (*uates*) which among the Augustans frequently denoted a profoundly serious exponent of heroic or public themes; it is sarcastically echoed by Cupid in line 24.

[11] See pp. xviii-xix.

[12] See e.g. Meleager, *AP* 12. 82, 126; cf. also Prop. 2. 29. 1-22.

[13] Meleager, *AP* 12. 126, 3.

[14] Meleager, *AP* 5. 176. 1-4.

[15] Posidippus *AP* 12. 98.

[16] Prop. 1. 7. 15-18.

[17] Prop. 2. 13. 1-8; see pp. 59-60. It has also been suggested that Philitas (see pp. xxii-xxiii) wrote of an inspirational encounter with Love; so Cairns (1979) 5-6. But, if so, it is surprising that no love poet before Ovid took up the idea.

[18] Cf. especially the tenor of Prop. 3. 3.

toying with the idea of writing a martial epic[19] or merely *dreaming* about it[20] for him: he had actually made a start – and a good one – with just the right material and technique (1-2, 17-18). Furthermore, when he does eventually capitulate, it is not in sober fashion to wise aesthetic counsel but cheerfully – for all his professions of pain – to *force majeure* of the most frivolous kind. Never was a poet's claim of coercion into a particular type of writing a more transparent façade for his determination to please himself *without scruple*. A refreshingly unguarded, unapologetic love elegist has evidently come on the scene. But while Ovid will have no truck – not even jocular truck – with the usual diplomatic pretence of being confined to elegy (or some other non-epic genre) by his own artistic limitations, neither does he make a case for the superiority of elegy on stylistic grounds. He may be no respecter of Augustan sensibilities (real or supposed), but here he is apparently no militant Callimachean either.

The manner in which Ovid claims to have become a lover is highly significant too. Love was something mechanically induced in him by Cupid. He says it is a searingly painful and dominating emotion, but the glib brevity of lines 25-6, with their tired old images of wounding, burning and enslavement, may make us doubt it. Of a *beloved* there is never a mention! The contrast with Propertius' first elegy[21] is particularly striking. There also the personified Love is alleged to have brought a defiant non-lover to heel; but his aim was to knock Propertius off an emotional, not a poetic, high horse. Love's activity there is merely theorised briefly (lines 3-6) from the more immediate subjugation of Propertius by his human beloved, the captivating but haughty Cynthia, whose very name gets first mention and around whose behaviour the whole poem is constructed. Being in love is presented by Propertius as an emotional experience which finds its expression in his elegy: for Ovid it is a stance to be assumed as a professional necessity – a prerequisite for the elegy to which he is already committed. Trivial details, such as the identity of the beloved, can be worked out later. Not even the semblance of emotional truth is to be expected from him.[22]

The preoccupation with metre in this opening poem gives clear indication that the technique of love elegy fascinates Ovid at least as much as its subject-matter. Not only does he base the whole thing on a clever conceit about metre, but he is also at pains to convey the essential nature of the

---

[19] Cf. Virgil, *Eclogue* 6. 3-6, Horace, *Odes* 4. 15. 1-4.

[20] Cf. Prop. 3. 3. 1-12.

[21] See pp. 35-44.

[22] Keith (1992) 340-44 further explores the relationship between Ov. *Am.* 1 1 and Prop. 1.1.

couplet – the unmatched length of its two lines (2-3, 30) and the satisfying sense of build-up, as it 'rises' (*surgat* [27]) in the hexameter, and resolution, as it 'falls' (*residat* [27]) in the pentameter (cf. also lines 17-18).[23] The pentameter was conventionally thought of as a come-down from the hexameter in more senses than one, and its poor-relation status is one of the main vehicles for the 'distinctive rococo wit' (Wilkinson [1962] 17) which characterises the whole poem. Sometimes this takes the form of hints at double meanings. For example, 'I had written the second hexameter' is certainly part of what Ovid means in line 3, but what he actually says is simply 'The lower line was equal', using a Latin word for 'lower' (*inferior*) which is also capable of exactly the same meaning as the English 'inferior', i.e 'of less high standing/quality'. The same words can thus describe both the original, pure epic form of Ovid's lines ('the line lower in position was as long as the other') and their present, humbler, elegiac one ('the line [now] lower in status was [before] just as good as the other'). The verbal play is enhanced here by the near-oxymoron of claiming that something 'inferior' is or was 'equal' (*par* [3]) to something else. There is a similar stroke of verbal wit involving the pentameter in line 18, where Ovid claims that the second line of his poem 'lowers the tone'. What he actually says here is 'That second line weaken*s* (*attenuat*) my strength'. The Latin verb *attenuare* literally means 'to make thin or slender'. 'Slenderness' was the stylistic ideal *par excellence* of the Alexandrian school, most strikingly represented by Callimachus; and so, although Ovid embarks on no aesthetic crusade in this poem, he does here slyly indicate that he has been converted from a traditional heroic to a Callimachean style of poet.

The poem's wittiest stroke of all, however, comes at the very beginning. First words of Latin poems were important. So frequently did they encapsulate the theme and tone of major works that they could even do duty as titles. Thus could Propertius' Book 1 be called his 'Cynthia' and Virgil's *Aeneid* be known as 'Arms and the man'. In the Latin *arma*, 'arms' (in Lee's translation 'wars') is the first word of this first poem of Ovid's *Amores*, and it is precisely the same first word as in the *Aeneid*. Never was there a potential title more mischievously misleading in the expectations it raises! That impish opening reminder of Virgil is hard to miss, but there is another, more subtle, almost at the end. 'Garland your hair with myrtle', Ovid tells the Muse of Elegy (27). That is exactly what the myrtle-loving goddess' son Aeneas did before gravely proceding to honour the ashes of his dead father at *Aeneid* 5. 72, and exactly what her distant descendant Octavian is envisaged doing on becoming a god at *Georgics* 1. 28. Ovid's

---

[23] See also p. xvi. Some detect a sexual *double entendre* here (and at other points in the poem): see e.g. Kennedy (1993) 58-63.

verbal reminiscence of these solemn Virgilian occasions suggests a tongue-in-cheek attempt to invest his lightweight Muse with the semblance of heroic dignity after all. The mock-solemnity is underlined by the sonorous quality of the final pentameter which results from its *recherché* diction[24] and unusually few words (the translation captures this well). Such a balance between opening and ending is a typical instance of Ovid's love of orderliness in structure and expression. Lines 7-12 constitute another. Ovid's stuffiest critics would judge three pairs of examples excessive, and yet they are integrated into the whole with great sophistication. The bone of contention is the trespassing on poetry by Cupid the love god (5-6). The first pair of hypotheses designed to deter him involves a love goddess, who is Cupid's own mother, and a war goddess (7-8). The central pair (9-10) is the least directly relevant, but Ceres' fame as a mother provides a link with the previous pair, while her opposite number Diana offers a link with the third pair in that she is the sister of Phoebus Apollo. He is god of poetry, and his opposite number is the god of war, Mars (11-12); this pairing foreshadows the next development – Cupid the love god's foray into warring of a sort as well as into poetry (21-4). Love, war, kinship and poetry: the intricate yet unobtrusive interweaving of these concepts is what both holds the passage 7-12 together and holds it in its place.

'A neat poetic joke' (Mack [1987] 55) is indeed what Ovid produces here. A joke ostensibly at his own expense, too, with a beautifully timed climax: first the pompous poet's own lengthy, blustering speech (5-20), then Cupid's menacingly deliberate preparations for retaliation (21-2), and finally his contrastingly laconic reply accompanied by the single unerring shot (23-4). But who or what does the joke really target? Poets and poetry in general, with their constant recycling of a few stock themes ('a brilliant perversion both of generic posture and of well-known literary motifs'; so Kenney [1987] 14)? Callimachus and his stylistic paranoia in particular? Propertius and his exaggerated sense of poetic self-worth? The romantic idea of love so important to Propertius and the others? Augustus and his supposed desire for traditional epic? Those contemporary poets who let Augustus' supposed desires bother them? Virgil in particular, who, depending one's perspective, either let the side down or came up trumps? Or is the joke perhaps on the reader, who may be fooled into thinking that this 'whimsical and illogical little drama' (Mack [1987] 56), which occcupies one of the most prominent and memorable places for a programmatic poem[25] – the very beginning of a collection – has no serious programmatic

---

[24] The verb *emodulari* is attested nowhere else.

[25] See p. xiv.

purpose whatever? 'A slight piece' it has been called (Wilkinson [1962] 17), and with reason; but is the weight of this elegy, with all its entertaining intertextuality[26] just disguised rather than lacking altogether?

Amores 1. 2

What's wrong with me I wonder? This mattress feels so hard.
  The blankets won't stay on the bed.
I haven't slept a wink – tossing and turning
  All night long. And now I'm aching all over.
Can it be love? Surely I'd know if it were?   5
  Or does love work under cover and strike unobserved?
Yes, those phantom arrows have pierced my heart
  And relentless Cupid is torturing me.
Shall I give in? Or fan the flame by fighting it?
  Better give in. Balance makes a burden light.   10
Shake a torch and it flares up –
  Leave it alone and it dies.
A bullock restive under the yoke
  Gets beaten more than his patient partner.
Spirited horses bruise their mouths on the bit;   15
  The docile seldom feel it.
The god of love hits rebels far harder
  Than his submissive slaves.
Then I submit, Cupid. I'm your latest victim,
  Standing here with my hands up.   20
The war's over. I'm suing for peace and pardon.
  There's no glory in shooting an unarmed man.
Bind your hair with myrtle. Harness your mother's doves.
  Vulcan will fit you out with a chariot.
Mount it and steer your doves through the crowd   25
  As they hail you victor.
You too can celebrate a glorious Triumph
  With young men and girls as your prisoners of war
And I'll be among them, wearing my new chains,
  Nursing this open wound – your abject slave.   30
Conscience and Common Sense and all Love's enemies

---

[26] For 'intertextuality' see p. xiv. Buchan (1995) 54-6 makes more ambitious claims for its role in this poem.

Will be dragged along with hands tied behind their backs.
You'll strike fear into all hearts.
The crowd will worship you, chanting *Io Triumphe*.
Your loyal irregulars Flattery Passion and Illusion   35
    Will act as bodyguard,
The forces that bring you victory over gods and men,
    Providing cover for your nakedness.
Your laughing mother will watch the Triumph from Olympus
    And clap her hands and shower you with roses   40
As you ride along, jewels flashing from wings and hair,
    A golden boy in a golden chariot,
Raising many a fire if I know you,
    Wounding many a heart as you pass by,
Your arrows willy-nilly never resting,   45
    The flame of your torch scorching at close range,
A god as mighty as Bacchus along the Ganges,
    Your doves terrible as his tigers.
Then spare me for your Triumph.
    Don't waste your strength on me   50
But imitate your conquering cousin Augustus –
    He turns his conquests into protectorates.

Love is something most people recognise when it hits them, but not, apparently, Ovid, who opens this poem with a poker-faced, almost academic weighing up of the chances of an sudden, undiagnosed attack of it being the cause of the horribly sleepless night he is having (1-6). Deciding that this must indeed be the problem – Cupid getting up to his usual tricks (7-8) – he goes on to debate, just as academically, whether it would be more sensible to give in or to resist (9-10), eventually concluding that giving in seems to be indicated (11-18). No sooner said than done: Ovid surrenders to Cupid in person, formally requesting an end to hostilities (21-4). He then invites Cupid to celebrate his victory in a 'Triumph'. This was a ritual honour, as formal as a modern military decoration, accorded to a Roman general in recognition of a notable campaign success. He was driven through the streets of Rome in a four-horse chariot to the temple of Capitoline Jupiter, accompanied by his loyal officers and with his prisoners-of-war and his booty paraded in his procession. Here Ovid imagines Cupid as the honorand on such an occasion, with himself one of the captives and crowds of spectators shouting acclaim (25-42). The show will also provide the opportunity for Cupid to make further conquests (43-8); and since Ovid could be such an ornament to it, it would be in Cupid's own best interests to show him mercy now. He should take a leaf out of the book of his 'cousin' (*cognati* [51], literally 'relative') Augustus, whose policy is to become the protector of those he has conquered (49-52).

How can Ovid claim not to know whether he is in love or not? How can he ask whether love steals up in secret? Didn't he just tell us in the previous poem that Cupid, in a face-to-face encounter, shot him with a passion-inducing arrow which had instantaneous effect? He did; but he also told us why it happened. Having embarked on what turned out to be the wrong poetic genre (epic) at the wrong time, he had needed to be made into a lover so that he could switch to the right one (love elegy). He had had love thrust upon him specifically to enable him to *start afresh* on a new footing. This is exactly what he is doing here in the second elegy of the *Amores* – starting afresh, and trying to show what a good job he is making of it by behaving as if the previously related encounter had never taken place. Lines 7-8 amount to a conspiratorial wink, however, in that they clearly recall that encounter for the reader.[27] Furthermore, anyone who was hoping that Ovid would really change his spots will be disappointed: the incongruously rational proposition and argument of lines 5-18, together with the speed and cheerfulness with which this elegiac lover accepts ser-vitude, confirm that even the veneer of emotional involvement is still out of the question. The slavery of love for him simply means acceptance of the lover's role and not the pose of subjection to the bitter-sweet tyranny of a uniquely attractive beloved. Indeed, there is still no beloved in sight. Not until the third poem of the book in fact does a woman come into the pic-ture, and not until the fifth is she named or described.[28] Here the protago-nists are again Ovid and Cupid alone,[29] and the love god is this time conscripted for the ingenious exercise which occupies lines 23-52.

Ovid may be interacting directly here with the epigrammatist Posidippus (*AP* 12. 120):

> I am well-armed, and I will fight you and not give in,
>   mortal though I am. Do not, Love, attack me any more.
> If you catch me drunk, carry me off defeated; but while ever I keep sober,
>   I have Reason drawn up against you.

---

[27] Moles (1991) offers a different explanation of the apparent contradiction between *Am.* 1. 1 and 1. 2; see also Boyd (1997) 147-9.

[28] Even though Ovid seems at *Am.* 1. 1. 20 to leave open the possibility of writing about ho-mosexual as well as heterosexual love, in the event he never does so.

[29] The same is true of *Am.* 2. 9A and 9B and essentially true of *Am.* 2. 12.

'Reason' is precisely what suggests to Ovid that he *should* give in! Cupid's attack, however, is one of the commonest motifs of Hellenistic epigram[30] and was probably the ultimate inspiration for the Augustan elegists' enthusiastic development of the idea of love itself as a type of warfare – the only type, in fact, in which they were happy to participate. But Ovid does not just use the notion of the warfare of love to distance himself from the real military ethos of the Augustan establishment. Rather he uses the idea to make a mockery of it, and the imaginary Triumph he creates for Cupid in this poem is a splendid case in point.[31] Turning the usual puckish aggressor into the honorand in this most prestigious of Roman military rituals, Ovid adapts its details to suit the god of love with much the same inventiveness and wit as he adapts the standard funeral dirge to suit a dead parrot in *Amores* 2. 6. Instead of the laurel wreath which conventionally crowned the head of the triumphing general Cupid will sport a garland of myrtle[32] (22), and his chariot will be drawn not by war-horses but by proverbially non-aggressive doves (23). The triumphal chariot itself will be supplied by Cupid's 'stepfather' (*uitricus* [24]), i.e. either Vulcan (so Lee in the present translation), the blacksmith god, who could engineer one,[33] or possibly Mars, the war god, who could loan one. Both of them were at different times credited with being Venus' husband,[34] but the identity of Cupid's father was notoriously uncertain, and the ambiguity of Ovid's expression is a witty allusion to that here. He then envisages Cupid's triumphal progress through the streets to the traditional cheer of *Io Triumphe* ('Hurrah, Triumph' [34]) from the awe-struck crowd (25-38). In his procession the place of conventional captives will be taken by young men and girls fallen victim to him, the freshly smitten Ovid among them (29-30). Also among the prisoners of war 'with hands tied behind their backs' (*manibus post terga retortis* [31]) will be the personified virtues 'Conscience' (*Pudor* [32]) and 'Common Sense' (*Mens Bona*[35] [31]). 'Flattery' (*Blanditiae* [35]) 'Passion'

---

[30] Further examples on pp. xviii-xix, 37. For the layout of the above non-metrical translation of Posidippus see p. ix.

[31] He may have been inspired by Prop. 2. 8. 39-40: 'Since Love is much my superior by virtue of both his mother and his weapons, / is there any wonder that he duly triumphs over me?' (*inferior multo cum sim uel matre uel armis, / mirum, si de me iure triumphat Amor?*). Athanassaki (1992) and Miller (1995) also detect intertextuality (see p. xiv) with Prop. 3.1 and read Ovid's poem, like Propertius', as a claim for the triumph of love elegy over epic. For the elegiac use of the triumph theme in general see further Galinsky (1969).

[32] Another frivolous use for this ornament so dignified on other occasions; see p. 135.

[33] He famously manufactured a shield on special order for Venus' *other* son, Aeneas, at Virgil, *Aeneid* 8. 370-453.

[34] Vulcan more frequently has the honour, but for Mars in this role cf. Ov. *Am.* 2. 9B. 23.

[35] Cf. Prop. 3. 24. 19, with discussion on p. 75.

(*Furor* [35]) and 'Illusion' (*Error* [35]) on the other hand will enjoy a privileged position among Cupid's lieutenants (35-6). Readers of Virgil's *Aeneid* will be struck here by the reversal of fortune for 'Passion' (*Furor*), whose subjugation, 'hands tied behind its back', is in *Aeneid* 1 a symbol for the peace and stability of the Augustan age.[36] Venus herself will look down from Olympus and savour the fun, says Ovid, but the mortal spectators will just present sitting targets for Cupid's relentless attack (39-46).

He then proceeds to compare Cupid with Bacchus (Dionysus), god of wine and civiliser of the world[37] (47-8). Hellenistic and Roman artists frequently depicted groups of Cupids in a chariot hauled by wild animals just like Bacchus'; but in Ovid's time Caesar Augustus himself had memorably been portrayed as emulator of Bacchus (by Virgil at *Aeneid* 6. 804-5), and so Cupid is in a way usurping his position here. Ovid, then, sets up the love god in competition with Augustus before suggesting that he follow Augustus' example (51-2). How could Augustus be Cupid's 'cousin' (in the loosest sense of 'distant relative')? Augustus liked to claim divine descent by tracing the Julian line back – through his adoptive father the deified Julius Caesar, Romulus the legendary founder of Rome, Iulus the son of Aeneas, and Aeneas himself – to Venus, daughter of Jupiter; this lineage is reverentially sketched by Virgil at *Aeneid* 1. 254-88. But if Augustus was indeed thus related to Aeneas, Venus' son by the Trojan Anchises, he was also related to Cupid, her *other* son of uncertain parentage, who was technically Aeneas' half-brother.

Whatever else, it is clear that at various points in this poem Ovid has, for fun, perverted the image of Augustus which was at least encouraged, if not invented, by the man himself and had been respectfully presented in Virgil's *Aeneid*. He has also systematically trivialised the Triumph, the public distinction by which his ruler set such store. Augustus was particularly proud of the Triple Triumph awarded him in 29 BC for the victories of Dalmatia, Illyria and Actium,[38] and after 19 BC he effectively restricted award of a Triumph to members of his own family. Both Ovid's stressing of Cupid's one impeccable qualification for the coveted honour now out of the reach of sober citizens – his kinship with Augustus – and his suggestion that Cupid should adopt his relative's much-advertised policy of mercy to

---

[36] *Aeneid* 1. 294-6: *Furor impius intus / saeua sedens super arma et centum uinctis aënis / post tergum nodis fremet horridus ore cruento*. Augustus had set up in his Forum Apelles' painting of *Furor* in chains at the victory-procession of Alexander the Great. For the destructiveness of *furor* in an amatory context cf. Prop. 1. 1. 7.

[37] The Indian conquest and triumphal progress from Asia to Europe which eventually became part of Bacchus' mythology was modelled on that of Alexander.

[38] See Augustus, *Res Gestae* 4.

the conquered[39] seem more likely to have been meant as a final outrageous joke rather than as the innocently off-beat compliment that some scholars imagine. At all events, if Ovid did think that the man who so stood on his dignity and was so careful of his public image would have been simply flattered by mention of his person and policies regardless of context, he probably should have known better.

This is another poem in which Ovid's creative intertextuality[40] and conceptual wit are matched by his virtuoso style. In line 38 he plays on the two meanings of 'naked' (*nudus*): both 'nude', which is the conventional state in which the god of love is depicted in art and literature, and 'defenceless', the state to which he would be reduced without the forces of Flattery, Passion and Illusion (witty substitutes here for his conventional weapons of bow and arrows). Again (cf. *Am.* 1. 1. 7-12) no less than three examples (11-16) illustrate a single point, and Ovid's liking for balance, antithesis and artistic repetition is never more evident than in lines 41-2. A glance at the Latin of the whole couplet, with a more literal translation, may here help to highlight these qualities:

> tu pinnas gemma, gemma uariante capillos
>   ibis in auratis aureus ipse rotis.

> Your wings with jewels, with jewels (*gemma, gemma*) your hair adorned,
>   you will ride on wheels which are gilded (*auratis*), golden (*aureus*) yourself.

A fresh start, then. But does this poem really prove to be in the end the fresh start that it logically should be? Or is it rather 'in many ways a continuation of the program elegy' (Galinsky [1969)] 92), re-enacting the confrontation in *Amores* 1. 1 and reinforcing some of its messages?[41] Logically it should be the first real love poem of the *Amores*, too, but would Catullus, Propertius and Tibullus have considered it a love poem at all?

---

[39] See e.g. Augustus, *Res Gestae* 3; cf. Virgil, *Aeneid* 6. 853. Prop. 2. 16. 41-2. The context of Ovid's allusion to imperial clemency here mischievously intimates that it was motivated by a substantial measure of self-interest. The same is of course true of many professedly 'protective' policies operated by authoritarian figures or bodies in the both the ancient and the modern world.

[40] See p. xiv.

[41] The poem's place in the 'programmatic' (see p. xiv) opening sequence *Am.* 1. 1-5 is examined by Buchan (1995) in a *tour de force* of deconstructive (see p. xlv) ingenuity; it mounts a particular attack on the 'realist' approach adopted here.

Amores 2. 7

So that's my role – the professional defendant?
  I'm sick of standing trial – though I always win.
At the theatre I've only to glance at the back rows
  And your jealous eye pin-points a rival.
A pretty girl need only look at me   5
  And you're sure the look is a signal.
I compliment another woman – you grab my hair;
  I criticise her – and you think I've something to hide.
If I'm looking well I don't love you;
  If pale, I'm pining for someone else.   10
I wish to God I had been unfaithful –
  The guilty can take their punishment.
As it is you accuse me blindly, believing anything.
  It's your own fault your anger cuts no ice.
Remember the donkey, putting his long ears back –   15
  The more he's beaten the slower he goes.
So that's the latest count against me –
  I'm carrying on with your maid Cypassis?
Good God, if I wanted variety
  Is it likely I'd pick on a drudge like her?   20
What man of breeding would sleep with a slave
  Or embrace a body scarred by the lash?
Besides, she's your coiffeuse – her skill
  Makes her a favourite of yours.
I'd be mad to ask a maid so devoted to you: 25
  She'd only turn me down and tell.
By Venus and Cupid's bow,
  I'm innocent – I swear it!

Ovid, we gather, is in the dock (1-2). Corinna[42] is the plaintiff and the
charge – as always, evidently – is infidelity. With a spirited show of right-
eous indignation Ovid dismisses as pure paranoia Corinna's habitual infer-
ences from (a) his casual glances (3-4) at the 'back rows' (*summa* [3]) of
the theatre (in the Augustan period this was where the women were made
to sit), (b) his chance encounters with pretty girls (5-6), (c) his passing re-
marks (7-8), and (d) his varyingly blooming or pallid appearance[43] (9-10).

---

[42] See pp. xliii-xliv.
[43] For amatory pallor see p. 36, n. 7.

Outrageously unjust and utterly self-defeating are his mistress' incessant accusations, he says (11-14); she should remember that beating a donkey (a beast as proverbial for uncooperativeness in antiquity as it is today) is counter-productive (15-16). The more mindless accusations she makes, he implies, the fewer comforting denials she can expect.

But one more, at least, is immediately forthcoming: Ovid vehemently denies Corinna's latest accusation (17-18) that he is having an affair with her personal maid, the hairdresser Cypassis. This girl's name wittily evokes both her actual appearance and its sex-appeal, since it is Greek for a kind of short frock and is as suggestive as calling her 'Mini-skirt'.[44] The leg-revealing garments which slave-girls wore instead of the full-length dress of well-born Roman women no doubt made them a particularly attractive proposition. First Ovid argues from probability: wouldn't he, a 'man of breeding' (*liber*[45] [21]), have better taste than to make love to a slave-girl (19-22)? His language conveys his apparent revulsion at the very idea. And wouldn't he have more sense than to proposition a woman so intimate with and so devoted to Corinna (23-6)? Then, on oath in the name of the goddess of love and her son Cupid's notorious bow, comes his formal plea of 'Not guilty' (27-8; the legal metaphor persists throughout the poem).

This is perhaps a dramatically a bit unrealistic in that no woman is very likely to have listened to it all in silence. But still, as denials go, it is convincing? It gives no reason to suppose that Ovid the lover here is not telling the truth, or that this is not the end of the matter? Read on!

Amores 2. 8

Cypassis, incomparable coiffeuse
   Who should start a *salon* on Olympus,
No country lass, as I know from our encounters,
   But Corinna's treasure and my treasure-hunt –
Who was it told her about us?   5
   How does she know we slept together?
I didn't blush though, did I? Said nothing by mistake
   To betray our secret?
I may have argued no one in his right mind
   Would have an affair with a maid,   10
But Achilles adored his maid Briseis

---

[44] Cf. the witty Greek names in Prop. 4. 7; also that of Pholoe in Tib. 1. 8 (see p. 114).
[45] Literally 'a free-born man'.

And Agamemnon fell for his slave Cassandra.
I can't claim to be greater than those two.
What goes for royalty is good enough for me.
Corinna looked daggers at *you* though.   15
    And how you blushed! I saw you.
But I saved the day, you must admit,
    By swearing my Venus oath.
(Dear goddess, bid the warm south winds
    Blow that white lie over the ocean!)   20
So in return, my black beauty,
    Reward me today with your sweet self.
Why shake your head? The danger's over.
    Don't be ungrateful. Remember your duty to *me*.
If you're stupid enough to refuse I'll have to confess   25
    And betray myself for betraying her.
I'll tell your mistress where and when we met, Cypassis,
    And what we did and how many times and how we did it.

So that's his game! The rotter! The cheek of it! Who would have thought
it? The first suspicion of earlier foul play arises when this poem opens with
an ingratiating direct address to the previously scorned Cypassis (1-4).
Now she is a *coiffeuse* fit only for goddesses (*comere...solas digna...deas*
[2])[46] and 'no country lass' (*non rustica* [3]), i.e. she is sexually sophisti-
cated.[47] This, Ovid says, he knows from their 'encounters' (*iucundo...furto*
[3], literally 'pleasant act of stealing'). The Latin clearly intimates that they
were 'encounters' of a sexual kind, and the word-play on *apta* ('suited') in
line 4 (literally 'you who are suited to your' [or 'my'] 'mistress, but suited
better still to me') sustains the salacious tone. In lines 5-6 the reader's
worst suspicions are unequivocally confirmed, but there are more shocks
lined up. First, Ovid has the nerve to congratulate himself on his own
cover-up performance (7-8). He breaks off his smug review (when
Cypassis begins to expostulate?) only to shrug off his earlier claim that no
one but a madman would make love to a slave-girl (9-14). Like many poets
defending slave-love, he cites mythological precedent, but hardly convinc-
ingly, for Briseis and Cassandra were not common slaves but high-born
captives, taken by the Greek heroes Achilles and Agamemnon respectively,
in the Trojan war. At the same time we discover that Cypassis was *there*

---

[46] Lee's 'should start a salon on Olympus' is an inspired way of putting it, even if some way
from the literal Latin.

[47] *rusticus*, 'countrified', is an adjective which Ovid regularly applies to the sexually gauche.

when Ovid was making his disparaging remarks about her and her kind. Not that this bothers him – he even accuses her of giving the game away (15-16). Only a brilliant bit of perjury on his part 'saved the day'[48] (17-18). Brilliant, because Venus, in whose name Ovid swore, was traditionally one of the deities who dispensed perjured lovers from punishment; hence the prayer to her in 19-20 to dispose of his 'white lie' (*animi periuria puri* [19], literally 'the perjuries of a pure heart'). The ultimate piece of cheek, however, is still to come: Ovid's request for another sexual favour from Cypassis as a 'reward' (*pretium* [21]) for protecting her (21-2)! Line 21 reveals that Cypassis was dark-skinned (*fusca*). Perhaps she was supposed to be black, perhaps a swarthy 'white',[49] but in any case this is almost certainly not intended to be shocking in itself. Miscegenation was evidently both practised and tolerated in Rome, and if the idea of sexual relations between a white man and a black girl had been shocking, Ovid would surely have included Cypassis' skin-colour among her shortcomings at *Amores* 2. 7. 19-22. More probably he refers to it here to re-emphasise his willingness to accept a slave-girl as a sexual partner, for darkness of complexion was firmly associated with servile status,[50] and when it occasionally connoted inferiority, it was only for that reason.[51] Finally, when Cypassis 'ungratefully' (*ingrata* [23]) refuses, Ovid reminds her that there are in her case two sides to 'duty'[52] (23-4) and reveals himself to be prepared to blackmail her into compliance (25-8; the legal metaphor surfaces again in line 25).[53]

So this poem and the previous one form a two-scene sequence. The second piece has in some ways more dramatic verisimilitude than the first, but then again its realism is arguably undermined by ostentatious shafts of wit. There are other pairings of a similar kind in the *Amores*,[54] but this one is unique in that the second poem shows up the first in an entirely different light.[55] All manner of writers throughout antiquity are to be found exploring

---

[48] Line 17 more literally: 'But if you happen to recall, how much more presence of mind *I* showed'.

[49] The Latin adjective *fuscus* covers both.

[50] See e.g. Cicero, *In Pisonem* 1.

[51] See Thompson (1989) 114, 142-4.

[52] Line 24 more literally: 'It is enough to have satisfied *one* of your masters'.

[53] Literally 'I shall turn informer and confess what happened earlier'.

[54] *Am.* 1. 11 and 12, 2. 2 and 3, 2. 13 and 14.

[55] The present selection of love elegy, however, offers evidence to suggest that Propertius and Tibullus may have experimented with something on similar lines. See pp. 91-2 and 118-19.

the implications of love between the free and the servile,[56] and the 'confrontation scene' arising from a triangular situation involving master, mistress and slave was a popular ingredient of comedy and mime.[57] Ovid's treatment of his chosen theme here, however, is entirely his own, and of all his elegies these two are possibly the most devastatingly revealing of his poetically unorthodox attitude to love. In itself, we are told, 'the drama implies more or more vivid things than a description or analysis would ever tell' (Lyne [1980] 271). What 'things', though? Things about Ovid? About men? About women? About you, the modern reader? No ultimate response from either Corinna in *Amores* 2. 7 or Cypassis in *Amores* 2. 8 is conveyed by the character who speaks in the poems: what do you think you are supposed to deduce from that?[58] And if you are shocked by the attitudes displayed in this pair of poems, which, if any, of the other authors in this volume do you believe would have shared your dismay?

Amores 3. 2

'It's not the horses that bring me here
  Though I hope your favourite wins.
To sit with you and talk with you is why I've come –
  I've come to tell you I'm in love.
If I watch you and you watch the races   5
  We'll both enjoy watching a winner.
How I envy your charioteer!
  He's a lucky man to be picked by you.
I wish it was me. I'd get my team
  Off to a flying start,   10
Crack the whip, give them their heads
  And shave the post with my nearside wheel.
But if I caught sight of you in the race
  I'd drop the reins and lose ground.
Poor Pelops was nearly killed at Pisa   15
  Gazing in Hippodamia's eyes,
But being her favourite of course he won –
  As I hope your driver and I will.

---

[56] Cf. especially Prop. 3. 15.

[57] See pp. xxii, xxiv-xxv, and cf. p. 116.

[58] James (1997) 72-3 offers an interesting, if contestable, interpretation of the significance of the two women's silence.

It's no good edging away. The line brings us together –
  That's the advantage of the seating here.   20
You on the right, sir – please be careful:
  Your elbow's hurting the lady.
And you in the row behind – sit up, sir!
  Your knees are digging into her back.
My dear, your dress is trailing on the ground;   25
  Lift it up – or there you are, I've done it for you.
What mean material to hide those legs!
  Yes, the more one looks, the meaner it seems!
Legs like Atalanta,
  Milanion's dream of bliss;   30
A painter's model for Diana
  Running wilder than the beasts.
My blood was on fire before. What happens now?
  You're fuelling a furnace, flooding the Red Sea.
I'm sure that lightweight dress is hiding   35
  Still more delightful revelations.
But what about a breath of air while we wait?
  This programme will do as a fan.
Is it really as hot as I feel? Or merely my imagination
  Fired by your sultry presence?   40
Just then a speck of dust fell on your white dress;
  Forgive me – out, damned spot!
But here's the procession. Everybody hush.
  Give them a hand. The golden procession's here.
First comes Victory, wings outstretched.   45
  Goddess, grant me victory in love!
Neptune next. Salute him, sailors.
  Not for me the ocean – I'm a landlover.
Soldiers, salute Mars. I'm a disarmer,
  All for peace and amorous plenty.   50
There's Phoebus for the soothsayers, Phoebe for the hunters,
  Minerva for the master craftsmen.
Farmers can greet Bacchus and Ceres,
  Boxers pray to Pollux and knights to Castor.
But I salute the queen of love and the boy with the bow.   55
  Venus, smile on my latest venture.
Make my new mistress willing – or weak-willed.
  A lucky sign – the goddess nodded
Giving her promise. And now I'm asking for yours.

With Venus' permission I'll worship you.   60
By all these witnesses, divine and human,
  I swear I want you to be mine for ever.
But the seat's a bit too high for you.
  Why not rest your feet on the railing in front?
Now, they've cleared the course. The Praetor's starting the first race.   65
  Four-horse chariots. Look – they're off.
There's your driver. Anyone *you* back is bound to win.
  Even the horses seem to know what you want.
My God, he's taking the corner too wide.
  What are you doing? The man behind is drawing level.   70
What are you doing, wretch? Breaking a poor girl's heart.
  For pity's sake pull on your left rein!
We've backed a loser. Come on everyone, all together,
  Flap your togas and signal a fresh start.
Look, they're calling them back. Lean your head against me   75
  So the waving togas don't disarrange your hair.
Now, they're off again – plunging out of the stalls,
  Rushing down the course in a clash of colours.
Now's your chance to take the lead. Go all out for that gap.
  Give my girl and me what we want.   80
Hurrah, he's done it! You've got what you wanted, sweetheart.
  That only leaves me – do I win too?'
She's smiling. There's a promise in those bright eyes.
  'Let's leave now. You can pay my bet in private.'

Ovid is at the races; and so are you! You are an eavesdropper on what he
says – mainly aloud and directly to, or for the benefit of, the girl in the seat
beside him,[59] but sometimes *sotto voce* to himself.

'I'm not here because I'm interested in the racing', he begins, 'though
I'm hoping that the driver you support is going to win. I'm here because
I'm interested in *you*. It's a great opportunity to let you know that I love
you, and we can both have the pleasure of looking at something we like'
(1-6). So are setting, subject and tone immediately established: Ovid's sole
aim is to seduce his pretty neighbour, and his strategy is to get into her
good books by backing her favourite charioteer. Many a man or woman, of
course, has feigned a shared enthusiasm to initiate or cultivate an amatory
relationship; but perhaps few would risk in a public place and on limited

---

[59] In the Roman Circus, unlike the theatre, the sexes were not segregated; cf. *Am.* 2. 7. 3.

acquaintance[60] an opening gambit as shamelessly direct as Ovid's. Importunate flattery immediately follows, as he imagines what driving a chariot in front of her would do for him: her favour would inspire him to go flat out to win[61] – unless he were distracted by her beauty, as Pelops was by Hippodamia's. Oenomaus, king of Pisa, famously declared that any successful suitor of his daughter, Hippodamia, would have to beat him in a chariot race, and he made Hippodamia herself ride with the contenders to distract their attention. He had killed a dozen who had failed the test before Pelops came along, but Hippodamia fell in love with him and helped him defeat her father by advising him to bribe Oenomaus' groom to remove the linchpins from his chariot. It was entirely due to Hippodamia's favour (*fauore* [17]), Ovid stresses (with a knowing leer, we may imagine), that Pelops was the winner (another leer, perhaps?), and he trusts that a lady's favour is going to produce *a couple* of winners that day. This at any rate seems to be the gist of his patter in lines 7-18. It is considerably stronger on salacious blandishment than on logic (Pelops is dragged in just to point the sexual angle), but the girl obviously gets his drift only too well. For Ovid's next remark makes it clear that she does what any self-respecting woman would do if she found the man sitting next to her behaving so outrageously: she tries to put some distance between them. As the tiresome fellow points out, though, this cannot be much because of the (un)luckily cramped nature of the seating; the 'line' (*linea* [19]) was a groove in the stone which marked off the individual places (19-20).

Evidently Ovid has blundered, but he boldly attempts to deflect attention from this by suggesting, with two splendidly aggressive barks at the occupants of the seats round about, that it is *their* proximity, not his, which is causing offence: 'You at the other side, watch it! And you behind, too!'[62] (21-4). Still, the rebuff has evidently been enough to compel Ovid to adopt a more oblique approach (though at this stage, one feels, only a fool would not see through it). He makes three supposedly chivalrous gestures excuses for physical contact. The first is to lift the girl's trailing dress off the ground for her (25-6); but the tantalisingly brief glimpse underneath

---

[60] My earlier assumption (in the 1995 edition) that the encounter in the poem was meant to be a very first meeting now seems to me unwarranted.

[61] A modern psychologist would no doubt find symptoms of sexual excitement in the frenzied driving he imagines.

[62] The Latin here teases the reader with hints of sexual impropriety. In lines 21-2 the spectator 'on the right' (*dextra*) is warned that 'contact with his side' (*contactu lateris*) is hurting the girl; *latus* ('side') is a common euphemism for the male genitals (see Adams (1982) 49). In lines 23-4 the spectator behind is told to 'pull up his legs' (*contrahe crura*), and not 'press her back' (*nec preme terga*) with his 'hard' (*rigido*) – 'knee' (*genu*): anticipation mischievously disappointed!

managed in this way brings another salacious compliment to his prattling lips (27-8): 'Nasty old dress you were to cover legs like that; / the more one looks...nasty old dress you were!' (a more literal translation). It sounds as if he may have held up the hem just a shade too long and consequently had the fabric sharply snatched away and pushed down again! The glimpse has been enough, however, to set off thoughts which are much too libidinous to be proffered openly, and can only be understood as a *sotto voce* reflection: 'Legs like Atalanta's or Diana's!' (29-32). In other words, fabulously, divinely, beautiful legs.[63] Some find these comparisons outlandish in their grandeur, if humorously so.[64] Is it really so very inappropriate, though, for thoughts of the fabled runner and the goddess of the chase to occur to one whose mind is supposed to be on racing and speed but is actually on hunting and capture? What is more, Atalanta and Diana are both suggestive of challengingly unsullied chastity, and Diana was often pictured wearing the sort of short, leg-flattering dress which Ovid's mind's eye lustfully substitutes for the respectable long skirts of his present neighbour. The salaciousness is reinforced by a *double entendre* in line 30, literally '[Legs like Milanion] would have liked to have *held up*' (*sustinuisse*), i.e. both in the race with her, which he needed to win, and in bed with her, when he had won it. He was bad enough before he saw those legs, Ovid reflects (still to himself), but now she's really started something. To think what else might be hidden under that frock! (33-6) He retains enough control, however, to confine his audible speech to a second supposedly innocuous politeness: an offer to fan the girl (37-8). But again the libidinous compliment follows: maybe all the heat is in his heart – fired by love of a lady. (39-40). This time no specific reaction is indicated: has she ignored him – or even given him hope by not actively resisting the fanning? At any rate he follows up quickly with the third ploy: a bit of dirt there (he says!) on her lovely 'white dress' (*alba...uestis* [41]) – what an opportunity! Yet another highly personal compliment (hidden in the translation) is slipped into the pentameter, for Ovid whips the speck of dirt not from her 'white dress' but 'from her snowy body' (*de niueo corpore*)![65] How this latest sally is received, however, we are again not told.

Anyway Ovid's attention is suddenly claimed by the entry of the procession marking the start of the Circus proceedings. Now he becomes the rather irritating self-appointed commentator which sporting or public events so often do produce; he even has the nerve to tell everybody else to be

---

[63] For Atalanta see p. 36, and for Diana, p. 132.

[64] See e.g. Lyne (1980) 256.

[65] A literal translation of line 42 is 'Get away from her snow-white body, dirty dust'.

quiet (43). Effigies of deities were conventionally carried from the Capitol on wagons into and around the Circus arena before the races started, and Ovid cannot let any of them pass without commenting on which deity it is, and who should be acclaiming it (as if nobody else knows, or the girl cannot see for herself), or why a particular deity does or does not have his personal support (as if everybody else is interested) (43-56). He gives or withholds approbation entirely on the basis of how lover-friendly a specific deity is – this in itself enough to indicate to his harassed neighbour what is still uppermost in his mind. Thus Neptune and Mars get the brush-off, seafaring and war traditionally being anathema to lovers, and Phoebus, Phoebe (Diana), Minerva, Bacchus, Ceres, Castor and Pollux all meet with indifference, but Victory, Venus and Cupid ('the boy with the bow')[66] are ecstatically applauded. The timely arrival of Venus' effigy prompts Ovid to ask for the goddess' blessing on his present suit, and he is evidently confident enough now to call the girl 'my new mistress' (*nouae...dominae* [57]) in her hearing (56-7). He interprets the swaying of the effigy as 'a lucky sign' (*signa secunda* [58]) and follows this slyly persuasive pretence to divine sanction ('What more could anyone want?' is the implication) with a direct request for the girl's favour. He adds further (supposedly winning) flattery (he will make her his Venus on earth), and an oath of eternal fidelity – which the reader who knows the amatory Ovid knows is not worth much (59-62).

Still, it looks as if, against all the odds, he may be getting somewhere with the girl, for we do not hear of any rejection. Furthermore, he is emboldened to risk another ploy to see those legs. Affecting concern for her comfort again, he suggests that she would be better with her feet up on the 'railing' (*cancellis* [64]); this may have been some sort of barrier dividing the tiers of seating (63-4). Once more he teasingly does not say whether she obliges him or not, but suddenly resumes his commentary as the real action on the race-course begins (65-6). At first all goes well, and Ovid attempts again, but with more finesse than at the start, to flatter the girl with claims of the extraordinary advantage her favour gives the selected charioteer and his team (67-8). But then, when the charioteer blunders and threatens to make a fool of him, with superb dramatic realism Ovid plays the excitedly involved spectator, who knows exactly what should be done and hurls angry questions, insult and advice at the hapless competitor (69-72). All seems lost, but the declaration of a false start saves the day (73-5). Even in the midst of all the excitement Ovid does not miss a trick with the girl

---

[66] In the Latin here, as often in Hellenistic art and poetry, there is a whole band of Cupids: *pueris...potentibus arcu* (55) literally means 'the boys powerful with the bow'. Cf. Prop. 2. 29. 3-6.

herself (75-6): 'So that the flapping togas don't upset your hair, / snuggle up close into my lap' (a more literal translation). Once again there is nothing to lead us to suppose that she demurs! For the moment Ovid the commentator is back in action (77-8), and then Ovid the partisan spectator, full of yet more excited advice and exhortation (79-80).[67] All over quickly, though, and with the favourite's victory comes a reminder of the master-plan which hinged on this outcome. Assuming his softening-up has had the desired effect, Ovid should now be able to exploit to his own advantage the girl's supremely good mood induced by her driver's win. And if the ruse doesn't seem to be going to work for the bounder after all! For he jubilantly exclaims 'She's smiling' (*risit* [83]), and the prospects for carrying off his own prize look very promising. There is some uncertainty, though, about the last line (84): 'That'll do here. You can pay the rest [of my dues] somewhere else'.[68] The manner and the place are, of course, only too eas-ily imagined. But are these words supposed to be (i) Ovid's own words addressed directly to her (the ultimate piece of lustful presumption)? Or (ii) his own unspoken thoughts (more or less the equivalent of 'It's in the bag!')? Or (iii) words which he actually hears, or hopefully imagines, coming from the girl's lips (to confirm wittily that her smile means what he thinks it means)?[69] Perhaps this question could only be answered defini-tively by seeing and hearing Ovid himself 'perform' the poem. In any case, none of the possibilities makes it absolutely clear whether Ovid did in the end achieve his object or not.

It is hard to imagine how this one-man enactment of 'Seduction at the Circus' could be bettered for the effectiveness with which it puts the reader in touch with all the sights and sounds of the occasion, all the antics of competitors and spectators,[70] and all the shameless ulterior motives in the speaker's libidinous mind.[71] Some scholars, ever suspicious of any whiff of real Roman inventiveness, have tried hard to find Hellenistic models for this poem. But although it is true that *Hymns* 1, 5 and 6 of Callimachus and

---

[67] Lee's translation of lines 79-80 captures well the effect of spluttering alliteration in the Latin hexameter and a succession of short, sharp words at the end of the pentameter.

[68] A more literal translation of the text printed; some editors prefer the reading *est* for *hic* in line 83.

[69] So Davis (1979) 67-8.

[70] With great skill the angle is gradually widened to bring more and more people into the picture; see further Davis (1979) 58-9.

[71] Ovid's own didactic rehash of the scene at *Ars Amatoria* 1. 135-64 (where the Circus is included in his guide to good places to pick up a girl in Rome), though lively and competent enough in itself, only highlights the masterliness of his manipulation of dramatic format here. For comparison of the two passages see Boyd (1997) 203-10.

Idylls 2 and 15 of Theocritus[72] contain at least partially monologic presentations of public rituals or spectacles, their connection with the present elegy would escape all but the most determined sniffers-out of precedents. Like all elegiac dramatic monologues,[73] the poem has some affinities with mime,[74] and it uses some traditional amatory material,[75] but if ever a Roman poem was inspired by life rather than by literature, this surely is it.

Without doubt 3. 2 is the most brilliantly sustained dramatic monologue in the *Amores*; yet it relies on a fair degree of artful contrivance. Dubiously *sotto voce* remarks have to be 'heard' from time to time, and in a number of places even the open chatter is unrealistically scripted. The girl would not, for example, need to be told what Ovid proposed to use as a fan (38) or what the effigy of Victory looked like (45); or that the thing she might rest her feet on was a railing (64); or that a 'clash of colours' (*discolor agmen* [78]) was visible when the horses started (the competing teams sported red, white, blue or green, and near-riots between rival groups of fans often developed).[76] All these things she would be able to see perfectly well for herself. Nor would sailors, soldiers, soothsayers, hunters, master craftsmen, farmers, boxers and knights (47-54) need to be told which deities they were supposed to support, and the chances of the whole lot of them being within earshot anyway are not very great. Nor would Ovid's fellow-spectators need to be told what was the standard signal for claiming a false start (74). All of these details are there purely to ensure that the reader is fully in the picture. It is unlikely, too, that the procession would actually have been organised in such an artistically convenient order. The false start seems little short of miraculous; its only purpose is to parallel Ovid's own initial blunder with the girl and hint, through the charioteer's second-attempt victory, that it is in all situations possible to recover after getting off on the wrong foot. But so well does the monologue come off as a whole that the liberties Ovid takes with dramatic realism largely pass unnoticed.[77] The poem's ostentatious wit is arguably another of its strengths. As well as the *double entendres* and understatements which give rise to a few moments of sexual innuendo (e.g. 21-4, 30, 39-40, 81-2), there are frequent manifestations of Ovid's penchant for other varieties of witty word-play, such as showy or emotive repetition (e.g. 5-6, 27-8, 43-4, 80-81) and striking alliteration

---

[72] See p. xxiv.

[73] See p. xiv.

[74] See pp. xxiv-xxv.

[75] E.g. the image of love as a fire (39-40) and the quasi-deification of the beloved (59-60).

[76] See Cameron (1976).

[77] See further Lyne (1980) 280.

(e.g. the repeated *p* in line 15, reproduced in the translation, is perhaps suggestive of Pelops' stammering admiration). All these verbal fireworks might also be thought to be unrealistic: quips so measured and scintillating rarely come to a speaker under pressure. On the other hand, are they not entirely in keeping with the figure Ovid is trying to cut here: irresistibly brilliant, suave and charming, and – in his own mind at least – God's gift to a woman?

Of course, we have all met his type: extravagantly theatrical, unbelievably pachydermatous, and never at a loss. Totally self-centred, too: absolutely nothing – not the person and ability of the charioteer, nor the procession and its incidents, nor the race itself and its outcome, nor even the girl's ultimate reaction to it – is seen or interpreted except through the eye of self-interest. Ovid gives the impression that the character he plays in this poem expected to get what he wanted in the end. But shall *we* also regard his success as certain and applaud? Some clearly do: 'Ingenious as it is true to life. [The ploy] deserved to succeed' (Wilkinson [1962] 23); 'The suit succeeds because he discovers that you just cannot compliment a girl too much' (Davis [1979]) 69). Or shall we cling to the hope that it did not come off (a possibility that Ovid does just leave open?), because we are, like some others, at least mildly repelled: 'An amusing, if rather obnoxious character' (Mack [1987] 68)? The turn of our individual sense of humour – not to mention our gender – may well be the deciding factor. At any rate, political correctness, sexual harassment and male chauvinist piggery are all things this race-goer has not heard of. But what about Ovid himself? Does the real Publius Ovidius Naso necessarily stand up here or not?

Ovid, *Amores*: Retrospect

When Ovid turned his attention to personal love elegy, it was alive and well, a fashionable and still developing genre; by the time he had finished with it, in its classic form[78] it was as good as dead – antiquity saw no more of any consequence, and when personal love poetry in Latin did reappear in the Middle Ages, it was cast in a different mould. So what was it about the *Amores* collection, successful and popular enough in its own time to go to a second edition,[79] which effectively ended the line of development stretching back through Tibullus and Propertius to Gallus,[80] Catullus and the Hellenistic

---

[78] See p. xi.

[79] See p. xliii.

[80] See pp. xxvii-xxviii.

Greeks? Above all it was Ovid's de-romanticisation of the amatory relationship. The *Amores* are love elegy in which elegy comes before love,[81] in which the beloved is almost an afterthought, and in which love itself, when it is not just a private skirmish between Ovid and Cupid, is no professed spiritual ideal or emotional torture but an undisguised quest for sexual satisfaction – as and when it may be available. It is a cheerful quest, too. Admittedly, Tibullus and Propertius allow occasional shafts of humorous irony to pierce their façade of Catullan seriousness, but Ovid dispenses with this altogether, systematically making a mockery of the conventions designed to present amatory entanglement as a serious matter. With what credibility could any male elegiac lover ever again pose as an anguished victim or a painfully degraded slave in the wake of *Amores* 1. 2, or as a model of unswerving fidelity after *Amores* 2. 7 and 8? The game was up for the romantic strain in love elegy once Ovid had made love itself a game.[82] To his modern readers the unembarrassed worldliness of his attitude may make him appear the most modern of the elegists. Yet within the ancient context he brings personal love poetry almost full circle, rehabilitating and developing, on an elegiac scale and against the sensitive background of contemporary politics, the frivolous spirit of Hellenistic epigram[83] from which Catullus and his immediate Augustan successors had turned away.

Not that Ovid necessarily had anything against romance in principle – any more than he necessarily had anything against Augustus. Both romantic love and Augustus' outlook and policies enjoyed established status, and that made them irresistible targets for the mocking humour of one who saw literary potential in nonconformity of every kind – even, paradoxically, in keeping his distance from nonconformity itself when it had become all but institutionalised, as was the case with the trumpeting of Callimachean aesthetics. Like Tibullus, however, Ovid is willing to practise the stylistic principles he declines to preach; and, although he may not have been anti-Augustan in any serious political sense, the generally anti-traditionalist label was an unwise one for him to acquire under a ruler happy to invoke tradition to promote his own public image and to consolidate his power. Little wonder that when Ovid eventually committed some kind of personal

---

[81] See p. 134.

[82] This is not to say, however, that Ovidian personal love elegy is therefore by definition *inferior* to earlier production; such is the distorted picture of much modern critical judgement presented by Boyd (1997) 1-18.

[83] See pp. xviii-xix.

indiscretion, Augustus seized upon it as a pretext to remove an irritatingly popular nuisance from the Roman poetic scene.[84]

The 'more playful' (*lasciuior*[85]) type of love elegy which Ovid initiated remains unique. Hardly surprising, given the sure-footed brilliance of its execution, which few, if any, could hope to emulate. The methodical and comprehensive exploration of a single theme in each poem (or dramatically related pair of poems), the exhaustive citation of example, the ingenious twist of argument, the deliciously *risqué* (but never verbally vulgar) pun and the generally witty turn of phrase, consistently enhanced by fluent and graceful manipulation of the couplet – all these features are incomparably Ovid's. And all of them his critics have held against him at one time or another as evidence of unbridled self-indulgence or over-reliance on techniques learned in the schools of declamation:[86] 'he was not unaware of his faults but in love with them',[87] 'he never knows when he would do well to leave off'[88] (Seneca the Elder, *Controuersiae* 2. 2. 12, 9. 5. 17); 'too much a lover of his own genius'[89] (Quintilian, *Institutio Oratoria* 10. 1. 88); 'more of a rhetorician than a poet' (Lord Macaulay). But Ovid's dexterity and wit are not substitutes for art: they *are* consummate art in themselves, for they are exactly what is called for by the stance he adopts. 'Great facility, bad end' was how the imaginary schoolmaster invented by Cyril Connolly[90] summed up Ovid, and the sourness of his supposed judgement is beautifully apt: Ovid was the type who is just too clever for his own good – or, more precisely, for the comfort of many of those who encounter him.

---

[84] See p. xliii.

[85] Quintilian, *Institutio Oratoria* 10. 1. 93; see p. xliv.

[86] See p. xlii with n. 133.

[87] *non ignorauit sua uitia sed amauit.*

[88] *nescit quod bene cessit relinquere.*

[89] *nimium amator ingenii sui.*

[90] Quoted by Luck (1969) 19.

Bibliography

Ancient Sources: fragmentary texts and epigrams

Where a translation is offered in the commentary, the reference given is to a standard original text. Where no translation is offered, the reference given is to an edition which includes an English version.

Anthologia Palatina: *The Greek Anthology*, translated by W.R. Paton. 5 vols, Loeb edition (Cambridge, Mass.-London, 1916-18).

Callimachus, *Aetia*: Callimachus, *Aetia, Iambi, Hecale and other fragments*, translated by C.A. Trypanis, revised Loeb edition (Cambridge, Mass.-London, 1978). The numbering of the fragments is the same as in R. Pfeiffer, *Callimachus* (Oxford, 1949-53).

Ennius, *Annals*: *The Annals of Quintus Ennius*, edited by O. Skutsch (Oxford, 1987).

Menander: Menander, *Reliquiae*, Vol. II, edited by A. Körte. Revised Teubner edition by A. Thierfelder (Leipzig, 1959).

Mimnermus: M.L. West, *Greek Lyric Poetry*, World's Classics edition (Oxford, 1993), 28-30. The numbering is the same as in M.L.West, *Iambi et Elegi Graeci*. Vol. II (2nd edn. Oxford, 1992).

Porcius Licinus: *Fragmenta Poetarum Latinorum epicorum et lyricorum praeter Ennium et Lucilium*, edited by K. Büchner, Teubner edition (Leipzig, 1982).

Sappho: *Greek Lyric*, Vol. I, translated by D.A. Campbell, Loeb edition (Cambridge, Mass.-London, 1977).

'Theognis': M.L. West, *Greek Lyric Poetry*, World's Classics edition (Oxford, 1993), 125-56. The numbering is the same as in M.L. West, *Iambi et Elegi Graeci*. Vol. I (2nd edn. Oxford, 1989).

Valerius Aedituus: *Fragmenta Poetarum Latinorum epicorum et lyricorum praeter Ennium et Lucilium*, edited by K. Büchner, Teubner edition (Leipzig, 1982).

Modern Works Cited

Adams, J.N., *The Latin Sexual Vocabulary* (London, 1982).

Ahl, F.M., 'Propertius 1. 1', *Wiener Studien* LXXXVII (1974), 80-98.

Allen, A., 'Armed camps in Propertius', *Rheinisches Museum* CXXXV (1992), 95-6.

Allen, A.W., 'Elegy and the Classical Attitude towards love', *Yale Classical Studies* VII (1950), 255-77.

——'Sincerity and the Roman elegists', *Classical Philology* XLV (1958), 145-60.

Anderson, R.D., Parsons, P.J. and Nisbet, R.G.M., 'Elegiacs by Gallus from Qasr Ibrîm', *Journal of Roman Studies* LXIX (1979), 125-55.

Athanassaki, L., 'The triumph of Love and Elegy in Ovid's *Amores* 1. 2', *Materiali e Discussioni per l'annalisi dei testi classici* XXVIII (1992), 125-41.

Booth, J., *Ovid, Amores II* (edition with translation and commentary) (Warminster, 1991. Revised reprint 1999).

——'Tibullus 1. 8 and 9: a tale in two poems?', *Museum Helveticum* LIII (1996), 232-47.

——'All in the mind: sickness in Catullus 76' in S.M. Braund and C.J. Gill (eds), *The Passions in Roman Literature and Thought* (Cambridge, 1997), 150-68.

Bowie, E.L., 'Theocritus' Seventh Idyll, Philetas and Longus', *Classical Quarterly* n.s. XXXV (1985), 67-91.

Boyd, B.W., *Ovid's Literary Loves: Influence and Innovation in the Amores* (Ann Arbor, 1997).

Bright, D.F., *Haec mihi fingebam. Tibullus in his World* (Leiden, 1978).

Brilliant, R., *Visual Narrative: Storytelling in Etruscan and Roman Art* (Ithaca-London, 1984).

Buchan, M., 'Ovidius Imperamator: beginnings and endings of love poems and empire in the *Amores*', *Arethusa* XXVIII (1995), 53-85.

Bulloch, A.W., 'Tibullus and the Alexandrians', *Proceedings of the Cambridge Philological Society* n.s. XIX (1973), 71-89.

Butrica, J.L., 'Hellenistic erotic elegy', *Papers of the Leeds International Latin Seminar* IX (1996), 297-322.

——'Editing Propertius', *Classical Quarterly* n.s. XLVII (1997), 176-208.

Cairns, F., *Generic Composition in Greek and Roman Poetry* (Edinburgh, 1972).

——'Some observations on Propertius 1. 1', *Classical Quarterly* n.s. XXIV (1974), 94-10.

——*Tibullus, a Hellenistic poet at Rome* (Cambridge, 1979).

Cameron, A., *Circus Factions. Blues and Greens at Rome and Byzantium* (Oxford, 1976).

——'How thin was Philitas?', *Classical Quarterly* n.s. XLI (1991), 534-8.

——*Callimachus and his Critics* (Princeton, 1995).

Coleman, R.G.G.,*Virgil, Eclogues* (edition with commentary) (Cambridge, 1977).

Commager, S., 'Notes on some poems of Catullus', *Harvard Studies in Classical Philology* LXX (1965), 83-110.

Copley, F.O., 'Emotional conflict and its significance in the Lesbia poems of Catullus', *American Journal of Philology* LXX (1949), 22-40 [= K. Quinn (ed.), *Approaches to Catullus* (Cambridge, 1972), 78-96].

Crowther, N.B., 'Cornelius Gallus. His importance in the development of Roman poetry', *Aufstieg und Niedergang der römischen Welt* II. 30. 3 (Tübingen, 1983), 1622-48.

Curran, L.C., 'Vision and reality in Propertius 1. 3', *Yale Classical Studies* XIX (1966), 189-207.

Davis, J.T., 'Dramatic and comic devices in Ovid, *Amores* 3. 2', *Hermes* CVII (1979), 51-69.

Dawson, C.M., 'An Alexandrian prototype of Marathus', *American Journal of Philology* LXVII (1946), 1-15.

Day, A.A. *The Origins of Latin Love Elegy* (Oxford, 1938).

Dover, K.J., *Greek Homosexuality* (London, 1978).

Elder, J.P., 'Tibullus: *tersus atque elegans*' in Sullivan (1962), 65-105.

Evans, S., 'Odyssean echoes in Propertius 4. 8', *Greece & Rome* n.s. XVIII (1971), 51-3.

Fairweather, J.A., 'Ovid's autobiographical poem, *Tristia* 4. 10', *Classical Quarterly* n.s. XXXVII (1987), 181-96.

Fantham, R.E., 'Mime. The missing link in Roman literary history', *Classical World* LXXXII (1988-9), 153-63.

Fisher, J.M., 'The structure of Tibullus' first elegy', *Latomus* XXIX (1970), 765-73.

Fitzgerald, W.F., *Catullan Provocations. Lyric Poetry and the Drama of Position* (Berkeley-Los Angeles-London, 1995).

Fowler, D.P and P.G. 'Literary theory and classical studies' in *The Oxford Classical Dictionary* (3rd edn., Oxford-New York, 1996), 871-5.

Galinsky, G.K., 'The triumph theme in the Augustan elegy', *Wiener Studien* LXXXII (1969), 75-107.

——*Augustan Culture. An Interpretive Introduction* (Princeton, 1996).

Goold, G.P., 'Problems in editing Propertius' in J.N. Grant (ed.), *Editing Greek and Latin texts* (New York, 1989), 97-119.

Griffin, J., 'Augustus and the poets: *Caesar qui cogere posset*' in F.G.B. Millar and E. Segal (eds), *Caesar Augustus: Seven Aspects* (Oxford, 1984), 189-218.

——*Latin Poets and Roman Life* (London, 1985).

Hallett, J.P., 'The role of women in Roman elegy: counter-cultural feminism', *Arethusa* VI (1973), 103-24.

Harrison, S.J., 'Drink, suspicion and comedy in Propertius 1. 3', *Proceedings of the Cambridge Philological Society* n.s. XL (1994), 18-26.

Harmon, D.P., 'Myth and fantasy in Propertius 1, 3', *Transactions of the American Philological Association* CIV (1974), 151-65.

Heyworth, S.J., 'Notes on Propertius Books I and II', *Classical Quarterly* n.s. XXXIV (1984), 394-405.

——'Propertius 2. 13'. *Mnemosyne* XLV (1992), 45-59.

——'Propertius: division, transmission and the editor's task', *Papers of the Leeds International Latin Seminar* VIII (1995), 165-85.

Hinds, S.E., *Allusion and Intertext. Dynamics of Appropriation in Roman Poetry* (Cambridge, 1998).

Hodge, R.I.V. and Buttimore, R.A., *The Monobiblos of Propertius. An Analysis of the First Book of Propertius* (Cambridge-Ipswich, 1977).

Holzberg, N. *The Ancient Novel* (London, 1995).

——'Playing with his life: Ovid's 'autobiographical' references', *Lampas* XXX (1997), 4-19.

——'Four poets and a poetess or a portrait of the poet as a young man? Thoughts on Book 3 of the *Corpus Tibullianum*', *Classical Journal* XCII.2 (1999), 169-91.

Horsfall, N.M., 'Some problems in the *Laudatio Turiae*', *Bulletin of the Institute of Classical Studies* XXX (1983), 85-98.

Hunter, R.L., *A Study of Daphnis and Chloe* (Cambridge, 1983).

Hutchinson, G.O., *Hellenistic Poetry* (Oxford, 1988).

Hubbard, M., *Propertius* (London, 1974).

James, S.L., 'Slave-rape and female silence in Ovid's love poetry', *Helios* XXIV (1997), 60-76.

Jenkyns, R.H.A., *Three Classical Poets. Sappho, Catullus and Juvenal* (London, 1982).

Keith, A.M., '*Amores* 1.1: Propertius and the Ovidian programme' in C. Deroux (ed.), *Studies in Latin Literature and Roman History* VI (Brussels, 1992), 327-44.

Kennedy, D.F., *The Arts of Love. Five Studies in the Discourse of Roman Love Elegy* (Cambridge, 1993).

Kenney, E.J., 'Virgil and the elegiac sensibility', *Illinois Classical Studies* VIII (1983), 44-59.

——General introduction and notes in *Ovid. The Love Poems*, translated by A.D. Melville (World's Classics edition) (Oxford, 1990).

Knox, P.E., 'Wine, water and Callimachean polemics', *Harvard Studies in Classical Philology* LXXXIX (1985), 107-19.

——'Philetas and Roman poetry', *Papers of the Leeds International Latin Seminar* VII (1993), 65-83.

Lake, A.K., 'An interpretation of Propertius 4. 7', *Classical Review* LI (1937), 53-5.

Leach, E.W., 'Poetics and poetic design in Tibullus' first elegiac book', *Arethusa* XIII (1980), 79-96.

Lee, A.G., 'The date of Lygdamus and his relationship to Ovid', *Proceedings of the Cambridge Philological Society* n.s. V (1958-9), 15-23.

——'*Tenerorum lusor amorum*' in Sullivan (1962), 149-79.

——'*Otium cum indignitate*: Tibullus 1. 1' in T. Woodman and D.A. West (eds), *Quality and Pleasure in Latin Poetry* (Cambridge, 1974), 94-114.

——*Tibullus: Elegies* (Latin text and translation with notes by R. Maltby) (Leeds, 1990).

——*The Poems of Catullus* (World's Classics edition) (Oxford, 1991).

——*Propertius: The Poems* (Oxford, 1994).

Lee-Stecum, P., *Powerplay in Tibullus: Reading Elegies Book 1* (Cambridge, 1998).

Ling, R.J., *Roman Painting* (Cambridge, 1991).

Luck, G., *The Latin Love Elegy* (London, 1969).

Lyne, R.O.A.M., 'Propertius and Cynthia. Elegy 1. 3', *Proceedings of the Cambridge Philological Society* XVI (1970), 60-78.

——'*Seruitium amoris*', *Classical Quarterly* n.s. XXIX (1979), 117-30.

——*The Latin Love Poets from Catullus to Horace* (Oxford, 1980).

——'Propertius 2. 10 and 11 and the structure of Books 2A and 2B', *Journal of Roman Studies* LXXXVIII (1998a), 21-36.

——'Introductory poems in Propertius: 1.1 and 2.12', *Proceedings of the Cambridge Philological Society* n.s. XLIV (1998b), 158-81.

Mack, S., *Ovid* (New Haven, 1987).

Maltby, R., see Lee (1990).

Michels, A.K., 'Death and two poets', *Transactions of the American Philological Association* LXXXVI (1955), 160-79.

Miller, J.F., 'Reading Cupid's triumph', *Classical Journal* XC (1995), 287-94.

Muecke, F., '*Nobilis historia*? Incongruity in Propertius 4. 7', *Bulletin of the Institute of Classical Studies* XXI (1974), 124-32.

Murgatroyd, P., *Tibullus 1. A commentary* (Pietermaritzburg, 1980).

McKeown, J.C., 'Augustan elegy and mime', *Proceedings of the Cambridge Philological Society* n.s. XXV (1979), 71-84.

Moles, J.L., 'The dramatic coherence of Ovid, *Amores* 1. 1 and 1. 2', *Classical Quarterly* n.s. XLI (1991), 551-4.

Nisbet, R.G.M., *Collected Papers on Latin Literature*, ed. S.J. Harrison (Oxford, 1995).

O'Neill, E.N., 'Cynthia and the moon', *Classical Philology* LIII (1958), 1-8.

Papanghelis, T.D., *Propertius, a Hellenistic Poet on Love and Death* (Cambridge, 1987).

Parca, M., 'The position of Lygdamus in Augustan poetry' in C. Deroux (ed.), *Studies in Latin Literature and Roman History* IV (Brussels, 1986), 416-74.

Parsons, P.J., 'Eine neugefundene griechische Liebeselegie' ['A recently discovered Greek love elegy'], *Museum Helveticum* XLV (1988), 65-74.

Pomeroy. S., *Goddesses, Whores, Wives and Slaves* (New York, 1975).

Postgate, J.P., *Select Elegies of Propertius* (text and commentary) (London, 1884).

Powell, J.G.F., 'Two notes on Catullus', *Classical Quarterly* n.s. XL (1990), 199-206.

Putnam, M.C.J., *Tibullus. A Commentary* (Norman, 1973).

Quinn, K., *The Catullan Revolution* (Heffer, Cambridge, 1969).

——*Catullus, the Poems* (edition with commentary) (London, 1970).

Ross, D.O. Jnr, *Style and Tradition in Catullus* (Cambridge, Mass., 1969).

——*Backgrounds to Augustan Poetry: Gallus, Elegy and Rome* (Cambridge, 1975).

Rudd, N., *Lines of Enquiry* (Cambridge, 1976).

——'Romantic love in classical times', *Ramus* X (1981), 140-55.

——*Horace; Epistles II and Epistle to the Pisones ('Ars Poetica')* (edition with commentary) (Cambridge, 1989).

——'Classical humanism and its critics', *Échos du monde classique* n.s. XV (1996), 283-303.

Small, G.P., *Catullus: A Reader's Guide to the Poems* (Lanham, Md., 1983).

Smith, K.F., *The Elegies of Albius Tibullus* (text and commentary) (New York, 1913).

Stahl, H-P., *Propertius: 'Love' and 'War'. Individual and State under Augustus* (Berkeley-Los Angeles-London, 1985).

Sullivan, J.P. (ed.), *Critical Essays on Roman Literature. Elegy and Lyric* (London, 1962).

——*Propertius. A Critical Introduction* (Cambridge, 1976).

Syme, R., *The Roman Revolution* (Oxford, 1939).

——*History in Ovid* (Oxford, 1978).

Thomas, R.F., *Virgil: Georgics* (edition with commentary in 2 vols.) (Cambridge, 1988).

——'The Old Man revisited: memory, reference and genre in Virgil, *Georgics* 4. 116-48', *Materiali e Discussioni per l'annalisi dei testi classici* XXIX (1992), 35-70.

Thompson, L.A., *Romans and Blacks* (London-Oklahoma, 1989).

Treggiari, S., *Roman Marriage: iusti coniuges from the time of Cicero to the time of Ulpian* (Oxford, 1991).

Veyne, P., *Roman Erotic Elegy. Love, Poetry and the West*, translated by D. Pellauer (Chicago-London, 1988).

Warden, J., '*Fallax Opus: Poet and Reader in the Elegies of Propertius* (Toronto, 1980).

Washington, P., *Fraud: Literary Theory and the End of English* (London, 1989).

Wilkinson, L.P., *Ovid Surveyed* [abridged from *Ovid Recalled* (1955)] (Cambridge, 1962).

——'The continuity of Propertius 2. 13', *Classical Review* n.s. XVI (1966), 141-4.

Wheeler, A.L., *Catullus and the Traditions of Ancient Poetry* (Berkeley, 1934).

White, P., *Promised Verse. Poets in the Society of Augustan Rome* (Cambridge, Mass.-London, 1993).

Williams, C.A, 'Greek love at Rome', *Classical Quarterly* n.s. XLV (1995), 517-39.

Williams, G., *Tradition and Originality in Roman Poetry* (Oxford, 1968).

——*Change and Decline. Roman Literature in the Early Empire* (Berkeley-Los Angeles, 1978).

Wiseman, T.P., *Catullan Questions* (Leicester, 1969).

——*Catullus and his World. A Reappraisal* (Oxford, 1985).

Wyke, M., 'Written women: Propertius' *scripta puella*', *Journal of Roman Studies* LXXVII (1987), 47-61.

——'Mistress and metaphor in Augustan elegy', *Helios* XVI (1989), 25-47.

——'Taking the woman's part: engendering Roman love elegy', *Ramus* XXIII (1994), 110-28.

Yardley, J.C., 'Cynthia's ghost. Propertius 4. 7 again', *Bulletin of the Institute of Classical Studies* XXIV (1977), 83-7.

——'Paulus Silentiarius, Ovid and Propertius', *Classical Quarterly* n.s. XXX (1980), 239-43.

——'Roman elegy and the funerary epigram', *Échos du monde classique* n.s. XV (1996), 267-73.

Zanker, P., *The Power of Images in the Age of Augustus*, translated by A. Shapiro (Ann Arbor, 1988).

Zetzel, J.E.G., 'Gallus, Elegy and Ross' [a review of Ross (1975)], *Classical Philology* LXXIV (1977), 249-60.